AS
PSYCHOLOGY
EXAM COMPANION

AS
PSYCHOLOGY
EXAM COMPANION

CLARE CHARLES
The Royal Latin School, Buckinghamshire

Psychology Press
Taylor & Francis Group

an informa business

Published 2010
by Psychology Press
27 Church Road, Hove, East Sussex BN3 2FA
Simultaneously published in the USA and Canada
by Psychology Press
270 Madison Ave, New York, NY 10016

Psychology Press is an imprint of the Taylor & Francis group, an Informa business

British Library Cataloguing in Publication Data
A catalogue record for this book is available from the British Library

ISBN: 978-1-84872-046-6

Typeset in the UK by RefineCatch Ltd, Bungay, Suffolk
Cover design by Andy Ward
Printed and bound in the UK by Ashford Colour Press Ltd, Gosport, Hampshire

CONTENTS

INTRODUCTION
How to Use this Exam Companion

Hello

Welcome to the *Exam Companion*! This guide will give you the inside knowledge you need to approach the AS-level psychology exam with confidence. That's because this guide includes:

- A range of model answers.
- Examiner advice per question. Look for the "Exam hint" box, which will look like this:
- AO advice where relevant to emphasise how the AO1, AO2, and AO3 skills are assessed. Look for the "AO advice box", which will look like this:

When you think about it, this is the most useful resource you could use right now because high grade answers are exactly what I'm sure you're aiming to write in the exam. The *Exam Companion* includes a wide range of model answers, but because the Specification is not prescriptive, other questions might come up. However, you should be able to adapt the model answers to most types of questions.

The model answers would gain top marks. So if you can't write quite as much as the answers don't panic; you do not need all of the content for a good grade. But note that practice makes perfect—you will be able to write more with practice. So do see this as an essential part of your revision. Write out a range of questions for a topic, put them into an envelope, and have a go at answering the questions. Then compare your answers with the model answers. This tried-and-tested technique does work!

THE EXAM FORMAT

Unit 1 (PSYA1)	Unit 2 (PSYA2)
1½ hours	1½ hours
AO1 16.66%	AO1 20.83%
AO2 16.66%	AO2 20.83%
AO3 16.66%	AO3 8.33%

Questions consist of short-answer and stimulus material questions (application of knowledge and how science works), which are variable in how many marks each question carries, but tend to range from 1–6 marks. The long-answer questions include at least one 12-mark question, which is split 50:50 between AO1 and AO2. Unit 1 will always contain only one 12-mark question and Unit 2 may contain one or more. Units 1 and 2 may also contain shorter 10- or 8-mark essay questions; again the split is 50:50 between AO1 and AO2. So note that you need to be ready for a 12-mark version of each answer, but also know what to edit if the question is a shorter 8- or 10-mark version.

THE EXAM SKILLS

The exam format above shows that AO1, AO2, and AO3 are all examined across both AS units but there are more AO3 questions in Unit 1 due to Research Methods being part of this exam paper. Below is a detailed description of what each of the skills means, but you may find it easier to remember each skill as:

AO1	AO2	AO3
Outline/describe	Evaluate/assess	Methodology

AO1 tests knowledge and understanding of science and of *How Science Works*

You may be asked to:

- Recognise, recall, and show understanding of content.
- Select, organise, and communicate content in a variety of forms.

AO2 Application of knowledge and understanding of science and of *How Science Works*

You may be asked to:

- Analyse and evaluate scientific knowledge and processes.
- Apply scientific knowledge and processes to content and issues raised.
- Assess the validity, reliability, and credibility of scientific information.

AO3 *How Science Works*

You may be asked to:

- Describe ethical, safe, and skilful practical techniques and processes, selecting appropriate qualitative and quantitative data.
- Know how to make, record, and communicate reliable and valid observations and measurements with appropriate precision and accuracy, through using primary and secondary sources.
- Analyse, interpret, explain, and evaluate the methodology, results, and impact of experimental research.

Quality of written communication (QWC)

There are two marks per Unit paper, for good use of grammar and punctuation, correct spelling, legible handwriting, appropriate style of writing, clear expression, and accurate use of technical terms. This should pose few problems for an AS-level student! It will be assessed in the extended 12-mark questions.

TYPES OF EXAM QUESTIONS

Each sub-section of the Specification is organised into different types of questions:

Definition questions—these require you to explain a key term so you are credited with AO1 marks.

Research questions—these require you to describe (AO1) or evaluate (AO2) key studies.

Explanation questions—these require you to outline a theory, or approach (AO1), or a criticism question may require you to explain a strength or weakness (AO2). Another type of explanation question may ask you to explain the differences between two concepts. Do make sure you draw a comparison; many candidates make the mistake of describing the two concepts without explaining the difference.

Essay questions—these require you to outline and evaluate whatever has been specified in the question. These require a 50:50 proportion of AO1 to AO2. You will see the easiest way to structure your essays is to write two paragraphs, one of AO1 and one of AO2.

Recognition questions—these questions require you to recognise information and impose some sort of order onto it. So you may be asked to recognise different definitions and match them up to the correct descriptor of the definition.

Application of knowledge questions—these questions require you to apply your knowledge of psychology to an unfamiliar situation and so are credited as AO2.

How Science Works **questions**—these questions require you to consider some aspect of research methodology, for example to explain or evaluate a research method, identify variables, or assess reliability, validity, or ethics, and so are credited as AO3.

Knowing what the question is asking

To understand what the exam question is asking you need to know what the injunctions used in the question require you to do, so make sure you are familiar with:

Outline, describe, identify: AO1 knowledge and understanding is being assessed.

Evaluate, assess: AO2 analysis and evaluation is being assessed, so give strengths and weakneses, evidence for and/or against, and commentary.

Explain: this one is not as straightforward. "Explain questions" tend to ask one of two things: "explain what . . ." is AO1 and "explain why or how . . ." is often used in the application of knowledge questions and so tests AO2.

Discuss/critically consider: these mean describe and evaluate and are used for essay questions, when of course you must include AO1 and AO2 in equal proportion.

Note the methodology questions could be preceded by these injunctions but the remainder of the question would clearly relate to methodology, such as "Identify the independent variable", and so these questions assess AO3.

How to achieve high marks

1) **Write the right amount—not too much, not too little.** You should be aiming to write approximately 100 words for a 6-mark question, and so 200 words for a 12-mark essay question, and 30–35 words for a 2-mark question. But this does depend on the nature of the question. If you are simply putting letters in a table for 2 marks then all you need to write is the letter!

2) **Know the exam injunctions and answer with the right skill.** So don't include "evaluate" in an "outline" question and vice versa.

3) **Elaborate.** An easy mistake to make is to identify the right answer or write about it very simply, which will only achieve at the basic level of the mark scheme. So do elaborate your description by including lots of detail and use the sandwich approach for AO2:

   - Identify the point (basic bread and butter).
   - Include evidence and/or explanation of the point (filling).
   - Include something extra. For example, discuss what the point means—so does it limit validity, or the usefulness of the research? (relish or sauce).

For example, an issue with the Asch study is sample bias (bread and butter). This is because it was androcentric (it had an all male sample). This means we cannot be sure the findings would generalise to other populations (filling) and so the research lacks external validity (relish).

4) **Don't write more than is needed.** Writing too much on one question can penalise how much you can write on later ones so please keep a sense of time. If the questions ask for one or two points don't include more than has been specified. Don't include more than 6 marks' worth of AO1 in the essay question or you will be wasting words because they cannot be credited.

5) **Time management.** You have 90 minutes for 72 marks, so there is thinking time and planning time for the longer answer questions (there is a planning box—use it, and don't cross it out as this can be credited).

6) **The marks for the question and the space provided for the answer provide a clue as to how much to write.** Try not to use the supplementary sheets but if you do, write "see extra sheet", so the examiner knows you've moved to there. You do need to be concise. Often candidates write more than is needed for the marks.

7) **Don't write in the margins.** Anything written there may not make it through the scanner and so may not be credited!

8) **Read the question carefully.** For example, a question that asks you to "Outline how research has investigated ..." is asking for procedures, not for any other part of the study. If it says "one" don't give two, etc. Read the stimulus questions very carefully, even the tick box ones, as many students make mistakes on these because they are careless.

For example, a question in a past exam described how you might obey a nurse in the workplace but not if you see her in a shop. Then it asked for an explanation of why you would be less likely to obey when you see her in a shop. Many wrote about why they would obey her in the workplace, which of course isn't relevant. You need to focus on why many would resist obeying her, e.g. her authority is decreased, she is out of uniform, just a member of joe public, etc. In the hospital she is a legitimate authority figure but outside you might question her authority.

Similarly, some candidates, on an implications for social change question, described studies by Asch and Milgram, which unsurprisingly didn't receive any marks because the question was on implications!

9) **Application questions.** If the question asks you to apply the knowledge, e.g. "Why might CBT be appropriate for . . ." i.e. a person described in the stimulus, then you must relate your answer to the person's difficulties, as a general description will receive little credit. Quote the question to make it clear you are applying it.

10) **Research methods questions.** These can appear anywhere on both exam papers but there will be more on PSYA1. If asked for a strength and a weakness of xxxxx research, think about whether the study was carefully controlled and so can be replicated, or not, perhaps the results are due to confounding variables, which reduce internal validity. OR consider artificial versus high mundane realism and how these affect external validity. If asked a question on ethical issues then the issue must be relevant, e.g. if participants don't know they are being studied then lack of protection is not an issue. They don't know they are being studied so how can they be distressed? So the real issues are deception and lack of informed content, unless they are being observed in a public space as the ethical guidelines say this is acceptable. If the research involves children or patients with psychopathological disorders the most obvious issue is informed consent—the need to get consent from parents or those acting in *locus parentis* for children, so this would be the family, and for patients this would be their doctors or care workers.

11) **Make up a mnemonic of key AO2 points:** control, cause and effect, extraneous variables, internal validity, external validity, reliability, sample bias, reductionism, determinism, correlational criticisms, observer bias, self-report weaknesses, lack of standardisation, participant variables, order effects, culture bias (ethnocentrism), individual differences, researcher effects, demand characteristics, social desirability, scientific/objective vs. subjective, operationalisation, etc . . . .

MARK SCHEMES

Note that these generic mark schemes would be adapted depending on whether the question was 3, 4, 5, or 6 marks.

Mark scheme for short answer AO1 questions

6 marks	*Accurate and reasonably detailed*
4–5 marks	*Less detailed but generally accurate*
3–2 marks	*Basic*
1 mark	*Very brief/flawed or inappropriate*
0 marks	*No creditworthy material*

Mark scheme for short answer AO2 questions

6 marks	*Effective explanation/evaluation*
4–5 marks	*Reasonable explanation/evaluation*
3–2 marks	*Basic explanation/evaluation*
1 mark	*Rudimentary explanation/evaluation*
0 marks	*No creditworthy material*

Mark scheme for short answer AO3 questions

There is no generic mark scheme for AO3 questions as the application of the mark scheme is variable depending on the way in which your understanding of how science works is being assessed.

Mark scheme for 12-mark questions

Simply combine the 6-mark schemes for AO1 and AO2 together for the long answer questions.

COGNITIVE PSYCHOLOGY
Memory

MODELS OF MEMORY

Definition question

Short-term and long-term memory

> **?** **Explain what is meant by the term . . .** **3 MARKS**

AO ADVICE

Questions that ask you to explain a term are asking for an outline of a key concept and so are AO1 questions because they require you to demonstrate knowledge and understanding.

EXAM HINT

You may be asked to define any of the Key Terms below. You do not have to write out the definitions word for word; just make sure you clearly communicate what the term means.

Memory: The mental processes used to encode, store, and retrieve information. Encoding takes many forms: visual, auditory, semantic, taste, and smell. Storage refers to the amount of information that can be held in memory. Retrieval refers to the processes by which information is "dug out" of memory, and includes recognition, recall, and reconstruction. It is useful to distinguish between two types of memory: short-term or immediate memory and long-term or more permanent memory.

Short-term memory: A temporary place for storing information during which it receives limited processing (e.g. verbal rehearsal). Short-term memory has a very limited capacity of 5+/–2 items and short duration of approximately 20 seconds, unless the information is maintained through rehearsal.

Long-term memory: A relatively permanent store, which has unlimited capacity and duration. Different kinds of long-term memory have been identified, including episodic (memory for personal events), semantic (memory for facts and information), and procedural (memory for actions and skills).

Encoding: Encoding is the transfer of information into code, which creates a memory trace that can be registered in the memory store. Baddeley's (1966) study of encoding found that STM and LTM use different codes. In STM encoding it is primarily acoustic (based on the sound of the word) and in LTM it is primarily semantic (based on the meaning of the word).

Capacity: Capacity is the measurement of how much information can be held in memory. The capacity of STM is limited to 7+/−2 items, i.e. there are between 5 and 9 possible items in the STM span, which was found by Jacobs (1887) using the digit span technique. This means the capacity of STM is very limited whereas LTM is thought to have unlimited capacity, but this is difficult to test.

Duration: This refers to how long a memory lasts. The existence of two distinct memory stores is supported by duration because this differs between STM and LTM. STM has a very limited duration of 18–30 seconds, whereas LTM potentially lasts forever and so memories may be permanent.

Research questions

EXAM HINT

The following answers mainly draw from research into duration and a little from encoding and capacity. Don't waste your revision time learning too many studies because the Specification does not specify that you need to know these, so what follows should be quite sufficient. Note how the two questions that follow ask for different aspects of the study; the first asks for the methods or procedures and the second for the findings. Do focus on the right part of the study and guard against starting with the methods when the findings have been asked for. This may seem obvious but it is a common mistake! Also note the procedures question may be phrased as "Explain how research . . . has been conducted". This is exactly the same question because it still requires you to write about the methods.

AO ADVICE

Note that, although these are research questions and they may ask you to outline methods, they are asking you to describe studies and so they are AO1 rather than AO3 questions. To achieve well you need detailed description.

? Outline the procedures of one study into the nature of short-term memory. OR Explain how research into the nature of STM has been conducted. **6 MARKS**

Peterson and Peterson's (1959) study into the duration of STM used what is known as the Brown–Peterson technique. On each trial, participants were presented with a meaningless trigram consisting of three consonants (e.g. BLM, CTG), which they knew they would be asked to recall in the correct order. Recall was required after a delay of 3, 6, 9, 12, 15, or 18 seconds. The participants counted backwards aloud in threes from a random 3-digit number (e.g. 866, 863, 860, and so on) between the initial presentation of the trigram and the time when they were asked to recall it. This was done to prevent rehearsal of the trigram, because rehearsal would have improved performance by keeping information in STM. Recall had to be 100% accurate and in the correct order (serial recall) in order to count. The participants were tested repeatedly with the various time delays. The experimenters varied the time delay, and the effect of time delay on memory was assessed in terms of the number of trigrams recalled.

> **?** **Outline the findings of one or more study(ies) into the nature of short-term memory.** **6 MARKS**

EXAM HINT
Note how this answer takes the approach of describing a number of studies in less detail, which is fine because the question says one or more. Another approach would be to write about only one study in detail.

Peterson and Peterson (1959), in their study into the duration of STM, found that there was a rapid increase in forgetting from STM as the time delay increased. After 3 seconds, 80% of the trigrams were recalled; after 6 seconds, 50% were recalled; and after 18 seconds, fewer than 10% of the trigrams were recalled. Thus, there was a rapid rate of forgetting, and very little information remained in STM for more than 18 seconds or so. Baddeley's (1966) research into encoding found that acoustic code was the preferred form of encoding in STM, which means that information is encoded based on sound. Jacobs' (1887) research into the capacity of STM using the digit span technique found that STM is limited to 7+/–2 items, i.e. there are between 5 and 9 possible items in the STM span.

> **?** **Outline the procedures of one study into the nature of long-term memory. OR Explain how research into the nature of LTM has been conducted.** **6 MARKS**

Bahrick et al.'s (1975) study into the duration of long-term memory used an opportunity sample of 392 American ex-high-school students aged from 17–74 years. They were tested in a number of ways:

1. Free recall of the names of as many of their former classmates as possible.
2. A photo recognition test in which they were asked to identify former classmates in a set of 50 photos, only some of which were of their classmates.
3. A name recognition test.
4. A name and photo-matching test.

These tests assessed very-long-term memory (VLTM), because the time since leaving high school was up to 48 years. Participants' accuracy (and thus duration of memory) was assessed by comparing their responses with high-school yearbooks containing pictures and names of all the students in that year.

> **?** **Outline the findings of one or more study(ies) into the nature of long-term memory.** **6 MARKS**

Bahrick et al.'s (1975) study into the duration of long-term memory found 90% accuracy in face and name recognition, even with those participants who had left high school 34 years previously. After 48 years this declined to 80% for name recognition and 40% for face recognition. Free recall was considerably less accurate: 60% accurate after 15 years and only 30% accurate after 48 years. The findings reveal that the duration of LTM is very long, hence VLTM was tested. Baddeley's (1966) research into encoding found that the semantic code was the preferred form of encoding in LTM, which means that information is encoded based on the meaning of the words.

Contrast/differences question

> **?** **Outline differences between short-term memory and long-term memory.** **6 MARKS**

One difference between STM and LTM is in the code that is preferred to lay down the memory trace. The preferred form of encoding in STM is acoustic encoding, which is based on the sound of the word. Whereas a different code is preferred in LTM as semantic encoding is used, which is based on the meaning of the word as found by Baddeley's (1966) study of encoding.

A second difference is in capacity (the amount that can be stored) as the capacity of STM is 7+/–2 chunks of information, i.e. there are between 5 and 9 possible items in the STM span (Jacobs, 1887; Miller, 1956). This means the capacity of STM is very limited whereas LTM is thought to have unlimited capacity, but this is difficult to test.

A third difference is in the duration of each type of memory. The duration of STM is very short, as demonstrated by Peterson and Peterson (1959). They used the Brown–Peterson technique to show that after 18 seconds less than 10% of the material was recalled and so STM has an approximately 18-second duration. Whereas the duration of LTM is very long as memories may endure forever, as supported by Bahrick et al.'s (1975) research into VLTM.

> **EXAM HINT**
> Remember encoding, capacity, and duration all reveal clear differences between the two memory stores. Identifying and explaining each of the three differences allows you to access all 6 marks, 2 per difference.

> **AO ADVICE**
> Note that you are asked to outline differences, so this is a knowledge and understanding question and tests AO1.

How Science Works questions

> **?** **Explain why research into short-term and long-term memory may be criticised as lacking validity.**
> **5 MARKS**

Research into the nature of memory, for example, Peterson and Peterson's (1959) study into the duration of STM is criticised because it lacked mundane realism (not like real life). This is because the test of memory, which was if participants could remember nonsense trigrams, is not like an everyday memory demand. The trigram is less meaningful and not particularly interesting and so may not have been remembered very well. This means the lack of realism of the study may have exaggerated the limited duration of STM, i.e. made it appear shorter than it actually is because the information was not very memorable. This means any findings may not be true of real-life memory and so may lack generalisability to other settings and so external validity may be limited.

> **EXAM HINT**
> The most obvious issue is that the memory tests in the laboratory are not the same as the way we use our memory in real life. Remember the key term is that research lacks mundane realism if it is not like real life.

> **AO ADVICE**
> Note that this question is about methodology because you are asked to assess the validity of the research and so it tests AO3.

? A psychologist has decided to test the effectiveness of chunking so two groups of participants have been given the same 30 letters to recall, which can be chunked into the following qualifications:

AS GCSE PHD BA MSC GNVQ BTEC GCE BSC MA

The participants were recruited through an advertisement that was displayed on university notice boards. Group 1 were given the chunked letters as above and Group 2 were given the same letters in a random order. The average number of letters is displayed in the graph below.

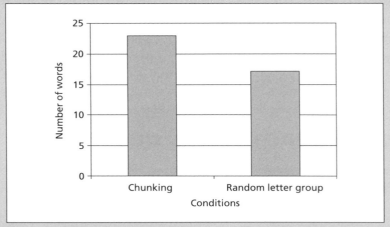

A bar chart to show the number of words recalled in the chunking and random letter groups

(a) (i) Which sample method has been used in this study? **1 MARK**

(ii) Give one weakness of this sample method. **2 MARKS**

(b) (i) What type of graph has been used to present the data? **1 MARK**

(ii) What does the graph show about the findings of the research? **3 MARKS**

(c) (i) Give a suitable hypothesis for this investigation. **2 MARKS**

AO ADVICE

Note that all of these questions are about methodology and so test AO3.

(ii) Is your hypothesis directional or non-directional? Explain why. `2 MARKS`

(d) What would be an appropriate measure of central tendency and why? `1 MARK`

(e) Identify one possible extraneous variable in this investigation. `2 MARKS`

(f) This was a laboratory experiment. Consider the usefulness of this study for explaining everyday memory. `4 MARKS`

EXAM HINT
A lot of these should be very straightforward if you know your research methods. Make sure you do! Do make sure on (b) (ii) you write enough for the 3 marks. C (ii) is handy because it gets you to think about if you worded your hypothesis correctly in (i). Make sure you do operationalise the hypothesis, i.e. write it so that it's clear how the dependent variable was measured. The question reveals exactly how many letters had to be recalled so you must include this.

(a) (i)   Volunteer sampling.

   (ii) The problem with volunteer sampling is that the people who volunteer are unlikely to be representative of the general population because they may be different from non-volunteers, for instance in personality, motivation, etc., and so may not be a truly representative sample. This makes generalising the findings to the non-volunteering population questionable.

(b) (i)   Bar chart.

   (ii) The bar chart shows that the group that chunked the information remembered on average six more letters than the group that didn't chunk the information.

(c) (i)   Participants where the letters are chunked will recall more from a maximum of 30 letters than participants where the same letters are presented randomly.

   (ii) The hypothesis is directional because previous research suggests that chunking will improve recall, and so a specific direction, so it can be predicted that the chunking group will do better than the random group.

(d) The mean would be an appropriate measure because it uses all of the data in the score distribution and so is the most sophisticated average.

(e) A possible extraneous variable is that participants in the chunking group may have drunk cups of coffee or eaten chocolate prior to the experiment. Therefore caffeine may improve their performance and the effects that appear to be due to the chunking could in fact be due to caffeine.

(f) The laboratory is a very controlled environment and so it is artificial. This means we cannot be sure how well any findings generalise to everyday life and so lab experiments lack external validity. The testing of how well participants recall letters is not like what we recall in real life and so this lack of mundane realism further limits external validity. Another weakness of the lab is that because it is such an artificial environment it is often easier for participants to guess the demand characteristics of the study, i.e. work out what the study is about. If they change their behaviour to give the experimenter the desired results then any findings are not valid because they are not genuine behaviour. This means the findings would have very little value for explaining everyday memory. On the other hand, the nature of laboratory studies means variables can be controlled, so enabling cause and effect to be investigated.

Recognition questions

EXAM HINT
This question requires you to summarise the differences between STM and LTM.

? Complete the gaps in the following table into the nature of STM and LTM. **4 MARKS**

	STM	LTM
Duration	Less than 30 seconds	*Infinite*
Encoding	*Acoustic code preferred*	*Semantic code is preferred*
Capacity	*7+/–2 items*	Unlimited

EXAM HINT
A straightforward question but do give yourself thinking time as candidates often make careless mistakes on what seem to be the easier questions.

? The following concepts relate to memory, only two of which have been defined below. Match the concepts to the appropriate definitions. **2 MARKS**

Encoding

Capacity

Duration

Retrieval

Definition	Answer
This is the measurement of how much information can be held in memory.	*Capacity*
This refers to how long a memory is held.	*Duration*

Application of knowledge question

> **?** James has been given a list of words that all sound very similar and Harry has been given a list of words that all have a similar meaning. James was asked to recall the words immediately within a 30-second period. Harry was asked to recall the words after an interval of 5 minutes. Explain which form of encoding will be preferred by James and Harry. **4 MARKS**

EXAM HINT
Note that this question relates to acoustic and semantic encoding and how which one is mainly used differs between STM and LTM.

James will encode the words using the acoustic code. This is because the words sound very similar and acoustic encoding is based on the sound of the words. It is also because he is asked to recall the words within 30 seconds and so this is within the duration of STM, and acoustic encoding is preferred by STM. Harry will encode the words based on the fact that they have a similar meaning and so he will encode them semantically. This is also because he was asked to recall the words after an interval of 5 minutes. This is beyond the duration of STM and so will require LTM, which prefers semantic encoding.

AO ADVICE
Note that this question requires you to apply your knowledge to a novel situation and so tests AO2. Remember you must clearly relate your answer to the situation and DO NOT just write about encoding generally because you must apply your knowledge to the situation.

Definition question

The multi-store model

> **?** Explain what is meant by the term the multi-store model. **3 MARKS**

Multi-store model: The notion that memory is divided into three kinds of store (sensory memory; short-term memory; and long-term memory). It is often assumed that attention is used to select

EXAM HINT

You may be asked to define both the multi-store model and the working memory model and so you need shorter descriptions than you would use in 6-mark questions. You need approximately 50 words for a 3-mark answer.

information from sensory memory for processing in the short-term store, whereas verbal rehearsal is involved when information is transferred from the short-term memory store to the long-term memory store. It is increasingly doubted that there is a single long-term memory store.

Explanation question

> **?** **Explain how information is transferred from STM to LTM according to the multi-store model.** **2 MARKS**

EXAM HINT

The answer is rehearsal but of course this will only get 1 mark so explain what it means for 2 marks.

According to the multi-store model, information is transferred via rehearsal, which is verbal repetition of the material. This helps us to encode the information into LTM.

Essay question

AO ADVICE

Note that essay questions always have an EQUAL split of AO1 to AO2 marks and so you need to equally balance how much description and evaluation you include. To do this for the 12-mark question aim for two large paragraphs, one of AO1 and one of AO2, each approximately 100 words. For the 10-mark question each paragraph should contain approximately 85 words, and for the 8-mark question each paragraph should contain approximately 70 words.

> **?** **Outline and evaluate the multi-store model of memory.** **8, 10, OR 12 MARKS**

EXAM HINT

Note that paragraph 1 is how you would answer a short answer AO1 explanation question that asks you to describe the multi-store model. The amount of marks allocated to the question can vary from 8 to 12 so do be prepared to shorten your answer for the 8- and 10-mark versions. Also note how AO1 and AO2 have been divided into separate paragraphs. This is a simple way of keeping a check that the proportion is 50:50.

10-mark question: Reduce the content on the differences between STM and LTM in paragraph 1 and leave out the criticism that they are not single stores in paragraph 2.
8-mark question: Leave out the content on the differences between STM and LTM in paragraph 1 and leave out the point about flashbulb memories and the criticism that they are not single stores in paragraph 2.

Paragraph 1 AO1

According to the multi-store model (MSM), there are three memory stores. Information first enters sensory memory and then the process of attention selects some of the information and transfers it to the short-term memory. Maintenance rehearsal refers to how the information is maintained in STM. It is then transferred to long-term memory (LTM) through elaborative rehearsal (verbal repetition). The rehearsal process is of key importance because information can't reach long-term memory unless it's rehearsed. The more it's rehearsed, the longer the memory will be as the trace becomes stronger and without rehearsal the memory trace will quickly decay. The MSM places emphasis on structure (the three stores: sensory memory, STM, LTM) and processes (attention and rehearsal). There are key differences between the two stores (STM and LTM) identified in the model, particularly in terms of capacity and duration. The capacity of STM is very limited to an average of seven items whereas LTM has potentially unlimited capacity. Similarly, the duration of STM is limited to as little as 30 seconds whereas the duration of LTM may be infinite.

structure

capacity

Paragraph 2 AO2

Support for the MSM of memory falls into two categories: research that supports the STM/LTM structure and research that supports rehearsal as a key process identified by the model. The primacy and recency effects provide support for both. These effects refer to how the first and last words in a list are remembered best and those in the middle are most likely to be forgotten. The first words (primacy effect) are remembered because they have been rehearsed and so transferred to LTM, and the last words (recency effect) are remembered because they are still in STM, and so the STM/LTM structure is supported. Glanzer and Cunitz (1966) provide further support as they found that an interference task wiped out the recency effect but had no effect on the words at the beginning and in the middle. This supports the STM/LTM distinction suggested by the multi-store model as the words at the end were easily forgotten because they were still in STM and the importance of rehearsal is supported because the interference task works by limiting rehearsal. However, rehearsal is not always necessary for memories to become permanent, e.g. flashbulb memory—information can be memorable because of the emotional significance of the event and so enter memory with very little rehearsal.

primacy / recency effect

interference

A counter-criticism is that often national events create flashbulb memories as these events are presented again and again in the news and so this is a form of rehearsal. The artificiality of research may

Methodological issues

have exaggerated the importance of rehearsal as word lists are not like real-life memory demands and so lack mundane realism. The information is not meaningful or motivational and so may require more rehearsal to be remembered. This may not be true of more interesting information and so the research lacks external validity, i.e. generalisability. STM and LTM are not single stores and so the multi-store model is oversimplistic in its presentation of memory as divided into single stores. In LTM, declarative and procedural memories have been identified. Similarly, the working memory model shows that there are different types of STM (visual, auditory, the central executive) and so it is also not a single store.

Recognition question

EXAM HINT

This is a straightforward question where you just have to label the multi-store model diagram.

? **Label the diagram of the multi-store model below.** **3 MARKS**

Sensory memory → Short-term memory → *Long-term memory*

rehearsal

Application of knowledge questions

EXAM HINT

This question is asking you to criticise rehearsal as the key process of transferring information from STM to LTM.

? **The multi-store model is criticised because it suggests that if Hannah learns and relearns her revision notes she should be able to recall the information well. However, instead she can remember perfectly what happened on her favourite TV programme last night but unfortunately not her revision notes. Explain how this shows a limitation of the multi-store model.** **4 MARKS**

Hannah's difficulty in remembering her revision notes, despite the fact she has learnt the information repeatedly, shows that rehearsal is not as important as the multi-store model suggests. According to the model, this is the way information is transferred to long-term memory (LTM). However, not all information needs the same amount of rehearsal, as shown by the fact that Hannah can recall her favourite TV programme much more easily than she can her revision notes. The programme may be remembered better because it is more interesting than her revision notes and so motivational factors need to be considered, which are ignored by the model. Also, the preferred form of encoding in LTM is semantic, which means that words are encoded based on the meaning of the word and so this may also explain why Hannah can remember the TV programme better than her revision notes. The TV programme provides information as part of a story and so this may be more meaningful and so better able to be encoded semantically than revision notes that may be quite abstract in content.

> **?** **Palwinder has just moved house and is trying to memorise his new postcode and telephone number. Using what you know about the multi-store model what advice can you give him?** **3 MARKS**

EXAM HINT
Key things include: the capacity of STM is limited; and, to transfer information to LTM, rehearsal is needed. Both of these can be used to answer this question.

AO ADVICE
Note that this question requires you to apply your knowledge. Make sure you do this in terms of Palwinder needing to learn his postcode and telephone number and don't make the mistake of writing in general rather than about the situation.

The multi-store model and research that supports it have shown that the capacity of memory is very limited to 7+/–2 items. The number of digits in Palwinder's new telephone number and postcode will exceed the average seven items that can be held. So what he needs to do is chunk the information together as this way more information can be held in his STM because each chunk counts as one item. For example, he can chunk the local dialling code into one number; similarly, the postcode is usually split into two chunks of information. The other thing he can do is make sure he rehearses his new number and postcode because, according to the multi-store model, this is the best way to transfer the information to LTM.

The working memory model

Definition question

> **?** Explain what is meant by the term the working memory model. **3 MARKS**

Working memory model: A model of memory proposed by Baddeley and Hitch as an alternative to the multi-store model. The model consists of a central executive (an attentional system, which has limited capacity, and which is involved in decision-making), together with two slave systems (the phonological loop, and visuo-spatial sketchpad). This model is concerned with both active processing and the brief storage of information, so in some ways it is a development of the concept of STM.

Essay question

> **?** Outline and evaluate the working memory model of memory. **8, 10, OR 12 MARKS**

Paragraph 1 AO1

The working memory model is a more sophisticated interpretation of short-term memory (STM) than the single store suggested by the multi-store model. According to the working memory model, STM is an active store made up of three components. The central executive is the organisational system and controls two slave systems, the phonological loop and the visuo-spatial sketchpad. The phonological loop processes auditory information, and so processes the information that we hear, and this information is saved in the phonological store, our "inner ear". The articulatory process allows us to sub-vocally (silently to oneself) process information, i.e. to use our "inner voice" to articulate information such as when reading. The visuo-spatial sketchpad processes visual and spatial information and so is also known as our "inner eye". Research that illustrates the model used the dual-task technique (Hitch & Baddeley, 1976). This technique involved two tasks that either made use of 1) the same component or 2) different components of working memory. Task performance was only inhibited when both tasks involved the central executive and both tasks were performed well when they used different components. The fact that two tasks can be performed simultaneously without inhibiting performance when different systems are used supports the multi-system structure suggested by the working memory model.

Paragraph 2 AO2

A negative criticism of the working memory model includes the fact that not a great deal is known about the central executive—it is difficult to verify an abstract concept. It is probably an over-simplification to see the central executive as one system. Only the phonological loop has been explored in any detail and so research is lacking on the visuo-spatial sketchpad and the central executive. This means the model is descriptive, not explanatory, because it does not fully explain how the multi-systems work. A key strength of the model is that the working memory model provides a less reductionist interpretation of STM than that proposed by the multi-store model because the working memory model accounts for STM as an active processor and a multiple system whereas the multi-store model suggests it is a single, passive store. It has face validity because it makes sense that different types of information (e.g. visual, auditory) should be processed by different systems. There are also practical applications of the model because it helps to explain verbal reasoning, mental arithmetic, reading, and planning, and so can help support the development of these abilities. However, it is logical to hypothesise that there would be additional slave systems to process input from the other senses as well as visual and auditory information.

Recognition questions

? Label the diagram of the working memory model below. **3 MARKS**

? Four of the following statements describe the different components of the working memory model. Decide which component the statement relates to and record the corresponding letter in the table below. **4 MARKS**

A   This is known as the "inner voice" because it involves the articulation of auditory information.

B   This is known as the "inner eye" because it involves the processing of visual and spatial information.

C   This is the capacity of memory because it refers to how much information can be held in memory.

D   This is known as the "inner ear" because it stores the sound of the information temporarily.

E   This component controls the other two slave systems.

Component of working memory	Letter/description
Central executive	_E_
Visuo-spatial sketchpad	_B_
Articulatory process	_A_
Phonological store	_D_

Application of knowledge question

> **?** Alex is drawing and listening to music at the same time, whereas Tom is listening to music and reading. Alex's drawing is very impressive and she is pleased with it whereas Tom's recall of what he has been reading is less so. Use the working memory model to explain these findings. **5 MARKS**

EXAM HINT
In this question you need to refer to the different components of working memory to explain why Alex is having more success multi-tasking than Tom. Using the components provides you with the detail needed for 4 marks. This question requires you to apply your knowledge to the stimulus so make sure you do this rather than describing working memory in general.

Alex and Tom are both multi-tasking and using components of their working memory. Alex's drawing will mainly rely on the visuo-spatial sketchpad because this slave system is used to process visual and spatial information. The music she is listening to will be processed by the phonological loop because this slave system processes auditory information. First she will process the information using her "inner ear" or phonological store, she may also be singing along to the music either aloud or sub-vocally (silently to herself) and this will involve the "inner voice" or articulatory process. This means Alex is using the two different slave systems. We know from research using the dual-task technique that performance is not inhibited on two tasks if they use different components of working memory, and so this explains why she is pleased with the progress of her drawing. In contrast, Tom will process the music in the same way as Alex but will also rely on the phonological loop whilst reading as he is also likely to use the articulatory process to sub-vocally say what he is reading. Working memory has difficulty performing two tasks successfully when they both use the same component and so Tom's performance is inhibited and this explains why his recall of what he has read is not that good.

MEMORY IN EVERYDAY LIFE

Research questions

Factors that affect eyewitness testimony: Age and anxiety

> **?** Outline the procedures of one study into a factor that affects eyewitness testimony (EWT). OR Explain how research into a factor that affects EWT has been conducted. **6 MARKS**

Loftus (1979) investigated the weapon focus effect by exposing participants to one of two conditions to show how anxiety is a factor that affects the accuracy of eyewitness testimony (EWT). Participants in the first condition overheard two people in a laboratory discussing the failure of an experiment in a neutral way and observed one of the people leaving holding a pen with grease on his hands. Participants in the second condition overheard an aggressive argument, crashing chairs, and breaking glass and observed one of the people leaving the laboratory holding a paper knife covered in blood. The participants were then given 50 photographs and asked to identify the man they had observed. Participants in the second condition were deliberately exposed to a more anxiety-provoking scene to see how their recall compared to participants in the low anxiety condition.

? Outline the findings of one or more studies into factors that affect EWT. 6 MARKS

Loftus (1979), in her study into the weapon focus effect as a source of anxiety, found a 49% successful identification rate in condition one, in which participants observed the man holding a pen with grease on his hands, whereas they found a lower 33% of correct identifications in the higher anxiety condition, in which the participants overheard an aggressive exchange and a man leave holding a paper knife with blood on it. Loftus's research found high levels of attention to (and good memory for) the criminal's weapon but not other information in the situation. The study found that anxiety in response to the weapon can have a negative effect on the accuracy of recall. Deffenbacher et al. (2004) researched the effects of high and low anxiety on eyewitness face identification and found that heightened anxiety and stress have a definite negative impact on EWT. They found an average of 54% correct identifications for low anxiety compared to 42% correct identifications for high anxiety conditions.

Essay questions

 Discuss research into age as a factor that affects the accuracy of eyewitness testimony.

8, 10, OR 12 MARKS

EXAM HINT

Note that paragraph 1 is also relevant to a short answer question that asks you to explain how age can affect EWT.

10-mark question: Leave out the description of the research from Wright and Stroud onwards and take out the criticism on demand characteristics.

8-mark question: Leave out the description of the research from Mueller-Johnson and Ceci onwards and take out the criticism on demand characteristics and reduce the content on positive applications.

Paragraph 1 AO1

Pozzulo and Lindsay (1998) carried out a meta-analysis combining the data from numerous studies on children and adults. They reported three main findings. First, young children up to the age of 5 were less likely than older children and adults to make correct identifications when the culprit was present in the line-up. Second, children over the age of 5 performed as well as adults at correct identifications when the culprit was present. Third, children up to the age of 13 were much more likely than adults to make a choice when the culprit was not present in the line-up. This may be because children are more affected by the social pressure to make a choice. Bruck and Melnyk (2004) suggest cognitive incompetence may explain the distortions of children. Young children may come to believe their own distorted memory reports because of limitations in processing, attention, or language. In their research they found that children continued to produce false memories even after having been warned that the interviewer may have been mistaken in his/her suggestions. This suggests that children are more suggestible than adult participants. Research also suggests that older eyewitnesses can be more easily misled. Mueller-Johnson and Ceci (2004) found that older adults (average age of 76) could be more easily misled about where on the body they had been massaged after a period of several weeks than younger adults (average age 20). Wright and Stroud (2002) found an "own age bias", where older and younger participants were more accurate at identification when the culprit was of a similar age to themselves. This suggests we pay more attention to the facial and other features of culprits the same age as ourselves.

Paragraph 2 AO2

A key weakness of the research is that the laboratory findings may exaggerate the inaccuracy of EWT. This may be due to the lack of mundane realism of the laboratory set-up. The event witnessed in artificial conditions will lack the emotional impact and stress of a real-life event and so recall may be less accurate. Therefore it is not a true reflection of EWT in real life, and so the findings lack external validity. Another factor is that the time eyewitnesses have is usually longer in real life than in the laboratory set-up, which may also affect recall and so not be true of real-life EWT. In the laboratory, participants know something is going to happen and so can focus, whereas eyewitnesses are taken by surprise in real life. Demand characteristics may play a part because participants may pick up on cues that they are expected to misremember and so the results lack internal validity. For example, demand characteristics rather than social pressure to make a choice may explain why children are more likely than adults to make an identification when the culprit is not in the line-up because maybe children respond more to the expectations of the researcher. The research into age has positive applications because it can be used to inform how to reduce the potential for younger or older participants to be misled. For example, Gross and Hayne (1999) suggest how the accuracy of EWT by young eyewitnesses can be improved through pictures. This is supported by their research findings, which showed that when children were asked to draw pictures about what they could remember about an event before being asked to provide a verbal report, the children who had produced drawings recalled about 30% more information in their verbal reports than did children who hadn't produced a drawing.

> **?** **Discuss research into anxiety as a factor that affects the accuracy of eyewitness testimony.**
> **8, 10, OR 12 MARKS**

EXAM HINT

Note that paragraph 1 is also relevant to a short answer question that asks you to explain how anxiety can affect EWT.

10-mark question: Condense the research by Deffenbacher et al. and end paragraph 2 with the point about the greater emotional impact of real-life EWT.

8-mark question: Leave out the research by Deffenbacher et al. and end paragraph 2 with the point about the lack of mundane realism.

Paragraph 1 AO1

Loftus et al.'s (1987) research on the weapon focus effect found high levels of attention to (and good memory for) the criminal's weapon but not other information in the situation. This shows that the anxiety caused by the presence of a weapon can further decrease the accuracy of EWT. Loftus (1979) presented a study in which some participants overheard an aggressive argument between two people followed by one of them emerging holding a paper knife covered with blood. Other participants overheard a harmless conversation between two people followed by one of them emerging holding a pen. When participants tried to identify the culprit from a set of photographs, only 33% of those in the weapon condition did so compared to 49% in the other condition. This shows the anxiety caused by weapon focus can decrease the accuracy of EWT. Deffenbacher et al. (2004) researched the effects of high and low anxiety on eyewitness face identification. They carried out meta-analyses combining findings from numerous studies on the effects of anxiety and stress on eyewitness memory. They found an average of 54% correct identifications for low anxiety compared to 42% correct identifications for high anxiety conditions. Thus, heightened anxiety and stress have a definite negative impact on EWT.

Paragraph 2 AO2

The research into the weapon focus effect is artificial because a weapon is completely unexpected in the laboratory set-up and this may have led to such a focus on the weapon, meaning the effect lacks validity in other contexts. It is possible that the weapon attracts attention because it is unusual (or unexpected) in most of the contexts in which it is seen by eyewitnesses, as well as because it poses a threat, and so we need to consider the context of where the weapon is seen. In support of this, Pickel (1999) found no evidence of weapon focus when eyewitnesses saw someone pointing a gun in a situation (a shooting range) in which guns are expected. Thus, the weapon focus has less of an effect if the context is where a gun might be expected. The importance of context is further supported by Valentine, Pickering, and Darling (2003) who considered the evidence from over 300 line-ups and found the presence of a weapon had no effect on the probability of an eyewitness identifying the suspect. This suggests real-life EWT has higher accuracy when a weapon is present than Loftus's findings suggest. The weapon focus effect found in the laboratory is limited to this setting and so the findings have little external validity. The lack of mundane realism of the laboratory set-up may explain why accuracy was greater in real life. In real life there will be greater emotional impact and stress, which may increase recall. The time eyewitnesses have to witness the event is usually longer in real life. Demand characteristics may play a part, participants being asked to see a video may pick up on cues that they are expected to misremember, and so the results may lack internal validity.

Application of knowledge questions

EXAM HINT

Don't make the mistake of focusing on which eyewitness is least reliable when the question asks you to consider which is most reliable.

> ❓ Two eyewitnesses of a robbery of a jewellery store have come forward; one of the eyewitnesses is aged 12 and the other aged 30. Use research to explain which of the two is likely to be the most reliable eyewitness. **5 MARKS**

The older eyewitness is likely to be considered as more reliable as there is evidence to suggest that younger eyewitnesses are more likely to make mistakes. For example, Pozzulo and Lindsay (1998) found that children over the age of 5 performed as well as adults at correct identifications when the culprit was present. However, children up to the age of 13 were much more likely than adults to make a choice when the culprit was not present in the line-up. The child eyewitness is age 12 and so falls into the category that is more prone to make a mistaken identification when the culprit is not present compared to adult eyewitnesses. This suggests the adult eyewitness will be more reliable that the child eyewitness.

Bruck and Melnyk (2004) provide further support that the older eyewitness is likely to be more reliable because they suggest younger eyewitnesses are more prone to cognitive incompetence and so may come to believe their own distorted memory reports because of limitations in processing, attention, or language. In their research they found that children continued to produce false memories even after having been warned that the interviewer may have been mistaken in his/her suggestions. This suggests that children are more suggestible than adult participants and so the older witness is likely to be seen as more reliable.

> **?** **Local residents of a small town are shocked by the crime wave that has overtaken their community. A number of houses and local businesses have had items burgled and the cashiers at the bank were subjected to a terrifying armed robbery. One woman, Jane, reported to police that she was so terrified she thought she was going to have a heart attack.**
>
> **What does research tell us about how Jane's anxiety may have affected the reliability of her eyewitness testimony?** **3 MARKS**

Loftus et al. (1987) have researched the effect of anxiety caused by a weapon. They found high levels of attention to (and good memory for) the criminal's weapon but not other information in the situation. This suggests that Jane's anxiety at the weapon used in the robbery will decrease the accuracy of her EWT. Loftus et al. (1987) found that participants who were witnesses to a scene with no weapon were more successful in identification of the culprit. This suggests that Jane's identification or photofit of the criminal, if she tries to give one, may not be that accurate.

Definition question

Eyewitness testimony: Leading questions

> **?** **Explain what is meant by the terms . . .** **3 MARKS**

EXAM HINT
You may be asked to define any of these Key Terms below.

Reconstructive memory: Reconstruction happens because we do not record things like a film and so reconstruction allows us to fill in the gaps in memory. Information from the to-be-remembered material and information from our knowledge and experience of the world are combined. Information based on our knowledge and experience of the world is contained in schemas, which are packets of knowledge. What often happens is that what we recall is not an accurate reproduction of the original material because our recall is distorted by our schemas, which have been used to fill in the gaps in our memory.

Eyewitness testimony: Evidence supplied by people who witness a specific event or crime, relying only on their memory. Statements often include descriptions of the criminal (facial appearance and other identifiable characteristics) and subsequent identification, and details of the crime scene (e.g. the sequence of events, time of day, and if others witnessed the event, etc.). There is good evidence that eyewitness testimony can be incorrect, because eyewitness memories of events tend to be fragile and easily distorted (e.g. be leading questions) and become reconstructed.

Leading questions: Leading questions are questions phrased in such a way as to lead witnesses to a particular answer, such as "Did you see THE broken glass?" instead of "Did you see ANY broken glass?" Such questions often include or imply the answer being sought. Another example would be Loftus and Palmer's (1974) study showing that speed estimates varied with the word (contacted, bumped, smashed, etc.) used in the question.

Research questions

> [?] **Outline the procedures of one study into EWT. OR Explain how research into EWT has been conducted.**
> **6 MARKS**

EXAM HINT
Loftus's research on leading questions seems the most appropriate if you are asked to describe a study into EWT. However, any study into EWT is appropriate including the one above on the weapon focus effect or you could use Loftus and Zanni's (1975) research on the effect of "the" versus "a".

Loftus and Palmer (1974) studied the effect of language on recall in eyewitness testimony. Forty-five American students formed an opportunity sample. Participants were shown seven short films, each showing a traffic accident. The films were taken from drivers' education films. After each film they were then asked to describe what had happened as if they were eyewitnesses. They were first asked to give a general account of what they had seen and then they were asked specific questions, including the critical question "About how fast were the cars going when they (hit/smashed/collided/ bumped/contacted—five conditions) each other?" This was a laboratory experiment with five conditions, only one of which was experienced by each participant (an independent measures design). Thus, the independent variable was the wording of the question and the dependent variable was the speed reported by the participants. The entire experiment lasted about an hour and a half. A different ordering of the films was presented to each group of subjects.

> **?** **Outline the findings of one or more studies into factors that affect EWT.** **6 MARKS**

> **EXAM HINT**
> Remember to compare the two key conditions "smashed" versus "hit".

Loftus and Palmer (1974), in their study into misleading information, found that estimated speed was influenced by the verb used. The verb implied information about the speed, which systematically affected the participants' memory of the accident. Those who were asked the question where the verb used was "smashed" thought the cars were going faster than those who were asked the question with "hit" as the verb. The mean estimate when "smashed" was used was 41mph, versus 34mph when "hit" was used. Participants in the "smashed" condition reported the highest speeds, followed by "collided", "bumped", "hit", and "contacted" in descending order. In answering the follow-up question, a higher percentage of participants who heard "smashed" said that they had seen broken glass (32%) than those who heard "hit" (14%) even though there was no broken glass.

How Science Works questions

? **Explain why studies of EWT have been criticised as lacking validity.** **5 MARKS**

The research into EWT has been criticised as lacking validity because it lacks mundane realism, as what the participants observed in the laboratory would not have had the same emotional impact as witnessing a real-life accident. It also differs from real life, in that the participants know that something is going to be shown to them, and so may pay full attention to it. In real life, eyewitnesses are typically taken by surprise and often fail to pay close attention. In real life they may have longer to observe the scene whereas the video clips shown in the laboratory happen very quickly. This means laboratory findings on EWT may not be true of real-life EWT. This is very evident in Loftus's research on the weapon focus effect as it has been shown that context is important because the weapon focus is less of a bias when the weapon is to be expected in the situation. The weapon focus effect may only happen because a weapon is so unexpected in the artificial laboratory setting, which means the findings are not representative of real-life events that involve a weapon. The findings lack generalisability and so external validity.

? **(a) Which research method is most commonly used to investigate eyewitness testimony?** **1 MARK**

(b) Give one strength and one weakness of this method. **2 + 2 MARKS**

(a) The method most commonly used by Elizabeth Loftus in her many studies of EWT was the laboratory experiment.

(b) A strength is the highly controlled environment of the laboratory allows for direct manipulation of the independent variable (IV) by the experimenter and this means cause and effect can be established, especially as other extraneous or confounding variables can be controlled. Causal relationships can be identified because, of all the experimental methods, this one provides the most confidence that the IV has caused the effect on the dependent variable (DV). For example, in her leading questions study, Loftus manipulated the verbs "smashed", "hit", etc. to test the effect on speed estimate. However, a weakness is that the laboratory is an artificial environment and consequently the research lacks mundane realism, i.e. it is not like real life. This means the findings may not generalise to settings other than the laboratory and so the research lacks external validity. For example, contradictory research suggests EWT in real life is more accurate than Loftus's research suggests, which may be because seeing a video clip of a car accident has less emotional impact and so is less memorable than seeing an accident in real life, or participants answer more carelessly than they would in real life.

Application of knowledge question

? **Identify which of the following is a leading question and explain why it is a leading question.**

A **"Did you see a child in the shop?"**

B **"Did you see the child in the shop?"** **1 + 2 MARKS**

EXAM HINT
You need to link this question to Loftus and Zanni's (1975) research.

AO ADVICE

The first mark is based on recognition of content and so is AO1. The second two marks are AO2 because explaining why requires you to apply your knowledge to a novel situation.

B is the leading question. This is because the definite article "the" is more misleading than the indefinite article "a" because "the" implies there was a child in the shop whereas "a" is not so clear-cut. "A" allows more for agreement or disagreement with the question whereas "the" leads the participant to answer "yes".

Essay question

? **Outline and evaluate research into eyewitness testimony.** **8, 10, OR 12 MARKS**

> **EXAM HINT**
>
> This answer focuses on Loftus's research into leading questions.
>
> 10-mark question: Condense the account of research by Loftus and Zanni (1975) to reduce paragraph 1 and condense the content on Yuille and Cutshall to reduce AO2.
>
> 8-mark question: Leave out the research by Loftus and Zanni (1975) to reduce paragraph 1 and leave out the content on Yuille and Cutshall to reduce AO2.

Paragraph 1 AO1

EWT is likely to rely on reconstructive memory (Bartlett, 1932) and this is one explanation for the unreliability as reconstruction involves filling in gaps in memory, and so the EWT account will not be 100% accurate. The language used in leading questions and post-event information may further distort the original memory and so lead to memory blending and confabulation (Loftus's research). Loftus and Palmer (1974) found that changing the wording of one critical question ("About how fast were the cars going when they (hit/smashed/collided/ bumped/contacted—the five conditions) each other?") posed to eyewitnesses of a car accident had a significant effect on the estimated speed of the vehicles. Further research on the effect of language (Loftus & Zanni, 1975) found that the definite article "the" was more leading than the indefinite article "a", as only 7% of those asked about *a* broken headlight said they had seen it, compared to 17% of those asked about *the* broken headlight, when in fact there was no broken headlight in the film.

Paragraph 2 AO2

Loftus's research on EWT has had a positive impact on police and court procedures, as it highlighted that leading questions should be avoided, and so the answer must not be implied in the question; and information should not be given away to the witness in questioning. The cognitive interview proceeds from a general account of what happened to open-ended questions to specific questions to minimise the potential for leading questions or post-event information. However, the validity of the above insights into EWT is questioned because the research was carried out in the artificial conditions of the laboratory and so mundane realism is low because laboratory experiments are not like real life. For example, video clips have less emotional impact than witnessing a real-life accident. This means the research findings lack generalisability to real-life EWT. Thus, the extent to which psychological research can improve the reliability of EWT is limited because of the methodological weaknesses of the research. The extent to which EWT testimony needs to be improved can also be questioned as real-life EWT has higher accuracy than the research would suggest. Yuille and Cutshall (1986) have found impressive accuracy in people's recall of the main events of a crime. Furthermore, research (Heath & Erickson, 1988) suggests that it is easier to distort minor details than key details. This raises further doubt as to how relevant the research is to real-life EWT, as the research tends to focus on insignificant details that can be easily distorted whereas key details are less likely to be as easily distorted.

Explanation questions

The cognitive interview

> **?** **How does the cognitive interview differ from the standard interview?** **6 MARKS**

The cognitive interview differs from the standard interview because it is structured in such as way as to limit the use of leading questions and the giving away of post-event information. Participants are first asked to give a general account of what happened because this open-ended questioning prevents the interviewer giving away post-event information or asking leading questions. The interviewer will then ask general questions based on the information that has been revealed and finally more specific questions, whereas the standard interview usually consists of specific, closed questions, which try to elicit facts but may provide information to the witness. The basic cognitive interview, unlike the standard interview, also draws upon cue-dependent theory because context reinstatement involves the witness recreating the environmental and internal (e.g. mood state) context. This means they may be asked to recall the weather, where they had come from, where they were going, and what they were thinking and feeling. Then the witness reports everything that comes to mind relating to the incident and then reports the details

EXAM HINT

You need to explain how the cognitive interview improves upon the standard police interview. Make sure you compare them because it is easy to make the mistake of just focusing on the cognitive interview.

in different orders and from various perspectives. For example they may be asked what somebody from another stand-point would have seen or to reverse the order of the event, so that these cues may trigger their memory, whereas the simple asking of questions in the standard police interview may not provide many contextual cues. Geiselman et al. (1985) compared the effectiveness of the basic cognitive interview with that of the standard police interview. The average number of correct statements produced by eyewitnesses was just over 10% better using the basic cognitive interview compared to the standard police interview.

EXAM HINT

Note how this question is not that dissimilar to the above question—you can bring out the same two strategies, structure and the use of cues.

> **?** **Identify and explain why two techniques in the cognitive interview improve the validity of EWT.**
>
> **2 + 2 MARKS**

(i) One technique used in the cognitive interview is the structure of the interview. Participants are first asked to give a general account of what happened because this open-ended questioning prevents the interviewer giving away post-event information or asking leading questions. The interviewer will then ask general questions based on the information that has been revealed, and finally more specific ones. This means the witness's account is less likely to be affected by the interview and so will be more accurate and have greater validity

(ii) Context reinstatement involves the witness recreating the environment and their mood when the event took place. This means they may be asked to recall the weather, where they had come from, where they were going, and what they were thinking and feeling, because these may act as cues and trigger recall. Reinstating the context is likely to trigger more accurate recall as the context provides cues and so the testimony is likely to have better validity.

Essay question

> **?** **Outline the cognitive interview and assess its effectiveness.** **8, 10, OR 12 MARKS**

EXAM HINT

10-mark question: To reduce AO1 leave out the last sentence on cue-dependent memory and in paragraph 2 condense the content on Fisher et al. (1990).

8-mark question: To reduce AO1 leave out the last two sentences on cue-dependent memory and in paragraph 2 leave out the content on Fisher at al. (1990).

Paragraph 1 AO1

The cognitive interview differs from the standard interview because it is structured in such as way as to limit the use of leading questions and the giving away of post-event information. Participants are first asked to give a general account of what happened because this open-ended questioning prevents the interviewer giving away post-event information or asking leading questions. The interviewer will then ask general questions based on the information that has been revealed, and finally more specific questions, whereas the standard interview usually consists of specific, closed questions, which try to elicit facts but may provide information to the witness. The cognitive interview also aims to minimise bias by encouraging free recall and encouraging the witness to report all details even if they seem trivial. The Home Office also advises not to delay EWT as this offers greater opportunity for reconstruction and the finding out of post-event information, which may distort the testimony. The basic cognitive interview also draws upon cue-dependent theory because context reinstatement is when the witness is asked to recreate the environmental and internal (e.g. mood state) context. This means they may be asked to recall the weather, where they had come from, where they were going, and what they were thinking and feeling. Cue-dependent memory is encouraged by asking the witness to mentally recreate the scene from different perspectives and in different orders, for example they may be asked what somebody from another stand-point would have seen, or to reverse the order of the event, so that these cues may trigger their memory.

Paragraph 2 AO2 with a little AO1 description of the enhanced interview

Geiselman et al. (1985) provide evidence for the effectiveness of the basic cognitive interview compared to the standard police interview. The average number of correct statements produced by eyewitnesses was just over 10% better using the basic cognitive interview compared to the standard police interview and so this supports the effectiveness of the interview method. However, the basic cognitive interview has been expanded upon. The enhanced cognitive interview (Fisher et al., 1987) has expanded upon the basic interview. Further techniques have been suggested, such as: distractions should be minimised; ask the witness to speak slowly; introduce pauses between questions; tailor language to the witness; follow response with interpretations; avoid interruptions; try to reduce witness anxiety; don't make judgmental or personal comments; and review the witness statement thoroughly. Fisher et al. (1987) found that the enhanced cognitive interview was more effective than the basic cognitive interview. Eyewitnesses produced an average of 20% more correct statements when given the enhanced interview compared to the basic cognitive interview. However, there were 28% more incorrect statements with the enhanced interview. However, Fisher et al.'s findings were obtained under artificial laboratory conditions. However, there is evidence that the enhanced interview is effective in real life as Fisher et al. (1990) trained detectives in the Robbery Division of Metro-Dade Police Department in Miami and found an average increase of 46% in the number of pieces of information elicited from eyewitnesses at interview. Where confirmation was possible, over 90% of these pieces of information were shown to be accurate. However, the Hawthorne effect may explain these improvements because interviewing techniques are being focused upon and so increased motivation may explain the improved performance.

Memory improvement

Essay question

> ❓ Discuss the usefulness of memory improvement techniques. **8, 10, OR 12 MARKS**

AO ADVICE

Note that discuss means both describe and evaluate and so as usual in the essay question you need an even proportion of both AO1 and AO2. Note that the content in the essay would also work for short answer questions. Paragraph 1 could be used if you are asked to outline memory improvement techniques and paragraph 2 could be used if you are asked to evaluate memory improvement techniques.

Paragraph 1 AO1

Memory improvement techniques are usually based on organisation and meaningful encoding, which means the information is related to prior knowledge, or the information is encoded with cues to increase retrieval. The method of loci is a visual imagery technique and involves associating to-be-learned information with a series of well-known locations. For example, 10 locations in the home could be chosen and the sequence of moving from one to the next should be obvious—for example, front door to entrance hall to kitchen to bedroom, and so on. It should be possible to move through these 10 locations in a consistent order without difficulty. Then 10 words or pieces of information can be associated with specific locations. For example, you could imagine bread in the kitchen and a candle in the lounge. The method of loci works because it provides a way to organise the information and uses pre-existing knowledge about sequences of locations, which allows the information to be encoded meaningfully and provides a detailed set of retrieval cues (i.e. the locations) to assist the memory. The pegword method is also a visual imagery technique in which you have to memorise 10 pegwords to rhyme with the numbers one to ten. For example, one = bun; two = shoe; three = tree; four = door; five = hive, etc. Then 10 unrelated words can be memorised by linking them to the pegwords. So if the first unrelated word is "boy" you could imagine the boy eating a bun. Organisation and mind-maps are also often used as memory techniques.

Paragraph 2 AO2

Evidence for the effectiveness of the method of loci is Bower's (1973) research in which he compared recall of five lists of 20 nouns. The group that used the method of loci recalled 72% of the nouns on average against only 28% for the group that didn't. The method of loci is so effective because it provides a way of organising random material in a way that makes use of pre-existing knowledge about sequences of locations and it provides a very detailed set of retrieval cues (i.e. the locations) to assist the memory. The technique has been criticised as lacking external validity because it has been suggested that it doesn't really work for more complex information and the word lists it was tested upon are not what we learn in everyday life. However, De Beni et al. (1997)

> **EXAM HINT**
>
> Try to include a general description of why memory improvement techniques work and some detail of specific techniques.
>
> 10-mark question: In paragraph 1 leave out the sentence, "The MOL works because . . ." and in paragraph 2 leave out the point about mind-maps and acrostics.
>
> 8-mark question: Condense the descriptions of how the techniques work and leave out the sentence, "The MOL works because . . ." in paragraph 1 and in paragraph 2 leave out content from, "This works for a list of unrelated words . . .".

provide contradictory evidence as they found it effective for a 2000-word story and so it does have some external validity. The method of loci is difficult to use if information is presented visually as this interferes with the visual imagery used in the technique and so this limits its usefulness. It is also less useful with abstract and complex/integrated information because it involves treating each item to be learned (e.g. words; facts) separately from the others. This works for a list of unrelated words, but is less effective if you want to integrate the to-be-learned information in some way. The pegword method also has questionable external validity because it can't be used with abstract information. The two techniques have limited applicability, so do mind-maps, or maybe acrostics, offer a better way to learn complex integrated information?

Application of knowledge questions

AO ADVICE

This question requires you to apply your knowledge to a novel situation and so tests your AO2 skills.

[?] **Georgia is struggling to remember the names of her new classmates. Suggest one memory improvement technique that she could use to help her do this and explain why it works.** **4 MARKS**

EXAM HINT
Remember to relate your answer to Georgia's situation rather than describing the technique in general. But do note how much of your answer can be drawn from the above essay, i.e. you can tailor the same information to different questions.

The method of loci is a visual imagery technique and involves associating to-be-learned information with a series of well known locations. So Georgia could select a number of locations in her home in a logical sequence of moving from one to the next—for example, front door to entrance hall to kitchen to lounge to bedroom, and so on. It should be possible to move through these locations in a consistent order without difficulty. Then each of her classmates can be associated with specific locations. For example, she could imagine so many in the kitchen doing different activities, like cooking, eating, or cleaning, and then more again in the lounge, reading, watching TV, listening to music, etc. The method of loci works because it organises the information and uses pre-existing knowledge about sequences of locations, which allows the information to be encoded meaningfully providing a detailed set of retrieval cues (i.e. the locations) to assist the memory.

> **?** **Karmvir is struggling to remember the anatomy of the skeleton—something he needs to learn as part of his training to be a doctor. Suggest one technique that he could employ to help improve his memory.**
> **3 MARKS**

EXAM HINT
Note that the technique needs to offer enough content for 4 marks, so select a technique that does give you enough to write about. The method of loci and the pegword techniques are the obvious choices as there is not a lot to write about the story technique. It would also be possible to use mind-maps but you would have to elaborate on how the mind-map could be organised.

Karmvir could use categorisation to help him learn the anatomy of the body. This means he could organise the to-be-learned information into categories, depending upon where they are in the body, so all of the backbones together, hip, shoulder, leg, arm, etc. The categories should then act as a cue as the bones will have been encoded in relation to the category and so remembering the category during recall will help trigger recall of the bones that fall within this category.

How Science Works questions

> **?** **Memory improvement strategies have been accused of lacking external validity. Explain why this might be the case.** **5 MARKS**

EXAM HINT
Think about why the techniques may be less useful when remembering information in real life.

A weakness of memory improvement strategies, such as the method of loci and the pegword method, is that they work best when learning lists of words, which is something that we rarely do in real life. The techniques are less effective with more complex and abstract information, which is more typical of the material we try to learn in real life, and so the generalisability of the techniques to real life is an issue. This means the techniques may not be as effective for tasks beyond the learning of unrelated words and so the techniques have limited usefulness with other types of information, which limits their external validity.

? A psychologist is testing which memory improvement strategy is more effective. One group is given the pegword method and another group is given the method of loci; both are given the same word list of 20 words.

(a) (i) Which experimental design is being used? **1 MARK**

(ii) Give a weakness of the experimental design. **3 MARKS**

(iii) How would you control for the weakness identified in (ii)? **3 MARKS**

(b) What should the psychologist consider when constructing the word list? **3 MARKS**

(c) What is the independent variable and what is the dependent variable in this study? **2 + 2 MARKS**

(d) How could the psychologist check if the results were reliable? **2 MARKS**

(a) (i) Independent measures design.

(ii) A weakness of the independent measures design is participant variables or individual differences because there are different participants in each condition. This means the results may be due to these individual differences, which would act as extraneous and maybe even confounding variables. For example, participants in one condition may be more intelligent than participants in the other condition, and so the results may be due to this rather than the memory improvement technique. This would limit internal validity as the study would not have measured what it set out to.

(iii) Random allocation controls for participant variables. This refers to how the participants are allocated to conditions in the independent measures design. As with the random sample it is best if every participant has an equal chance of being allocated to the condition. This reduces bias and minimises participant variation/individual differences because it ensures that they are randomly distributed, which increases internal validity. It minimises bias in the allocation process as this can lead to participants with certain characteristics being favoured for one condition over another, which would distort the findings.

(Note: Matched participants can also be used as a control. It's the same as independent but the participants are matched on key variables as determined by the nature of the study, in this case intelligence, and so this design controls for participant variables.)

(b) The psychologist would have to consider standardisation of the word list. If the test of recall is to be reliable, the words should be of similar level of difficulty to recall and so should have the same number of letters and be of similar familiarity, thus should be in common usage rather than less well known. Standardisation means the difficulty of recalling each word should be relatively consistent and it is this consistency that makes the measure of memory more reliable.

(c) The independent variable is the type of memory technique used: the pegword technique versus the method of loci.

(d) Reliability refers to the consistency of the research and this can be checked by seeing if the same findings are obtained when the two memory techniques are used again. So the reliability of the results can be checked by doing a test–retest. This involves testing once and then again at a later date, i.e. replication of the original research. The findings are compared for consistency using statistical analysis as consistency is an indicator of reliability.

DEVELOPMENTAL PSYCHOLOGY
Early Social Development

ATTACHMENT

Explanation questions

> [?] **Outline the behavioural theory of attachment.**
> **5 MARKS**

AO ADVICE

This is an "outline" question so requires AO1 content. You should aim to write about 85 words for a 5-mark question.

According to the behavioural explanation, attachment, like all behaviour, is learned from the environment. The attachment is learned through classical and operant conditioning. According to classical conditioning (CC), the child learns to associate the mother with food and the satisfaction of the hunger drive. Food is the unconditioned stimulus (UCS), which automatically results in pleasure, the unconditioned response (UCR). The mother, before CC, is a neutral stimulus. After CC she is associated with the food being the main provider, and so becomes the conditioned stimulus (CS) and pleasure in response to the mother is the conditioned response (CR). According to operant conditioning, the mother is a source of positive reinforcement because she provides food. The food is a primary reinforcer and the mother is a secondary reinforcer. The child is attached to the mother because she rewards the child with food and so there are positive consequences to the attachment.

EXAM HINT

Do make sure you have a clear understanding of the differences between classical conditioning (learning through association) and operant conditioning (learning through consequences) as these are often muddled up.

EXAM HINT

Think about if attachment is just based on food and the reductionism of the theory.

? Give two criticisms of the behavioural theory of attachment. **2 + 2 MARKS**

AO ADVICE

Criticisms are AO2 so make sure you include only evaluation and no description.

(i) Harlow's research with monkeys provides a criticism of the behavioural theory of attachment because it challenges "cupboard love" as an explanation of attachment—it shows that social interaction rather than food is an important factor in attachment. The fact that the deprived monkeys in Harlow's study preferred the substitute mother that provided "contact comfort" rather than food shows that the theory that attachment is based on food is too reductionist. Attachment is more complex than this and probably has a multiple basis.

(ii) Learning theory is a reductionist (oversimplified) explanation because it only accounts for one factor: learning. Its focus on nurture ignores nature (the influence of genes), yet babies may be "hardwired" to attach. Cognition is also ignored as learning theory only considers what is observable and measurable. These are significant omissions that make it a reductionist explanation.

EXAM HINT

Do make sure that you focus on evolutionary theory in its own right and not just the evolutionary aspects of Bowlby's theory.

? Outline the key features of the evolutionary explanation of attachment. **4 MARKS**

According to the evolutionary explanation of attachment, behaviours that are adaptive help us to survive and are selected into the next generation through natural selection, and so due to the universality of attachment we can conclude it is adaptive. If attachment is evolved then it is genetic, an inherited biological mechanism meaning that babies are "hardwired" to attach. Imprinting illustrates this as, according to imprinting, animals have an innate ability to recognise their caregivers. Lorenz showed that geese line up behind the mother because they imprint onto the first large moving object they see. Human babies may imprint onto faces and this may explain their preference for human faces. Imprinting must occur within a critical period. In geese it must occur within 36 hours and so there may be a fixed period during which attachment must occur.

? **Give two criticisms of the evolutionary explanation of attachment.** **2 + 2 MARKS**

EXAM HINT
Two different scientific criticisms are covered here. Be careful to make sure you write enough for two marks. A VERY common mistake is to state a relevant criticism but not elaborate it for the second mark.

(i) Evolutionary theory is post hoc; this means after the event because the theory was proposed after the time when our genes evolved. This means we do not have proof that natural selection actually happens; we can only assume that this is a valid explanation. It cannot be verified or falsified because there is insufficient evidence to do either. We cannot tell from fossils how they were attached, and so the theory has limited scientific validity because it cannot be tested. Therefore the evolutionary explanation has been criticised as mere speculation.

(ii) Extrapolation of research on imprinting and the critical period to humans is questionable because in animals attachment is mainly a biological process but in humans attachment is more complex and involves more psychological factors. Attachment is likely to be more than just imprinting in humans and so the research lacks generalisability to humans.

? **How does the behavioural explanation of attachment differ from the evolutionary explanation?** **4 MARKS**

EXAM HINT
Focus on nature versus nurture and the evidence versus lack of it for the theory.

The evolutionary and behavioural explanations differ in terms of the approach they take in terms of nature–nurture. The evolutionary approach takes an approach based on nature because it suggests that attachment is instinctive and so biological (nature), which differs from the behavioural approach that suggests that attachment is not biological but learned through life experience (nurture). Thus according to evolution, attachment is an internal genetic (and therefore innate) mechanism that is instinctive, whereas according to behaviourism, it is external, being learned from the environment, which is external to the individual. They also differ in the evidence for the theories as evolution lacks evidence because the theory is post hoc (made up after the event). This means we have to rely on fossils for evidence and these physical remains provide no real evidence of attachment behaviour. The behavioural explanation, however, takes a scientific approach and so is well-supported with evidence for classical and operant conditioning.

Recognition questions

EXAM HINT
Read carefully and tick the correct ones.

AO ADVICE
This question requires you to recognise and show understanding of content, and so assesses AO1.

? **Tick the two boxes below that relate to behavioural theory.** **2 MARKS**

Babies are "hardwired" to form attachment. ■

Attachment is learned through classical and operant conditioning. ✓

Attachment is monotropic. ■

"Cupboard love explains attachment; the mother is associated with food". ✓

? **Outline Bowlby's explanation of attachment.**
6 MARKS

EXAM HINT
You could be asked to outline this theory for 4 or possibly 3 marks, so do think about which bits you could leave out to shorten the answer, e.g. the internal working model and monotropy, and so leave out the last two sentences if 3 marks and just the last sentence if 4 marks.

Bowlby's (1951) explanation of attachment draws from the evolutionary and psychodynamic approaches, as he supports the evolutionary perspective that attachment is innate and adaptive. According to Bowlby, its main purpose is to provide safety and so promote survival, as the attachment acts as a "stay-close" mechanism where the mother is used as a secure base. Bowlby proposed that attachment is a biological mechanism and so it must occur within a critical period (7 months–2½ years). If an attachment has not formed within this time then it is unlikely to. Bowlby also proposed that the primary attachment provides the child with an internal working model (a template of expectations about relationships), which is based on the prototype of the psychodynamic explanation. He expanded on this with the concept of monotropy, which means that attachments form a hierarchy where the infant has one main primary attachment, and this is a special bond qualitatively different from all other attachments.

Essay question

> **?** Outline and evaluate *one or more* explanations of attachment. **8, 10, OR 12 MARKS**

AO ADVICE

Remember you need a 50:50 split of AO1:AO2 in the essay questions.

EXAM HINT

Any of the explanations can be used if the question does not specify which one but it is perhaps sensible to use Bowlby given that his theory provides such a lot to write about for the 12-mark answer, and it means you can focus on just the one theory.

10-mark question: For AO1 condense the description of monotropy and the last evaluative point about the contributions of Bowlby's theory.

8-mark question: Remove the description of monotropy and the last evaluative point about the contributions of Bowlby's theory.

Paragraph 1 AO1

Bowlby's (1951) explanation of attachment draws from the evolutionary and psychodynamic approaches, as he supports the evolutionary perspective that attachment is innate and adaptive. According to Bowlby, its main purpose is to provide safety and so promote survival, as the attachment acts as a "stay-close" mechanism where the mother is used as a secure base Bowlby proposed that attachment is a biological mechanism and so it must occur within a critical period (7 months–2½ years). If an attachment has not formed within this time then it is unlikely to. Bowlby also proposed that the primary attachment provides the child with an internal working model (a template of expectations about relationships), which is based on the prototype of the psychodynamic explanation. He expanded on this with the concept of monotropy, which means that attachments form a hierarchy where the infant has one main primary attachment, and this is a special bond qualitatively different from all other attachments.

Paragraph 2 AO2

The claim that attachment is based on evolution (survival) accounts for the intensity of mother–child bonds. However, weaknesses of the evolutionary explanation challenge Bowlby's theory because he draws heavily from evolution. For example, evolution is a speculative theory of attachment because there is a lack of evidence, i.e. we cannot tell from fossils how they were attached. Therefore the theory has limited scientific validity because it cannot be tested, and so the evolutionary explanation has been criticised as just being a story because it cannot be verified or falsified. On the other hand, a key strength of Bowlby's theory is that he introduced the idea that psychological and emotional care are as important for the child's mental health as vitamins are for physical health. The internal working model can be criticised for determinism because later relationships are not just a product of the first attachment. This ignores the individual's free will to overcome a poor early attachment. Schaffer and Emerson (1964) provide evidence of multiple attachments that may not be hierarchical because it is not always possible to identify which attachment is strongest. This contradicts monotropy, which states that the first attachment is more special than all the others. Monotropy may be valid for some but is not generalisable to all. Whilst Bowlby's theory has many negative criticisms, it has made important contributions to our understanding of attachments as the universal characteristics of attachment are consistent with the fact that we have all evolved in the same physical way, so it is logical to assume in the same psychological way too.

Recognition questions

? Tick the two boxes below that relate to Bowlby's theory of attachment. **2 MARKS**

Babies are "hardwired" to form attachment. ☑

Attachment is learned through classical and operant conditioning. ◼

Attachment is monotropic. ☑

"Cupboard love explains attachment, the mother is associated with food". ◼

EXAM HINT
This question is very straightforward but do double check that you have ticked the correct box!

? Concepts within Bowlby's theory are defined in the table below. Match the concept to the appropriate definition. **3 MARKS**

A Attachment occurs in a critical period

B Internal working model

C Monotropy

D Attachment is adaptive

EXAM HINT
Double check you have included the correct letters.

Definition	Answer
Attachments form a hierarchy.	_C_
Attachment must occur within a fixed period of about 3 years.	_A_
Attachment acts as a template for future relationships.	_B_

Types of attachment

Definition question

> **?** **Explain what is meant by the term attachment.**
> **3 MARKS**

EXAM HINT
You may be asked to define a key term. You do not have to write out the definitions word for word; just make sure you clearly communicate what the term means.

Attachment: This is a strong, reciprocal, emotional bond between an infant and his or her caregiver(s) that is characterised by a desire to maintain proximity. Attachments take different forms, such as secure or insecure. Infants display attachment through the degree of separation distress shown when separated from the caregiver, pleasure at reunion with the caregiver, and stranger anxiety.

Research questions

EXAM HINT
Ainsworth's Strange Situation test is the key research on types of attachment. Remember that even if the question is worded as it is in the second question it is the procedures that explain how attachment can be assessed.

> **?** **Outline the procedures of one study into individual differences in attachment. OR Explain how attachment type can be assessed.** **6 MARKS**

Ainsworth and Bell's (1970) study of individual differences in attachment using the Strange Situation test lasts for just over 20 minutes and was used on American infants aged between 12 and 18 months. It takes place in the laboratory and the method used is controlled observation. The Strange Situation consists of EIGHT stages or episodes as follows:

Stage	People in the room	Procedure
1 (30 seconds)	Mother or caregiver and infant plus researcher	Researcher brings the others into the room and rapidly leaves
2 (3 minutes)	Mother or caregiver and infant	Mother or caregiver sits; infant is free to explore

3 (3 minutes)	Stranger plus mother or caregiver and infant	Stranger comes in and after a while talks to mother or caregiver and then to the infant. Mother or caregiver leaves the room
4 (3 minutes)	Stranger and infant	Stranger keeps trying to talk and play with the infant
5 (3 minutes)	Mother or caregiver and infant	Stranger leaves as mother or caregiver returns to the infant. At the end of this stage, the mother or caregiver leaves
6 (3 minutes)	Infant	Infant is alone in the room
7 (3 minutes)	Stranger and infant	Stranger returns and tries to interact with the infant
8 (3 minutes)	Mother or caregiver and infant	Mother or caregiver returns and interacts with the infant, and the stranger leaves

There are two separations and reunions. Separation protest, stranger anxiety, reaction to reunion with the caregiver, and the infant's willingness to explore the environment are the key behaviours used to assess the security/insecurity of the attachment relationship.

> **?** **Outline the findings of one or more study(ies) into individual differences in attachment.** **6 MARKS**

Ainsworth and Bell's (1970) and Ainsworth et al.'s (1978) research into individual differences in attachment produced several important findings. There were considerable individual differences in behaviour and emotional response in the Strange Situation. Most of the infants displayed behaviour categorised as typical of secure attachment (70%), whilst 10% were insecure resistant, and 20% insecure avoidant. The securely attached infants were distressed when separated from the caregiver, and sought contact and soothing on reunion. They were easily soothed by the mother and happy to explore the environment using the mother as a secure base. Resistant attachment was characterised by ambivalence (conflicting emotions), both seeking and rejecting the caregiver on reunion. They were very distressed at separation but not easily comforted as they appeared angry with the mother. Avoidant attachment was characterised by detachment as the infants kept their distance and so the infants did not seek contact with the caregiver, they showed little distress at separation, little or no stranger anxiety, and little interest in the caregiver at reunion.

EXAM HINT

Ainsworth and Bell (1970) and Ainsworth et al. (1978) found clear differences between secure and insecure attachment, so detail these as the two individual differences.

? Outline two individual differences in attachment.
3 MARKS + 3 MARKS

(i) Secure attachment type is experienced by the majority of infants (70%). The secure attachment type is evident in a child's protest at separation, pleasure at reunion, and preference for the caregiver over the stranger. Also, they play happily in the mother's presence and are willing to explore the environment as they use the mother as a secure base.

(ii) Insecure attachments are experienced by approximately 30% of infants. Avoidant is the most common insecure type in Western cultures (20%) and is evident in children that are not distressed (little or no separation anxiety) when the mother leaves and show little pleasure when she returns. There is no preference for the mother as the infant's main behaviour is avoidance of both the mother and the stranger. The infant appears distant and detached.

? Give two differences between insecurely and securely attached infants. **6 MARKS**

EXAM HINT

When you read the research answers that follow on the next two pages note how this answer has drawn from this research and make sure you are clear on the differences between resistant and avoidant infants as these are often confused. Remember avoidant means to avoid, i.e. be detached from the caregiver.

(i) Responses to the caregiver: Secure infants show a clear prefer-ence for the caregiver over the stranger, which is evident in their distress when the caregiver leaves, and their stranger anxiety, whereas insecure infants do not have such a clear pref-erence for the caregiver. The contrast with secure infants is particularly apparent in the avoidant infants as there is no preference for the caregiver, they are not distressed when the caregiver leaves, and they do not show pleasure on her return. The resistant child shows ambivalence, which means mixed emotions to the caregiver, so that they are very distressed when the caregiver leaves and both seek the caregiver and push her away when she returns.

(ii) Separation anxiety: The secure infants show a moderate level of separation anxiety and so do show distress when the care-giver leaves, and their response to this falls somewhere in the middle between the two insecure attachment types. The avoid-ant child shows little or no distress at the mother leaving, whereas at the other extreme the resistant infant shows the greatest amount of distress of all three types.

? **Give two behaviours characteristic of an infant with:**

(i) **Secure attachment**

(ii) **Insecure avoidant attachment**

(iii) **Insecure resistant attachment**   **2 + 2 + 2 MARKS**

EXAM HINT

Draw once again from the findings of Ainsworth and Bell (1970) to answer this question. Note you can only comment on two behaviours, not all of the measures of attachment, so stranger anxiety has been left out in these answers. You do not need to write at length; be concise.

(i) Infants with secure attachment are confident exploring the new environment of the Strange Situation, using the mother or caregiver as a secure base. They show pleasure at reunion with the mother when she returns after going out of the room.

(ii) Infants with insecure avoidant attachment show little sepa-ration distress when the mother or caregiver leaves the room and do not seek comfort from her when she returns.

(iii) Infants with insecure resistant attachment show the highest levels of distress at separation from the mother or caregiver. When the mother returns to the room they both seek and reject her and so are not easily soothed as they remain angry at her absence.

EXAM HINT

The question is asking you to explain HOW the attachment type develops. The obvious choice is either maternal sensitivity or the temperament hypothesis.

? Explain why some infants have a secure attachment type and others have an insecure attachment type.

3 MARKS

Attachment type can depend on the caregiver's behaviour. The sensitivity hypothesis suggests that sensitive caregivers have secure infants and less sensitive caregivers have insecure infants. Sensitive caregivers respond accurately and consistently to their child's needs whereas a less sensitive caregiver may be less consistent or may be less able to identify the infant's needs correctly.

Essay question

? Discuss research into types of attachment.

8, 10, OR 12 MARKS

EXAM HINT

Reduce the content on the method if the question is the shorter 8 or 10 marks, and focus on validity rather than reliability and validity for AO2. Note how paragraph 1 draws from the research answers above and paragraph 2 draws from the How Science Works answers below. So it's the same information being structured in a different way—keep in mind how similar questions may appear in different forms.

10-mark question: Condense the content on how the different types react. For example, leave out how they react to the stranger. To reduce AO2, leave out Wartner et al.'s evidence for reliability.

8-mark question: Condense AO1 by leaving out how the three types react to the stranger and condense the description of their reactions to separation and reunion. To reduce AO2 leave out the first section on reliability.

Paragraph 1 AO1

Ainsworth and Bell (1970) studied types of attachment through a test called the Strange Situation. The Strange Situation test is a controlled observation; it lasts for just over 20 minutes and was used originally on American infants aged between 12 and 18 months. It consists of eight stages or episodes and includes two separations and reunions with the caregiver, in this research the mother, and reaction to a stranger. The security/insecurity of the attachment is assessed through four measures: separation distress, stranger anxiety, reaction to reunion with the caregiver, and the infant's willingness to explore the environment. Ainsworth's research found the most common attachment type to be secure (70%), whilst 10% were insecure resistant, and 20% insecure avoidant. The securely attached infants were distressed when separated from the caregiver, and sought contact and soothing on reunion. They were easily soothed by the mother and happy to explore the environment using the mother as a secure base. Resistant attachment was characterised by ambivalence (conflicting emotions), both seeking and rejecting the caregiver on reunion. They were very distressed at separation but not easily comforted as they appeared angry with the mother. Avoidant attachment was characterised by detachment as the infants kept their distance and so did not seek contact with the caregiver, they showed little distress at separation, little or no stranger anxiety, and little interest in the caregiver at reunion.

Paragraph 2 AO2

The Strange Situation is easy to replicate and so the Strange Situation test has been repeated (test–retest) to see if the same attachment type is found in the same infant at different times; and if the distribution of attachment types is the same within and across cultures. Many studies have found similar results, suggesting the Strange Situation is a reliable measure of attachment. Replication tests reliability because if the attachment types are consistent then the Strange Situation is reliable. Wartner et al. (1994) provide evidence for the reliability of the Strange Situation as they assessed infants' attachment at the age of 12 months and then again at the age of 6 years. A significant 82% of the children remained in the same category over the 5-year period—this indicates great consistency. However, validity is not as well supported as reliability. We cannot be sure the Strange Situation provides a true (i.e. valid) measure of attachment type. First, the strange environment of the Strange Situation means the research lacks mundane realism and so the infants and caregivers may not have behaved as they would in real life, and so external validity is limited. External validity is an issue because the Strange Situation is an imposed etic; this means it imposes American standards of attachment (because that is where the test was devised) onto other cultures where the Strange

Situation test has been used. This means the research is ethnocentric (culture-biased). We cannot be sure of the real nature of how attachments vary across cultures. The mother may have experienced evaluation apprehension because she knew her child and her parenting were being assessed and so she may have interacted differently with the child, not showing her normal behaviour and so affecting the child's behaviour too. This means the research would lack internal validity because the research would not have measured what it set out to if the behaviour was not genuine. Validity is a further issue—Main and Solomon (1986) have suggested a further attachment type D (disorganised) because some infants cannot be categorised, which shows the original classification of just three types is too simplistic (reductionist), and so does not measure attachment accurately.

Explanation question

EXAM HINT

The differences in insecure attachment types across Western and non-Western cultures offer the clearest two cultural variations.

> **?** **Outline two cultural variations in attachments.**
> **3 MARKS + 3 MARKS**

(i) Avoidant insecure attachment behaviour is most common in Western cultures. This is linked to the individualistic nature of Western cultures, as the emphasis on independence may lead to infants being classified as avoidant. For example, Grossmann et al. (1985) suggest that it is because the German culture requires distance between parents and children and so "the ideal is an independent, non-clinging infant", which has been interpreted as avoidant attachment type, although this labelling may not reflect the actual emotional bond.

(ii) Resistant insecure attachment type is most common in non-Western cultures. This is linked to the collectivistic nature of these cultures. The emphasis is on extended kinship networks or an alternative collective as in the Kibbutz system in Israel, where children are cared for in communal childcare and parents are with their children for a few hours per day, meaning that children in these cultures rarely experience complete strangers. Their resistant behaviour is perhaps due to the absence of the familiar caregiver figure, plus the presence of the stranger, and so leads to the infants being classified as resistant.

Research questions

> **?** **Outline the procedures of one study into cultural variations in attachment. OR Explain how research into cultural variations in attachment has been conducted.**
>
> **6 MARKS**

EXAM HINT
The Strange Situation has been replicated across many cultures and the following meta-analysis of these findings provides a useful summary of cultural variations.

Van IJzendoorn and Kroonenberg's (1988) study of cross-cultural variation in attachment involved a meta-analysis that compared the findings of 32 studies that had used the Strange Situation procedure to measure attachment and to classify the attachment relationship between the mother and the infant. A meta-analysis is a tool that takes the findings from studies that have investigated the same area and identifies patterns in the results. Research from eight different nations was compared, including Western cultures (e.g. USA, Great Britain, Germany) and non-Western cultures (e.g. Japan, China, Israel). Van IJzendoorn and Kroonenberg researched various databases for studies on attachment that had used a similar method, the Strange Situation.

> **?** **Outline the findings of one or more study(ies) into cultural variations in attachment.** **4 MARKS**

EXAM HINT
Remember the universal findings about secure attachment as well as the differences.

Van IJzendoorn and Kroonenberg's (1988) study of cross-cultural variation in attachment found considerable consistency in the overall distribution of attachment types across all cultures. Secure attachment was the most common type of attachment in all eight nations. However, significant differences were found in the distributions of insecure attachments. For example, in Western cultures the dominant insecure type is avoidant, whereas in non-Western cultures it is resistant, with China being the only exception, as avoidant and resistant were distributed equally. A key finding was that there was 1.5 times greater variation *within* cultures than between cultures.

Recognition questions

? Complete the gaps in the following table on the characteristics of the types of attachment. **5 MARKS**

Attachment type	Separation anxiety	Stranger anxiety	Reaction at reunion
Secure	Show distress	_Some anxiety_	_Pleasure_
Insecure avoidant	_Little distress_	No interest	_Little interest_
Insecure resistant	Very distressed	_Very anxious_	Ambivalence

? The types of attachment are defined in the table below. Match the types of attachment below to the appropriate definition. **3 MARKS**

A Insecure avoidant

B Secure

C Insecure resistant

D Disorganised

Definition	Answer
The infant shows distress on separation from the caregiver but is easily soothed by her when she returns.	_B_
The infant shows no clear pattern of attachment behaviour.	_D_
The infant seems to be angry at the mother and so both seeks her and rejects her on reunion.	_C_

Application of knowledge question

> ? You have been asked to contribute to a website for new parents. Based on what you know about attachments what advice can you give for the nurturing of a strong attachment bond? **4 MARKS**

EXAM HINT
This question is asking you to apply what you know about attachment and so is more difficult than a question that just asks you to outline information. So do pause to think and don't write everything you know about attachment. Make sure it is appropriate, i.e. advice, not just information about attachment in general and that you write the right amount rather than too little or too much.

The key piece of advice is that you should respond sensitively and consistently to your child's needs because, according to the maternal sensitivity hypothesis, this is the best way to nurture a secure attachment bond. Bowlby's theory of attachment reveals that infants provide social releasers such as smiling, cooing, and crying to elicit care. So you need to monitor these social releasers and you will learn what your child needs. For example, your child may have different cries for food, a dirty nappy, or just wanting a cuddle. Research also shows that babies are more interested in people than in things, so this is an extra reason to talk to and play with them, and this is important as it will help them learn. Another piece of advice is not to worry and let nature take its course because, according to Bowlby, babies are programmed to attach and adults are programmed to care and so the development of a secure loving bond is a completely natural thing; so use your instinct and do what comes naturally.

How Science Works questions

> ? What type of observation was employed by Ainsworth in the Strange Situation test? Give one advantage and one weakness of this method. **1 + 3 + 3 MARKS**

EXAM HINT
The method is controlled observation and so the rest of the answer is a straightforward evaluation of this method.

AO ADVICE
Methodology questions all count as AO3.

Controlled observation is the method used, which has the advantage that richer and more complete information is often obtained than from experiments in which participants produce limited responses. This is true of the Strange Situation because a range of behaviours were observed to categorise attachment whilst the child was with the mother (caregiver), when she leaves, when a stranger is present, and when the mother returns. However, a weakness is the artificiality of the situation may make it hard to generalise the findings to more natural situations. The strange environment of the Strange Situation may mean that the behaviour was not true of the infants' and caregivers' normal behaviour and so the study may lack external validity and generalisability to real-life settings.

EXAM HINT
Remember reliability means consistency.

> **?** How can the reliability of the Strange Situation be tested? **2 MARKS**

Replication tests reliability because if the attachment types are consistent then the Strange Situation is reliable. A test–retest can be performed by repeating the Strange Situation to see if the same attachment type is found in the same infant at different times, for example, 12 months and 6 years old, and if the distribution of attachment types is the same within and across cultures.

EXAM HINT
You need to think about what limits the truth of the attachment types (internal) and why they may lack generalisability (external validity).

> **?** Why has the Strange Situation been accused of lacking validity? Refer to both internal and external validity. **6 MARKS**

The strange environment of the Strange Situation may mean that the behaviour was not true of the infants' and caregivers' normal behaviour, which means the results may not generalise to real life and so this limits external validity. The mother may have experienced evaluation apprehension as she knew her child was being assessed, and so interacted differently with the child, not showing her normal behaviour and so affecting the child's behaviour too. This means the attachment type measured may not be true and so the research would lack internal validity. External validity is also an issue because the Strange Situation was developed in America and therefore reflects that culture's norms and values, meaning it acts as an imposed etic when it is used to assess attachment in other cultures. It imposes American standards of attachment and so the research is ethnocentric (culture-biased). We cannot be sure of the real nature of how attachments vary across cultures. The cross-cultural findings that China has the highest rate of insecure attachment and that other Eastern cultures have a higher rate of resistant attachment compared to Western cultures may not be valid because the Strange Situation may not be a valid measure of attachment in these cultures. Validity is a further issue. Main and Solomon (1986) suggested a further attachment type D (disorganised) as some infants cannot be categorised into the original three types, which shows the classification is too simplistic (reductionist) and so lacks internal validity because the original three types of attachment lack accuracy.

? **Explain how the artificiality of the Strange Situation procedure might affect the validity of the attachment types.** **4 MARKS**

EXAM HINT
This is quite similar to the question above—note how the content overlaps, which means less for you to learn! You just need to be able to extract and apply the same content to different questions.

The strange environment, the laboratory setting, and the presence of the stranger in the Strange Situation mean that the situation is artificial and so the behaviour shown may not be true of the infants' and caregivers' normal behaviour in their everyday environment. This means the results may not generalise to real life and so limits external validity. The artificial situation and assessment taking place may have led the mother to experience evaluation apprehension (fear about how she and her child would be assessed) and so she may have interacted differently with the child, for example she may have been more attentive to her baby than she might normally be. This means the attachment type measured may not be true and so the research would lack internal validity.

? **(a) Why might demand characteristics have limited the validity of Mary Ainsworth's research into the types of attachment?** **3 MARKS**

(b) How can the researcher control for demand characteristics in research? **3 MARKS**

EXAM HINT
This question is very specific; it is asking you to consider how cues in the research may have been given away that affected the participants' behaviour. For (b) remember standardisation is a very useful control.

(a) The mothers may have tried to guess what the researchers were looking for. Almost certainly they would have realised their interactions with their child were being assessed in some way and so they may have changed their behaviour and so perhaps been more attentive to the baby than they might normally be and so the researchers might not be able to measure what they wanted to measure, i.e. the attachment, therefore the internal validity of the research is reduced.

(b) Standardised instructions can be used to control for demand characteristics because these limit any cues being given to the participants as the researcher will have planned in advance and written down exactly what will be said. If the participants are given them to read this also controls for the tone of voice acting as a cue. In observations the only way to limit demand characteristics might be to do natural observations, but this then brings in ethical concerns.

EXAM HINT
The most obvious problem is the classification system itself because this may lack validity.

? **Explain one difficulty psychologists may have in assessing attachment type.**   **2 MARKS**

One difficulty is that the classification system proposed by Ainsworth is too simplistic because there are only three types and it may not be possible to categorise attachment into only three types. In fact, Main and Solomon (1986) suggest a fourth type, type D, disorganised attachment, because some infants do not show any clear pattern of behaviour, thereby making it difficult to assess their attachment type.

EXAM HINT
The obvious issue is the distress of the infants; which ethical guideline does this relate to?

? **(a) Why does the Strange Situation procedure raise ethical issues?**   **4 MARKS**

(b) What justifications can be made for the research?
3 MARKS

(a) Protection of the participants is an issue because the unfamiliar environment of the Strange Situation, separation from the mother, and presence of the stranger are distressing for infants and they should be protected from this. Nowadays UK researchers have to ensure no more stress than everyday stress should occur, but if a child has never been left alone in a strange place or with a stranger then the child's stress is likely to be great. This raises the issue of protection of participants from psychological harm. Informed consent is another issue because the child is unable to understand the true nature of the research and so cannot give this and if the mother knows the purpose of the research she may not behave normally. It is also questionable whether the mother would know just how distressing the procedure may be for the child and so her consent in locus parentis may not be fully informed.

(b) The research can be justified in spite of the issue of protection from psychological harm because it can be argued that any distress only lasted as long as the duration of the study; there would be no long-lasting effect on the infants, and so they would have left the experiment in the same psychological state that they arrived in. Another justification is that the brief separations from the caregiver and interactions with strangers are no different from those experienced by many babies if they enter day care and so the procedure is not that different from the level of stress they would experience in everyday life. Some would also argue that the importance of understanding attachment outweighs the relatively minor ethical concerns, so the findings justify the means.

> **?** **Psychologists have identified the importance of maternal sensitivity in the formation of secure attachment. Mothers and children at a playgroup were rated by observers for both maternal sensitivity and how secure the attachment was and the results were correlated as displayed in the graph below.**

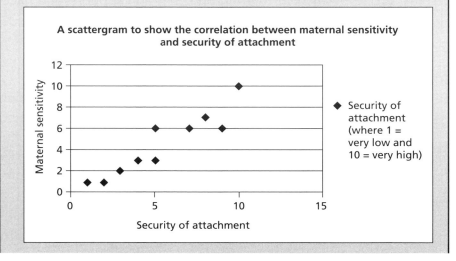

A scattergram to show the correlation between maternal sensitivity and security of attachment

Maternal sensitivity (y-axis)

Security of attachment (x-axis)

◆ Security of attachment (where 1 = very low and 10 = very high)

(a) What sort of graph is this? **1 MARK**

(b) What sort of correlation is shown on the graph? **2 MARKS**

(c) What can you conclude from the findings shown on the graph? **2 MARKS**

(d) Identify the two variables being studied. **1 + 1 MARKS**

(e) For behaviour to be genuine it would help if the participants were not aware they were being observed. Suggest two ways the researchers could have carried out the study without the participants being aware it was taking place. **2 MARKS**

(f) What ethical issues would arise from carrying out the observation in a covert way and how could these issues be resolved? **3 + 3 MARKS**

(a) Scattergram.

(b) The scattergram shows a strong correlation because the points on the graph nearly form a straight line, and so they show a correlation of approximately 0.7. It's a positive correlation because both variables rise and fall together.

(c) The strong positive correlation on the graph supports the background theory that maternal sensitivity is linked to secure attachment, and so it can be concluded that training parents to show sensitivity will increase the emotional security of their children.

(d) Maternal sensitivity and secure attachment.

(e) The researcher could film the playgroup session using a hidden camera so that the participants were not aware they were being studied. Or they could pretend to be one of the mothers in the group. This is called participant observation because the researcher joins the participant group being studied so that again the participants would not realise they were being studied.

(f) Deception is an issue because if a hidden camera or participant observation was used then the participants would not even know they were taking part in research, and deception should be avoided in research. The deception links to another issue. The participants would not be able to give informed consent, which they should give before the research takes place. To resolve these issues a debrief could be given in which the researcher explains the full nature and purpose of the research, and so this deals with the deception. They could also obtain retrospective consent after the debrief, during which the participants are given the choice to withhold their data if they are unhappy with any aspect of the research, and so this deals with the lack of informed consent. Deception involving children is a serious concern and the researchers' ethical committee and peers should give thought as to the rights and wrongs and costs and benefits of the proposed research. The parents or guardians of the children should be asked to provide consent on behalf of the children involved in the study.

Research question

Disruption of attachment and failure to form attachment (privation)

> **?** **(a)** Outline one study into the disruption of attachment (note this occurs when the child is separated from the caregiver during early childhood). **5 MARKS**
>
> **(b)** What are the weaknesses of the study you have described in (a)? **5 MARKS**

(a) Bowlby (1944) investigated disruption of attachment as he aimed to establish a cause and effect relationship between separation from the caregiver and emotional maladjustment. Eighty-eight children selected from the clinic where Bowlby worked formed an opportunity sample. Bowlby interviewed the children and their families. He compared the early life experiences of 44 juvenile thieves and 44 "controls" who had been referred because of emotional problems. Bowlby diagnosed 32% of the thieves but none of the controls as "affectionless psychopaths". Most of the 32% had experienced separation for at least one week before the age of 5. Bowlby concluded that the disruption of attachment caused emotional damage, which he called "affectionless psychopathy", characterised by lack of concern for others, lack of guilt, and inability

EXAM HINT

In this answer I have used Bowlby's study of the 44 juvenile thieves as a study of disrupted attachment. You could alternatively use Robertson and Bowlby's (1952) work on the short-term effects of separation.

to form meaningful and lasting relationships. He claimed that once the attachment bond was broken the negative effects could not be reversed or undone and so the lack of emotional development would be permanent.

(b) Rutter (1981) criticised the above research because Bowlby failed to distinguish clearly between deprivation (loss of an attachment) and privation (lack of an attachment). Many of Bowlby's juvenile delinquents had experienced several changes of home/ principal caregiver during their early childhood. This indicated to Rutter that their later problems were due to privation rather than deprivation and that this is a very different type of experience from deprivation. Another weakness is that Bowlby confused correlation with causation. The results are correlational and so we cannot prove cause and effect. Bowlby assumed that the early separation had caused the later disturbance, but many other factors could be responsible. For example, children from poor backgrounds are more likely to be hospitalised. Children from poor families are also more likely to become delinquent. Attachments may not be the cause, instead poverty may be. This means the research lacks validity because Bowlby did not measure what he set out to, i.e. the effect of separation on development, because other factors will have been involved.

How Science Works question

EXAM HINT
These are very precise questions about observation design so do make sure you know your non-experimental designs. You are not assessed for the quality of your written answer so don't worry about sentences—answer and move on to questions that require more time.

? A young child is experiencing disruption of attachment because his mother has been taken into hospital.

A psychologist has used naturalistic observation to assess the boy both before his mother was admitted to hospital and after she had returned home.

(a) How can the psychologist categorise the behaviour observed? **2 MARKS**

(b) How can the psychologist record the behaviour observed? **2 MARKS**

(c) How could the psychologist use content analysis to analyse the observation? **3 MARKS**

(a) The amount of crying when the mother leaves the room. How much the child clings to the mother.

(b) The psychologist can use a tally chart to record the observed behaviours, for example:

	Crying at separation	Clinging
Before hospital		
After hospital		

This compares the behavioural categories before and after the visit to hospital. The psychologist simply ticks the relevant box every time the behaviour is shown.

(c) Content analysis involves making qualitative data quantitative. The behavioural patterns observed are qualitative as they describe the behaviour in words. To make it quantitative behavioural categories are needed, as shown in the table above, and the researcher can quantify the data by counting the number of items that fall into each category.

Definition question

 Explain what is meant by the term privation.

3 MARKS

EXAM HINT

Another key term to learn. Remember you cannot define a term with the same term so you must move beyond privation to say what it means.

Privation means the lack of any attachments, as distinct from the loss of attachments (deprivation). This is due to the lack of an appropriate attachment figure and/or neglect so that a bond does not form between the child and caregiver. Privation is more likely than deprivation to cause permanent emotional damage or "affectionless psychopathy", the condition diagnosed by Bowlby as involving permanent emotional damage.

Research questions

? Outline the procedures of one study into failure to form attachment (privation). OR Explain how research into failure to form attachment (privation) has been conducted. **6 MARKS**

Hodges and Tizard's (1989) study into the failure to form attachment involved 65 children who had been taken into care before the age of 4 months who formed an opportunity sample. This was a natural experiment, using a matched-pairs design, as the institutionalised children were compared with a control group raised at home. It was a longitudinal study (age on entering care to 16 years). Each child had been looked after on average by 24 different caregivers by the age of 2. By the age of 4 years, 24 had been adopted, 15 restored to their natural home, and the rest remained in the institution. The children were assessed at ages 4, 8, and 16 on emotional and social competences through interview and self-report questionnaires. These included: an interview with the adolescent; an interview with the mother (and father in some cases); a self-report questionnaire concerning social difficulties; a questionnaire completed by their teacher about relationship at school; and the Rutter 'B' scale which is a type of psychometric test which identifies psychiatric problems such as depression.

? Outline the findings of one or more study(ies) into failure to form attachment (privation). **6 MARKS**

At age 4, the institutionalised children had not formed attachments. By age 8, significant differences existed between the adopted and restored children. At age 8 and 16 most of the adopted children had formed close relationships with their caregivers and were as attached as the control group; 17 out of 21 of the adoptive mothers felt their child was deeply attached to them. These attachments were closer than those of the children restored to their natural homes, i.e. the adopted group showed better emotional adjustment. There were no differences regarding the number of contacts with opposite-sex friends, or whether the 16-year-old currently had a boy/girl friend compared to non-institutionalised adolescents. However, the ex-institutional children had greater problems with siblings than did a comparison group, and negative social effects were also evident at school, as they were attention-seeking and had difficulty forming peer relationships.

Essay question

 Discuss research into failure to form attachment.
8, 10, OR 12 MARKS

> **EXAM HINT**
>
> Note how this draws from the research questions above. Be prepared to edit this version for the shorter 8- and 10-mark answers.
>
> 10-mark question: Leave out the last sentence of paragraph 1 to reduce AO1 and leave out some of the other factors in the last evaluation point of paragraph 2.
>
> 8-mark question: Leave out the last two sentences of paragraph 1 to reduce AO1 and leave out all of the content on other factors from Clarke and Clarke onwards.

Paragraph 1 AO1

Hodges and Tizard's (1989) research into the failure to form attachment involved 65 children who had been taken into care before the age of 4 months who formed an opportunity sample. This was a natural experiment, using a matched-pairs design, as the institutionalised children were compared with a control group raised at home. It was a longitudinal study (age on entering care to 16 years). Each child had been looked after on average by 24 different caregivers by the age of 2. By the age of 4 years, 24 had been adopted, 15 restored to their natural home, and the rest remained in the institution. The children were assessed at ages 4, 8, and 16 on emotional and social competences through interview and self-report questionnaires. At age 4, the institutionalised children had not formed attachments. By age 8, significant differences existed between the adopted and restored children. At age 8 and 16 most of the adopted children had formed close relationships with their caregivers and were as attached as the control group; 17 out of 21 of the adoptive mothers felt their child was deeply attached to them. These attachments were closer than those of the children restored to their natural homes, i.e. the adopted group showed better emotional adjustment. However, the ex-institutional children had greater problems with siblings than a comparison group, and negative social effects were also evident at school, as they were attention-seeking and had difficulty forming peer relationships.

Paragraph 2 AO2

Hodges and Tizard's study has positive implications because it shows that the critical period for attachment (a period of 7 months to 3 years when attachment must be formed) may not be so critical as the long-term effects of privation/institutionalisation can be reduced. This contradicts a critical period because institutionalised children did form attachments after the age of 4 years. Thus, a sensitive period rather than a critical period may be more accurate and this is positive as it provides more hope that the effects of poor early care can be overcome. However, the research findings on failure to form attachment are contradictory, i.e. do not show a reliable (consistent) effect. For example, the case studies of privation, such as Genie, support the argument that the effects of privation are irreversible. These case studies provide weak evidence because the sample sizes mean the generalisability of such studies is limited. Another weakness is the lack of control the case studies have because the children have usually not just experienced privation or failure to form attachment but also physical maltreatment and/or social isolation and/or lack of stimulation as well. This means any effects are not just due to emotional privation, and so the research lacks validity because we cannot conclude privation alone has caused the effects. The multiple outcomes of failure to form attachment can be linked to the weakness of the correlational method. First, there is the issue of cause and effect: because privation cannot be manipulated, we cannot conclude that privation has caused any effects and so conclusions are limited to associations. Second, there are other factors other than privation that influence later social development. Clarke and Clarke (1998) emphasise: the importance of middle and later childhood, so not just early childhood needs to be considered; individual differences in the resilience of the child; length of privation; and quality of subsequent care. These many factors show that the correlation between privation and later effects is too simplistic.

Recognition question

> **?** Privation or failure to form attachment is described in two of the statements below. Tick the two boxes below that relate to privation. **2 MARKS**

EXAM HINT
Remember privation means lack of attachment not loss of.

The lack of an attachment bond. ☑

The loss of an attachment bond. ■

Separation can break the attachment bond. ■

Neglect, abuse, or prolonged separation could explain why an attachment does not form between the child and the caregiver. ☑

Application of knowledge questions

> **?** A young child aged 4 has been found in a state of neglect and abuse. The mother is an alcoholic and the father rarely present. The child was left tied up in his bedroom for long periods of time, and shows no signs of attachment to the mother or father.
>
> Explain what the effects this failure to form attachment is likely to have had on the child's emotional development. **4 MARKS**

EXAM HINT
This could have been referring to disruption of attachment or failure to form attachment. That is until the last sentence, which makes it clear this question is about failure to form attachment (privation). Make sure you do accurately distinguish between these two types of experience when deciding what the question is looking for.

Privation is more likely than separation/deprivation to cause permanent emotional damage or "affectionless psychopathy", the condition diagnosed by Bowlby as involving poor emotional development. It is characterised by a lack of concern for others, a lack of guilt, and inability to form meaningful and lasting relationships. The extent of the effects of privation is partly determined by the length of the privation and whether it extends beyond Bowlby's critical period (7 months–2½ years). Hodges and Tizard (1989) found that some, although not all, of the effects of early privation were reversible with good subsequent care, as the children attached to their foster families, and so this indicates that privation does not necessarily have permanent effects. There are multiple outcomes that depend on the severity of the privation, the quality of subsequent care, and resilience of the individual child.

EXAM HINT
This question is asking you to compare two very different experiences, i.e. having attachment and losing it versus never having it in the first place.

? **Emily has been affected by the early death of her mother. Charlie has been in and out of care homes and so has no constant attachment figure. Using the concepts disruption of attachment and failure to form attachment, explain which of these experiences is likely to have the most severe long-term effects.** **4 MARKS**

Emily has experienced loss and so disruption of attachment, whereas Charlie lacks an attachment and so has experienced failure to form an attachment. Because he has had no constant caregiver he is unlikely to have formed an attachment bond. According to Bowlby, disruption to the attachment through separation from the caregiver, particularly within the critical period of 7 months to 2½ years, can lead to social and emotional problems. Both of these experiences can lead to poor emotional development or "affectionless psychopathy", the condition diagnosed by Bowlby as involving permanent emotional damage. It is characterised by a lack of concern for others, a lack of guilt, and inability to form meaningful and lasting relationships. The failure to form an attachment is more likely to have severe long-term effects because never having an attachment and so having no internal working model of attachment is more severe than having an attachment and losing it. The latter is very distressing but at least the internal working model will have formed and so Emily is more likely to have healthier emotional development than Charlie.

> **?** In Africa many children have been orphaned by the
> AIDS epidemic. Often they have no family left willing
> or able to care for them.
>
> **(a)** Using your knowledge of disruption and failure to
> form attachment explain how being orphaned
> might affect these children's development.
> **6 MARKS**
>
> **(b)** To what extent might the children recover from
> being orphaned? **4 MARKS**

EXAM HINT
Note that the effects on development are variable as it depends at what age the children were orphaned, whether they had formed a bond with the caregiver, or whether the illness prevented this. So do consider the variability of outcomes in your answer. Also note that even if you go wrong on (a) you could still get marks on (b). So you can earn marks even if you have made a mistake. Use research in (b) to support how the negative experiences can be overcome.

(a) The effect of being orphaned will vary depending on the age of the child and the amount of caregiving they had prior to the illness of the caregiver. These factors will determine whether an attachment formed. If the illness meant that little caregiving was provided it's likely that no real attachment bond was formed, meaning a failure to form attachment. If there was caregiving, the death could mean a disruption to the attachment. According to Bowlby, disruption to the attachment through separation from the caregiver can lead to social and emotional problems. Both disruption and failure to form attachment can lead to "affectionless psychopathy", a condition of permanent emotional damage, characterised by a lack of concern for others, a lack of guilt, and inability to form meaningful and lasting relationships. The children who have experienced failure to form an attachment are more likely to have severe long-term effects because never having an attachment and so having no internal working model of attachment is more severe than having an attachment and losing it. The children who were able to form a close bond with the caregiver before he/she became sick will have an internal working model and are likely to have healthier emotional development and be able to form future relationships.

(b) Research by Hodges and Tizard (1989) into institutionalised children who experienced failure to form an attachment until after the age of 4 showed that they were able to overcome this and form meaningful relationships with their foster parents. This suggests that the children who failed to form an attachment will be able to recover from this bad experience, which means that so should those with disrupted attachment as this is not as damaging an experience as privation. Rutter concluded from his Isle of Wight study that divorce was four times more likely to lead to maladjustment than separation as a result of physical illness or death of the mother. This suggests that the death need not cause permanent damage to the children's development; whether it does or not will depend very much on the quality of the care received both before and after the death, as shown by the children in the Hodges and Tizard study who recovered because they had loving foster parents.

How Science Works questions

EXAM HINT

External validity is limited by the small samples, and internal validity is limited by the lack of control and retrospective nature of the studies.

? **Explain why the research into failure to form attachment can be criticised as lacking validity.** **4 MARKS**

Much of the research into failure to form attachment has been based on single case studies due to the ethical impossibility of manipulating privation and this means the research lacks external validity. The findings do not necessarily generalise to other case studies of privation because case studies are highly specific and so the nature and effects of privation will be very different across case studies. Another weakness is the lack of control the case studies have because the children have usually not just experienced privation or failure to form attachment but also physical maltreatment and/or social isolation as well. This means any effects are not just due to emotional privation and so the research lacks validity. Another issue is that case studies are retrospective and so involve looking backwards into the individual's past, which can lack validity as the individual's recall may lack accuracy due to reconstructive memory.

EXAM HINT

A straightforward question for (a) asking you to analyse a research method. You should know two strengths and two weaknesses of each method just in case you are asked for two strengths or two weaknesses instead of one of each.

? **Research into failure to form attachment consists of a number of case studies such as Genie and the children of the Holocaust.**

(a) Give one advantage and one weakness of the case study method. **2 + 2 MARKS**

(b) What sort of data do case studies yield? Explain why it is this form of data. **2 MARKS**

(a) An advantage of the case study method is that it can provide far more in-depth information about a specific individual than is usually obtained from studies involving groups of individuals. For example, very detailed information about Genie's intellectual and social development was obtained over a period of several years. A key weakness is the issue of generalisability. The case study involves a very small sample and so the individual is not likely to be representative of individuals of the same age and gender. Even if the individual studied is representative, it is unlikely that they are representative of a wider population. This means conclusions cannot be drawn about the wider population and so external validity is limited.

(b) Qualitative data is obtained from case studies because they consist of a number of clinical interviews with the subject, and so the data provided is words, which cannot easily if at all be quantified.

Research questions

Institutionalisation

> **?** Outline what research has shown about the effects of institutionalisation. **5 MARKS**

Many studies have shown that institutionalisation can have a damaging effect. Rutter and the ERA Study Team (1998) followed 111 Romanian orphans adopted in the UK before the age of 2. When the orphans first arrived in the UK they were physically and mentally underdeveloped, which shows the immediate effects of being raised in an institution. This research also shows that the effects can be long-term because even when adopted out of the institution some did not recover fully if they were adopted at an older age. Similarly, O'Connor et al. (2000) studied Romanian children exposed to very severe deprivation and neglect in Romania before being adopted by caring British families. They compared those children adopted between 24 and 42 months (late-placed adoptees) and those adopted between 6 and 24 months (early-placed adoptees). Both groups showed significant recovery from their ordeal in Romania. However, the late-placed adoptees had greater difficulty in achieving good cognitive and social development than early-placed adoptees.

EXAM HINT
There have been a number of studies into Romanian orphans and how they recovered from this early experience once adopted.

EXAM HINT
Both methodology
and ethics provide
sources of evaluation.

? Evaluate the research evidence into the effects of institutionalisation. **6 MARKS**

A problem in assessing the improvements children make when they are removed from the institution is that the researchers such as Rutter have not been able to obtain much information about the conditions of the institution, and so it is hard to assess the extent of the privation and consequent recovery. Another issue is the lack of control in such research, which means cause and effect cannot be established. There is a lack of control because the effects of institutionalisation are not just due to the emotional privation: there may also be physical and social deprivation and a lack of stimulation, which will also contribute to the effects and so it is impossible to establish what caused what. The longitudinal nature of the research leads to another issue because often participants drop out; this is called sample drop-off, and this means the sample that is left is less representative and so the research has less validity. The fact that there is such sample drop-off raises ethical issues because it shows that some families would prefer not to have the intrusion of being in a research study and so researchers need to be sensitive to this and ensure that all participants are aware of their right to withdraw from the research.

Essay question

? Outline and evaluate research evidence into the effects of institutionalisation. **8, 10, OR 12 MARKS**

EXAM HINT
Simply combine the two above answers to get an essay answer.

10-mark question: Leave out the last sentence on the outline question to reduce AO1 and reduce the point about ethical issues to reduce AO2.

8-mark question: Condense the O'Connor et al. study and leave out the last point about ethical issues.

ATTACHMENT IN EVERYDAY LIFE

Definition questions

Day care

> **?** **Explain what is meant by the term day care.**
> **3 MARKS**

Day care is care, usually not in the child's home, that is provided by people other than the parent or relatives of the infant, for example, nurseries, childminders, play groups, etc. It is different from institutionalised care, which provides permanent substitute care; day care is a temporary alternative to the caregiver.

> **?** **Explanation question**
>
> **Give two effects of day care on social development.**
> **6 MARKS**

EXAM HINT
Note that one effect is on peer relations and the other on aggression. These are both identified in the Specification and various possible questions could be asked on these effects, so make sure you know these well.

(i) Shea (1981) found nursery has a positive effect on peer relations because it provides children with the opportunity to interact with their peers, which they may not have at home. Children's sociability increased during the first 10 weeks of nursery school. The physical distance between the children decreased, as did aggression, and there was an increase in play with peers and distance from the teacher. The fact that sociability was greater in those who attended nursery the most shows that this was responsible, not maturation.

(ii) Research also suggests the more time spent in day care the more aggressive behaviour is shown when the child goes to school. Bates et al. (1994) found that children who spent more time receiving any type of day care during their first 5 years of life had more behaviour problems, peer-rated aggression, and observed aggression than those receiving less day care.

EXAM HINT
Remember you only get assessed for the quality of written communication in the essay question(s) so you do not need long wordy sentences. Keep it simple and clear.

Research questions

? Outline research evidence into the effects of day care on peer relations. **6 MARKS**

Shea (1981) found nursery has a positive effect on peer relations because it provides children with the opportunity to interact with their peers, which they may not have at home. Children's sociability increased during the first 10 weeks of nursery school. The physical distance between the children decreased, as did aggression, and there was an increase in play with peers and distance from the teacher. He found that children who attended more regularly were more active, more sociable in that they went looking for people to talk to, and made more contact with others. The fact that sociability was greater in those who attended nursery the most shows that this was responsible, not maturation. Clarke-Stewart et al. (1994) studied 150 children between the ages of 2 and 3 and found more advanced peer relations in children who attended day care. Day care is beneficial because it encourages social learning (it provides more role models to observe and imitate) and the children have experience of coping with peers. They have more opportunity to acquire social skills such as how to negotiate, e.g. with their peers to get the toy they want.

? Outline research evidence into the effects of day care on aggression. **6 MARKS**

A number of studies have linked day care to aggression and behaviour problems. Research suggests the more time spent in day care the more aggressive behaviour shown when the child goes to school. Vandell and Corasaniti (1990) found that 8-year-olds who had spent their early years in day care were rated as more "non-compliant" by both their teachers and their parents compared to children who had spent less time in day care. Bates et al. (1994) found that children who spent more time receiving any type of day care during their first five years of life had more behaviour problems, peer-rated aggression, and observed aggression than those receiving less day care. Belsky (1999) found that more time in day care over the first five years of life was associated with more aggression and other behaviour problems. Belsky et al. (2007) have linked the aggression to centre-based care involving large groups of peers, suggesting that the size of the day care setting and amount of contact time with the carers are key factors linked to aggression. On the other hand, day care may decrease aggression because children in group day care have more opportunities to learn effective ways of resolving interpersonal conflict without resorting to physical aggression.

> **?** **Give three weaknesses of the research into day care.**
> **2 + 2 + 2 MARKS**

EXAM HINT
Each weakness is worth 2 marks so make sure you elaborate each one for the second mark.

(i) Day care research lacks control as day care cannot be manipulated as an independent variable. Consequently, cause and effect cannot be established which means we cannot conclude that day care causes effects on social development; associations only can be identified which limits conclusions on the effects of day care.

(ii) Children's social development is influenced by many factors, of which day care is just one, and so it is difficult to assess its overall effects. The type, quality, time spent in, and age on entering day care, as well as the quality of the home environment, all interact. These limit the validity of the findings because we cannot be sure if the effects are due to day care or something else.

(iii) Due to children entering day care so early the research is retrospective, not prospective, i.e. they are studied after they begin day care rather than before. It would be useful to compare children's physical aggression before they go to day care and during the period they go to day care. Without this comparison we cannot be sure if the aggression existed before entry to day care or if it is an effect of the day care.

Application of knowledge question

? Imagine you have been asked by a parent to advise them on what you know about day care and aggression. What advice would you give the parent? **5 MARKS**

Overall research suggests that quality of day care is the vital factor. Based on research by Belsky et al. (2007) that has linked aggression to centre-based care involving large groups of peers, I would advise the parent by suggesting that the size of the day care setting and the amount of contact time with the carers are key factors linked to aggression, and so a day-care centre where the children play in small groups with more carers would be preferable to a large group setting with fewer carers. I would also advise them that effects may be positive rather than negative because an NICHD study found that levels of assertiveness at 54 months were higher in children who had spent more time in day care. Thus, day care may be associated with assertive behaviour and so this is a positive effect.

Essay questions

? Outline and evaluate what research shows about the effects of day care on peer relations.
8, 10, or 12 MARKS

EXAM HINT
You may be asked about social development in general but equally it may specify just peer relations, so better to be ready for separate questions on peer relations and aggression.

10-mark question: Leave out Clarke-Stewart et al. to reduce AO1 and leave out the factors of high quality day care at the end of paragraph 2.

8-mark question: Leave out Clarke-Stewart et al. and condense the description of Shea et al. and leave out the last two sentences of paragraph 2.

Paragraph 1 AO1

A range of research suggests that day care can have positive effects on peer relations. For example, Shea (1981) found nursery has a positive effect on peer relations because it provides children with the opportunity to interact with their peers, which they may not have at home. Children's sociability increased during the first 10 weeks of nursery school. The physical distance between the children decreased, as did aggression, and there was an increase in play with peers and distance from the teacher. Shea found that children who attended more regularly were more active, more sociable in that they went looking for people to talk to, and made more contact with others. The fact that sociability was greater in those who attended nursery the most shows that this was responsible, not maturation. Clarke-Stewart et al. (1994) studied 150 children between the ages of 2 and 3 and found more advanced peer relations in children who attended day care. Day care is beneficial because it encourages social learning (it provides more role models to observe and imitate) and the children have experience of coping with peers. They have more opportunity to acquire social skills, such as how to negotiate, e.g. with their peers to get the toy they want.

Paragraph 2 AO2

The above research for positive effects is contradicted by the research evidence that day care can have negative effects on social development. There is no direct evidence that day care can have a negative effect on peer relations. However, Belsky and Rovine (1988) and Sroufe (1990) suggest that day care can increase the risk of insecure attachment with the caregiver and this in turn will affect the child's confidence and expectations when forming peer relations. However, the overall effects of day care are not clear cut because there are so many factors that affect peer relations and all interact, such as the type, quality, time spent, and age on entering day care, as well as the quality of the home environment and individual differences such as temperament of the child. These limit the validity of the research because we cannot be sure if the effects are due to day care or something else. These factors also mean that it is difficult to compare the findings of different studies because we are not comparing like with like. If the findings from one nursery where the home background of the children was very stimulating were compared with those of children from a disadvantaged background then conclusions could lack validity. Furthermore, as the research is correlational, then it cannot be concluded that day care causes effects on peer relations; associations only can be identified, which limits conclusions on the effects of day care. But given the evidence that day care can be positive then the focus should be on transferring this to cases in which day care still has negative effects. Thus, the good practice of high-quality day care needs to be identified—factors such as consistency of caregivers, low child: staff ratio, training of child-care staff, and the number of interactions and sensitivity of staff to the children in their care.

EXAM HINT

You need to think about which content you will leave out if the question is the shorter 8 or 10 marks.

10 mark question: Leave out the last sentence of paragraph 1 to reduce AO1 and the last sentence of paragraph 2 to reduce AO2.

8 mark question: Condense Blesky et al. (2007) and leave out the last sentence of paragraph 1 to reduce AO1 and leave out from Clarke-Stewart onwards for AO2.

> **?** Outline and evaluate what research shows about the effects of day care on aggression. **8, 10, or 12 MARKS**

Paragraph 1 AO1

A number of studies have linked day care to aggression and behaviour problems. Research suggests the more time spent in day care the more aggressive behaviour shown when the child goes to school. Vandell and Corasaniti (1990) found that 8-year-olds who had spent their early years in day care were rated as more "non-compliant" by both their teachers and their parents compared to children who had spent less time in day care. Bates et al. (1994) found that children who spent more time receiving any type of day care during their first five years of life had more behaviour problems, peer-rated aggression, and observed aggression than those receiving less day care. Belsky (1999) found that more time in day care over the first five years of life was associated with more aggression and other behaviour problems. Belsky et al. (2007) have linked the aggression to centre-based care involving large groups of peers, suggesting that the size of the day-care setting and amount of contact time with the carers are key factors linked to aggression. On the other hand, day care may decrease aggression because children in group day care have more opportunities to learn effective ways of resolving interpersonal conflict without resorting to physical aggression.

Paragraph 2 AO2

A criticism of the above research is that physical aggression reaches a peak in the preschool years, the years during which the great majority of day care takes place. Thus, it may appear that day care is making the children aggressive when in fact this is a meaningless association because aggression would increase during this time anyway. This links to the criticism that the research is correlational and so it cannot be concluded that day care causes aggression; associations only can be identified, which limits conclusions on the effects of day care. Another problem is that the effects of day care are not clear cut because there are so many factors that affect aggression. It is difficult to assess the overall effect of day care, as the type, quality, time spent in, and age on entering day care, as well as quality of the home environment and individual differences such as temperament of the child, all interact. This limits the validity of the research because we cannot be sure if the effects are due to day care or something else. These factors also mean that it is difficult to compare the findings of different studies because we are not comparing like with like. If the findings from one nursery where the home background of the children was very stimulating were compared with those of children from a disadvantaged background, then conclusions could lack validity. For example, Belsky et al. (2007) suggest the home environment and the sensitivity of the mother have more impact than day care on aggression. Clarke-Stewart et al. (1994) argue that much of the research into aggression fails to distinguish assertiveness from aggression in instances of non-compliance. This means what is being reported as more aggressive behaviour in the day-care children could simply be children that have greater confidence and have learned to assert themselves better.

How Science Works questions

> **?** **Day care has been linked to increased aggressive behaviour in children. A psychologist decides to investigate this further be observing children in five different day care settings.**

EXAM HINT

You need to think critically about the observation method. Remember reliability means consistency. You also need to know about the correlational method, and so be ready to apply your knowledge of research methods.

(a) **Why is reliability an issue with this method?**
2 MARKS

(b) **How could the reliability of the observation be checked?** **2 MARKS**

(c) **What kind of correlation is being investigated?**
1 MARK

(d) **Give one advantage and one weakness of the correlational method.** **2 + 2 MARKS**

(a) Reliability is an issue because the psychologist may be inconsistent in the categorising of the aggressive behaviour, and so any comparisons between centres will lack validity if the aggressive behaviour has not been assessed in exactly the same way.

(b) To increase reliability of the observation a technique called inter-observer reliability should be used. This involves two or more observers and if the same behaviour is rated the same by two different observers then the observations are reliable.

(c) Positive correlation (you don't need to explain why but, just to make this clear, it's because the relationship being investigated is the longer the time spent in day care, the more aggressive the child is likely to be, and so the variables increase together, therefore positive).

(d) A correlation is a useful method to use when manipulation of the variables is impossible, and so a great advantage is that it can be used when an experiment cannot. A weakness is that cause and effect cannot be shown because the variables are not directly manipulated and so some other factors may be causing the aggression rather than the day care. This means we cannot conclude that x caused y as we can with an experiment, and so conclusions are limited.

? **Another psychologist has decided to interview mothers about how day care has affected their child's sociability.**

(a) **Give one advantage and one weakness of the interview method.** **2 + 2 MARKS**

> **(b)** Suggest a question that would generate quantitative data and a question that would generate qualitative data and explain why the questions are appropriate to quantitative or qualitative data. **2 + 2 MARKS**
>
> **(c)** Why might the interview method have limited validity? **3 MARKS**
>
> **(d)** Explain how the qualitative data can be analysed. **3 MARKS**

EXAM HINT
A range of methodology is being assessed here, which really shows that a good understanding of research methods is the key to success in this exam. Remember that quantitative means numbers and qualitative means words, and that you analyse qualitative data by looking for themes and patterns in the data.

(a) The interview can yield rich detailed data, which has high validity because it reveals more about the participant and so is more meaningful. Interviewer bias is a weakness because question setting is subjective and the data analysis is vulnerable to misinterpretation by the researcher, either deliberately or unconsciously. The researcher may be drawn to data that support the research hypothesis and may disregard data that don't and so validity will be reduced.

(b) Please rate your child's sociability before entering day care and after entering day care, on a scale of 1–10, where 1 is very unsociable and 10 is very sociable. This generates quantitative data because the data will be in the form of numbers.

How do you think day care affected your child's sociability? This generates qualitative data because it is an open question that requires the participant to answer at length and so the data will be in the form of words.

(c) The interview method may have limited validity because interviewer bias may lead to the asking of leading questions to influence the participants' answers to suit the researcher's own ideas. Participant reactivity is also a problem as answers may be biased by evaluation apprehension and social desirability. This means participants may be worried about how they will be judged and so will answer to place themselves in the best possible light. This means the answers may not be true and so validity would be low.

EXAM HINT
The first two parts are straightforward and test your knowledge of the naturalistic observation. With part (c) think about what affects the truth of the results. Part (d) is a very open question. You could write about a range of things and receive credit. The trick is to write enough for the 4 marks and no more and make sure you include a high level of observation design features.

? An educational psychologist is studying children across five primary schools in a city to assess the effects of day care on the children's social behaviour. The psychologist has interviewed parents to take a record of the children's attendance of day care and has asked the teacher to assess the children's social behaviour. The psychologist is also doing this through observation of the children at play.

(a) What sort of observation is this and why?
2 MARKS

(b) Give one advantage and one weakness of the method you identified in (a). **2 + 2 MARKS**

(c) Identify and explain two factors that might limit the validity of the research. **2 + 2 MARKS**

(d) Explain how the psychologist could design the observation. **4 MARKS**

(a) Naturalistic observation because it takes place in the participants' natural setting, the primary schools.

(b) An advantage is that naturalistic observation involves looking at behaviour as it occurs naturally and so has greater mundane realism than more artificial methods. Consequently, it may have greater generalisability to real life and so high external validity. A possible weakness is observer bias; this may lead to imprecise recording or interpretation of what is observed. Consequently, the observation may lack reliability (lack of consistency) and validity.

(c) The parents' interview reports may lack validity because their answers may be biased by participant reactivity, e.g. evaluation apprehension and social desirability. This means the participant may be worried about how their child's sociability will be judged and so will answer to place themselves and their child in the best possible light. This means the answers may not be true and so validity would be low.

(d) The psychologist should decide observation criteria in advance to reduce observer bias during the observation. The observation criteria need to be carefully devised so that they allow the children's aggressive behaviour to be categorised clearly and consistently. The psychologist could employ a colleague to conduct the observations as well and this way inter-observer reliability could be used to check the accuracy of the observations. If the same behaviour is rated the same by two different observers then the observations are reliable. The psychologist could also compare the children's behaviour against a control group of children who didn't go to day care so that there is a baseline. The psychologist might also design the observation as a longitudinal study so that the long-term effects of day care could be researched. This would involve observing the same children's behaviour at 5 and then again perhaps at 8 and 10 years of age.

Application of knowledge questions

Implications of research into attachment and day care for child-care practices

> **?** Imagine you have been asked to advise parents on what to look for in a day-care centre. Suggest four things they should look for as indicators of high-quality day care. **2 +2 + 2+ 2 MARKS**

(i) Consistency of caregivers: The parent should ask about staff turnover because children need a stable attachment figure to attach to if they are to be secure in the day-care environment.

(ii) Low child:staff ratio: Optimally this should be 1:3 so the parent should look for how many staff there are to children. A low ratio allows for more individual attention, and so longer and more interaction between staff and children, and this helps a secure bond develop and provides more stimulation for the child.

(iii) Training: Day care provided by well-trained caregivers is typically of higher quality than day care provided by poorly trained or untrained caregivers, so the parent should ask about the level of training of the staff.

(iv) Stimulation: The parent should look for evidence of lots of stimulating toys and educational materials, as well as the length of time the carers spend interacting with the children, as this is an important source of stimulation.

EXAM HINT

Pick four things to identify and explain briefly what they are, as each is only worth 2 marks. On the other hand, don't just identify as you will not get the second mark.

EXAM HINT
Note that these are similar but different questions so you must use research findings on attachments for (a) and research findings on day care for (b).

? (a) Explain two implications of research into attachment for child-care practices. **2 + 2 MARKS**

(b) Explain two implications of research into day care for child-care practices. **2 + 2 MARKS**

(a) (i) One positive implication of research into attachment is the changes to hospital visiting procedures. Up until the 1960s, there were strict rules and limits placed on how long parents could spend with their children. Following research findings, such as Bowlby's, that children require continuing emotional care and as much contact as possible with parents, visiting hours were extended and most hospitals now have unlimited visiting access.

(ii) Another positive implication is parenting skills training. Knowledge of attachments has been used to train new parents in emotional sensitivity so that they are better able to respond to their child's needs, and findings show this increases secure attachment.

(b) (i) One positive implication of research into day care is that it is possible to consider the child–environment fit. For example, as day centres where children are cared for in large groups have been linked to aggression it may be better if a child displaying aggressive tendencies is cared for in a home setting such as with a childminder or in-home care.

(ii) Another positive implication is that day care can compensate for social disadvantage. Borge et al. (2004) found that very socially disadvantaged children were less aggressive in group day care than when looked after full-time by their mother, and so group day care may be more beneficial for children from very socially disadvantaged backgrounds than for those from less disadvantaged backgrounds.

Essay question

? Discuss the implications of research into attachment and day care for child-care practices.

Paragraph 1 AO1

Research into attachment and day care has revealed a number of positive implications. Bowlby's research into attachment identified the importance of emotional care. This was a groundbreaking insight because child care up until this point had focused more on physical care. As a consequence of his research showing that children need continuing emotional care, hospital visiting procedures were changed to provide parents with much greater access to their children. Research into maternal sensitivity also has positive implications, both in terms of parenting skills training and the training of child-care specialists, because this training is linked to an increase in secure attachment. Another implication is that children need consistent care. Hodges and Tizard's (1989) research into privation showed that the institutionalised children did not form attachments prior to foster care due to the high turnover of staff; each child averaged 50 carers before the age of 4, which shows the need for low staff turnover and a key worker scheme to increase the consistency of day care. Other implications of research into day care include the need for a low child:staff ratio; optimally this should be 1:3 because a low ratio allows for more individual attention and so longer and more interaction between staff and children and this helps a secure bond develop and provides more stimulation for the child.

Paragraph 2 AO2

The implications seem overwhelmingly positive and so have made a significant contribution to improving the quality of child-care provision, whether this is in hospitals or day-care centres. However, we can argue that how much the changes to day-care provision have made a difference is not really testable. This is because the effects of day care are multiple and difficult to predict. There are so many factors that affect aggression and sociability, two much investigated effects of day care, that it is difficult to assess the effect of any one implication. This limits the validity of the research because we cannot be sure if the effects are due to day care or something else, and so the implications are difficult to measure. On the other hand, there are some more controlled studies: for example, Bakermans-Kranenburg et al. (2003) found that it is possible to make infants more securely attached by interventions designed to increase maternal sensitivity. Thus, what is needed is more controlled research in which centres where provision has been changed are compared against control centres. However, such comparisons are difficult to make because often it is not possible to compare like-for-like centres because one centre may have children with more secure attachment types because the home environment is more sensitive than another centre, or in one centre there may be lower staff turnover than another, and so any findings would lack validity because they would not just be due to the change to provision. A further issue is that it may not always be possible to implement the implications because they may be optimal but are not necessarily practical. For example, there will usually be some staff turnover, and the 1:3 staff:child ratio is not followed by all day-care centres due to the cost and practicality of providing more staff.

RESEARCH METHODS
4

TYPES OF EXAM QUESTION

Unlike the other AS units we cannot provide complete model answers to the Research Methods questions as you will need to CONTEXTUALISE your answer in terms of the stimulus given in the question. Instead we have given guidance on appropriate content for the various types of Research Methods question. So having a good knowledge of the following types of question is a good starting point for being able to answer the "How Science Works" questions in the exam.

Do compare the guidance here with the "How Science Works" questions within the topic chapters to see how the types of answers here have been used to answer these types of questions. This will give you a better idea of how the guidance here can be adapted to the questions you will get asked in the exam.

- *The Method question*
- *The Aims and Hypothesis question*
- *The Research Design question*
  - *Experimental research designs*
  - *Non-experimental research designs*

- *The "Factors Associated with Research Design" question*
  - *Operationalisation of the IV/DV*
  - *Conducting pilot studies*
  - *Controlling extraneous variables*
  - *Assessing and improving reliability*
  - *Internal and external validity*
  - *Ethical issues*

- *The Selection of Participants question*
- *The Relationship Between Researchers and Participants question*
  - *Participant reactivity and demand characteristics*
  - *Investigator effects*
  - *How to control investigator effects/participant reactivity*

- *The Data Analysis question*
- *The Graphs and Charts question*
- *The Data Response question*
- *The Quantitative vs Qualititative Approach question*

QUANTITATIVE AND QUALITATIVE RESEARCH METHODS

The Method question

? **What is the research method used in this investigation?** **1 MARK**

You will be able to determine from the question whether the research is experimental (testing for a difference) and which type (laboratory, field, or natural), correlational (testing for a relationship), a naturalistic observation, questionnaire, interview, or case study. Look for cues in the question—was the study in controlled conditions? So it's likely to be a laboratory experiment. Did it involve observing participants in a natural setting? So it's likely to be naturalistic observation.

EXAM HINT

We present information on each of the possible methods below, with two advantages and two disadvantages for each, which can be applied to this question.

? **Give one advantage and one weakness of this method . . .** **2 + 2 MARKS**

Give two advantages OR two weaknesses . . . **2 + 2 MARKS**

Laboratory experiments

Advantages:

1. The highly controlled environment of the laboratory, in particular the direct manipulation of the IV by the experimenter and control of extraneous and confounding variables, enables cause and effect to be established. Causal relationships can be identified because, of all the experimental methods, this one provides the most confidence that the IV has caused the effect on the DV because other extraneous or confounding variables can be controlled.

2. Laboratory experiments take the traditional scientific approach and the strength of this is that they are objective. That is, they involve precise measurements and so are not as subject to researcher bias as subjective methods, which are open to different interpretations.

Weaknesses:

1. The laboratory is an artificial environment and consequently the research lacks mundane realism, i.e. it is not like real life. This means the findings may not generalise to settings other than the laboratory and so the research lacks external validity.
2. Laboratory experiments are reductionist as they focus on only two variables, and cannot completely control extraneous or confounding variables, when in real life there are usually many interacting variables and multiple cause and effects involved in behaviour. Therefore, the laboratory experiment is oversimplified.

Field experiments

Advantages:

1. The field experiment takes place in a natural setting and so usually has greater mundane realism than laboratory experiments, and consequently may have greater generalisability to real life, and so high external validity.
2. There is control over the IV, and so cause and effect can be established to some extent, but not necessarily due to the disadvantage of lack of control of the many situational variables. This limits internal validity because if a confounding variable has biased the results then the research has not measured what it set out to.

Weaknesses:

1. There is less control in a field experiment, which means confounding variables, rather than the IV, may be causing the effect on the DV. This means internal validity is lower and it is difficult to conclude cause and effect, as we cannot be sure the results are due to the IV.

2. Many field experiments cannot involve informed consent, right to withdraw, or debriefing, and so the ethical implications are a weakness.

Quasi-experiments

Advantages:

1. A quasi-experiment enables us to research behaviours that could not otherwise be investigated experimentally because it involves a naturally occurring IV. This means it can be used to investigate phenomena that would not be practical or ethical to manipulate in a laboratory or field experiment, where the IV is controlled.
2. The experimental environment is controlled by the experimenter, which enables better control of confounding variables, and greater confidence that the IV has been isolated, and so there is greater confidence that the IV has caused the effect on the DV, which supports internal validity.

Weaknesses:

1. Cause and effect can only be inferred when the experimenter directly manipulates the IV, and so in a quasi-experiment association only can be identified, which limits the conclusiveness of the findings.
2. Quasi-experiments are reductionist as they focus on only two variables when in real life there are usually many interacting variables and multiple cause and effects involved in behaviour. Thus, the quasi-experiment is oversimplified.

Natural experiments

Advantages:

1. A natural experiment enables us to research behaviours that could not otherwise be investigated experimentally, either because it involves a naturally occurring IV or because there are ethical concerns with trying to manipulate the behaviour being studied. This means it can be used to investigate phenomena that would not be practical or ethical to manipulate in a laboratory or field experiment, where the IV is controlled.

2. The natural experiment takes place in a natural setting and so usually has greater mundane realism than the controlled environments of laboratory and quasi-experiments, and consequently may have greater generalisability to real life and so high external validity.

Weaknesses:

1. Cause and effect can only be inferred when the experimenter directly manipulates the IV, and so in a natural experiment association only can be identified, which limits the conclusiveness of the findings.
2. There is less control in a natural experiment, which means confounding variables, rather than the IV, may be causing the effect on the DV. This means internal validity is lower and so findings can be difficult to interpret and it may not be possible to infer associations.

Correlational analysis

Advantages:

1. Correlational analysis shows the direction and strength of relationships and so its greatest use is prediction. The strength of one variable can be predicted from the other.
2. It is a useful method to use when manipulation of the variables is impossible, and thus a great advantage is that it can be used when an experiment cannot, and so a wider range of behaviour can be investigated because we can study behaviour that cannot be controlled.

Weaknesses:

1. Cause and effect cannot be established because the variables are not directly manipulated and consequently we cannot conclude that *x* caused *y*, we can only conclude that they are related and so conclusions are limited.
2. Only two variables are investigated, but other factors may be involved that were not known of or were not accounted for in the research. This means the inferred association would lack validity.

Naturalistic observation

Advantages:

1. The naturalistic observation involves looking at behaviour as it occurs naturally and so has greater mundane realism than more artificial methods. Consequently, it may have greater generalisability to real life and so high external validity.
2. Naturalistic observation is less biased by participant reactivity, e.g. demand characteristics, which means the behaviour observed is more genuine and so the research may have greater internal validity.

Weaknesses:

1. Observer bias may lead to imprecise recording or interpretation of findings. Consequently, they may lack reliability (lack of consistency) and so lack validity (lack truth), and so extra observations are useful.
2. Observations *describe* behaviour but do not *explain* it, so what they tell us is limited as further research is required to be able to draw useful conclusions.

Controlled observation

Advantages:

1. If the situation is well controlled, there is less risk of unwanted extraneous variables influencing participants' behaviour than is the case with naturalistic observations, so the findings have good validity.
2. Richer and more complete information is often obtained from studies using controlled observations than from conventional experimental studies in which participants are only required to produce limited responses.

Weaknesses:

1. The artificiality of the situation may make it hard to generalise the findings to more natural situations, and so the study may lack external validity—generalisability to real-life settings.

2. Problems such as investigator effects (due to experimenter expectations) and demand characteristics (due to participant expectations) may arise in studies using controlled observations. Both of which may limit internal validity as they will affect the truth of the research.

Interviews

Advantages:

1. The interview can yield rich detailed data, which has high validity because it reveals more about how participants make their experiences meaningful, particularly if open questions are used.
2. The interview can be more flexible as the more unstructured interviews can be participant-led rather than researcher-led, which means the direction of the interview can be adapted to fit with the answers given by the participant. More insight is likely to be gained if the interview is adapted to suit the participant and so the data is more likely to be valid (true).

Weaknesses:

1. Interviewer bias is a weakness because question setting is subjective and data analysis is vulnerable to misinterpretation, either deliberately or unconsciously. The researcher may be drawn to data that corroborate the research hypothesis and may disregard data that don't and so validity will be reduced.
2. Participant reactivity is a problem as answers may be biased by evaluation apprehension and social desirability, whereby the participants are worried about being judged and so answer to place themselves in the best possible light, which means validity would be low as the answers would lack truth.

Questionnaires

Advantages:

1. The questionnaire is very flexible as open and closed questions can be used, thus both quantitative and qualitative data can be gathered, and consequently a wide range of phenomena can be investigated.

2. On a practical level questionnaires are quick and economical to conduct and consequently a large sample can be obtained with little expense as relatively untrained people can administer the questionnaires.

Weaknesses:

1. Researcher bias in question setting, implementation, or analysis can reduce validity as the researcher may be drawn to data that corroborate the research hypothesis and may disregard data that don't.
2. Participant reactivity is a problem as answers may be biased by evaluation apprehension and social desirability, which means validity would be low, as the answers would lack truth.

Case studies

Advantages:

1. Case studies can provide far more information about a specific individual than is usually obtained from studies involving groups of individuals. For example, in the case study on Genie, very detailed information about her intellectual and social development was obtained over a period of several years.
2. Case studies (even limited ones) can nevertheless provide useful insights that influence future theoretical developments. For example, the case study of Little Albert (Watson & Rayner, 1920) influenced the development of behaviour therapy—it showed that fears can be classically conditioned and suggested to behaviour therapists that fears can perhaps be eliminated through conditioning as well.

Weaknesses:

1. A key weakness is the issue of generalisation and drawing general conclusions from case studies. There are two kinds of problem with respect to generalisation. First, the individual may not be representative of individuals of the same age and gender. Second, even if the individual studied is representative, it is still likely that other individuals of the opposite gender and/or a different age would behave differently. For example, strictly speaking, the case

study of Little Albert only tells us about fear conditioning in a boy of 11 months—it is perfectly possible that younger or older boys or girls or adults would show different effects.

2. Another weakness with case studies is that of subjective selection, i.e. researcher bias (Coolican, 1994).The therapist often only reports a small fraction of the information obtained from the individual being studied, and what is selected may be influenced by his/her preconceptions.

RESEARCH DESIGN AND IMPLEMENTATION

The Aims and Hypothesis question

? **Give an aim for the investigation described in the stimulus.**

Give a directional (or non-directional) hypothesis for the investigation described in the stimulus.

? **Give a null hypothesis for the investigation described in the stimulus.** **2 MARKS PER QUESTION**

EXAM HINT
This may be experimental or correlational depending upon what is being tested in the stimulus.

EXAM HINT
As above this may be experimental or correlational depending upon what is being tested in the stimulus.

EXAM HINT
You need to practise these to get a better idea of these hypothesis templates.

Experimental/alternative (difference) hypothesis:

Non-directional: There is a significant difference between group/condition 1 and group/condition 2 in DV, as measured by . . . (remember to operationalise, i.e. say how the DV was measured).

Directional: Group/condition 1 DV: self-report measure (on scale of . . .), number of words recalled, time taken (remember to operationalise) are significantly higher/is greater than group/condition 2.

Null hypothesis: There is not a significant difference between group/condition and group/condition in DV, and any differences that do exist are due to chance and/or random variables.

Correlational (correlation/relationship/association): There is a significant correlation between V1 (variable 1) and V2 (variable 2), as measured by . . . (remember to operationalise).

Directional: There is a positive/negative correlation between V1 and V2, as measured by . . . (remember to operationalise).

Null: There is not a significant correlation between <u>V1</u> and <u>V2</u>, and any association that does exist is due to chance and/or random variables.

? **Can you decide whether a hypothesis is directional or non-directional** **1 MARK** **and justify your choice** **2 MARKS** **?**

Clue: What would background research predict?

Can you explain what the null hypothesis means? **2 MARKS**

The null hypothesis is the prediction that there is no significant difference (experimental) or no relationship/association (correlation) and that any difference/relationship that is observed is due to chance alone and/or random variables AND so it is not due to a systematic cause/association. In terms of an experiment, it is the prediction that the independent variable will have no effect on the dependent variable, and in a correlation it is the prediction that two or more variables are not related.

The Research design question

Experimental research designs

EXAM HINT

Any of the research methods could come up—either experimental (independent groups, repeated measures, and matched participants) OR non-experimental (naturalistic observations, questionnaires, interviews).

? **What is the research design used in this investigation?** **1 MARK**

Give one advantage and one disadvantage of this design . . . **2 + 2 MARKS**

How would you control for the weaknesses of the . . . design? **2 MARKS**

Outline the procedures that could be used to investigate the research aim using a different method . . . **6 MARKS** **OR**

How could the research be investigated using a different method from that used in the question? ◀ **6 MARKS** ▶

Independent measures (two different groups of participants).

Advantage:

An advantage of the independent measures design is that it avoids order effects because the participants only experience one condition and so are less likely to guess the demand characteristics. They are also less likely to experience other order effects such as boredom, fatigue, and practice effect.

Disadvantage:

A disadvantage of the independent measures design is participant variables, which means there may be consistent individual differences between the two groups of participants. For example, if one group was more alert than the other this would systematically distort results on a quick response test. Random allocation counters this weakness.

How would you control for the weaknesses?

The random allocation question: Random allocation controls for participant variables. This refers to how the participants are allocated to conditions in the independent measures design. As with the random sample it is best if every participant has an equal chance of being allocated to the condition. This reduces bias and minimises participant variation/individual differences because it ensures that they are randomly distributed, which increases internal validity. It minimises bias in the allocation process as this can lead to participants with certain characteristics being favoured for one condition over another, which would distort the findings.

Repeated measures (one group of participants who experience both conditions)

Advantage:

An advantage of the repeated measures design is that it minimises participant variables. Because the same participants are in each

> **EXAM HINT**
> You should know the difference between the various types of experimental research design, an advantage and disadvantage of each, and also be prepared to explain how you would control for the weaknesses of each. You should also draw from the "Factors Associated with Research Design" section.

> **EXAM HINT**
> Matched participants can also be used as a control. It's the same as independent but the participants are matched on key variables as determined by the nature of the study and so controls for participant variables.

condition, participant variation is reduced, but it is not eliminated as there will still be some individual differences between the participants.

Disadvantage:
A disadvantage of the repeated measures design is order effects: practice effect, fatigue, or boredom may all affect the second condition, so differences may be due to this rather than the action of the IV, and so the internal validity of the research is constrained, because the research will not have measured what it set out to. Demand characteristics are another order effect. As the participants experience two conditions they are more likely to guess the purpose of the study and so demand characteristics may reduce the internal validity of the research.

How would you control for the weaknesses?
The counterbalancing question: Counterbalancing is a form of randomisation and refers to how the participants are allocated to conditions in the repeated measured design. It controls for order effects such as guessing the demand characteristics, practice or fatigue, which may occur if all participants experienced the two conditions, A and B, in the same order. The ABBA design controls for this because half experience A then B and the other half experience B then A. Consequently, any order effects are balanced out (but not eliminated) and so any differences are more likely to be due to the action of the IV and internal validity is higher.

Matched participants design (two different groups of participants but matched on key variables)

Advantage:
An advantage of the matched participants design is that it minimises participant variables. Participants are matched on important variables and so there is less participant variation (individual differences) between participants, meaning that extraneous or confounding variables are less likely to occur, and so findings have greater internal validity because there is greater confidence the research measured what it set out to.

Disadvantage:
A disadvantage of the matched participants design is that it is difficult to achieve a good match. It can be difficult to find participants who match on a number of key variables because to do so a large pool of participants is needed to draw from, making this time consuming and less practical than the other designs.

Non-experimental research designs

> **?** **Outline the procedures for carrying out naturalistic observations/questionnaires/interviews.** **6 MARKS**
>
> **Suggest two ways the design of the study can be improved.** **3 + 3 MARKS**

> **EXAM HINT**
> You should know how to implement and evaluate naturalistic observations, questionnaires, and interviews. You will most likely draw from the "Factors Associated with Research Design" section for the second question (see the standardisation, randomisation, pilot study, how to control investigator/participant effects, sample, and ethics questions below) as you can draw from many areas—but most likely you will be asked for two improvements so will have to select two only.

> **EXAM HINT**
> Note that many aspects of the design are covered and you would NOT have to write about all of them necessarily—match the amount of content to the number of marks.

Naturalistic observation
Overt or covert observation: The researcher needs to decide whether to conceal themselves (covert) or not (overt), which depends on what is being investigated.

Participant or non-participant observation: Participant observation is when the researcher becomes a member of the group they are observing in order to observe more natural behaviour, e.g. Donal MacIntyre's report on football hooligans. However, participant observation is not always possible and for some investigations non-participant observation may be more practical and ethical, e.g. when investigating alcohol or drug abuse.

Event, time, and point sampling: To avoid data overload these different forms of sampling are used. Event sampling is when only relevant events or behaviours are recorded. Time sampling is when observations are recorded only during specific time periods. Point sampling is when one individual is observed and their current behaviour categorised, and then a second individual, and so on.

Observation criteria: This is a very important design consideration of an observation because the criteria need to be very clear and precise to ensure the observer categorises the behaviour in a consistent, and so reliable, way.

Recording the data, e.g. frequencies, observation criteria, notes, video or audio recordings: There are many ways to record the data, some of which involve interpretation in order to categorise the behaviour into frequencies or observation criteria, e.g. moving forward could be recorded as an action or interpreted as an aggressive behaviour, depending on what is being investigated.

Inter-observer reliability: Two or more observers are usually used to control for subjectivity, i.e. personal bias in the observations. Inter-rater reliability is used to test the accuracy of the observations. If the same behaviour is rated the same by two different observers then the observations are reliable. Observers must be well trained and have precise, clear observation criteria. A number of measures are taken and correlated to test for reliability.

Ethical considerations: Naturalistic observations often cannot involve informed consent, right to withdraw, or debriefing.

Questionnaires
Closed and open questions: Closed questions involve a fixed response, which the participant must choose from, e.g. a Likert scale. This is easier to score and analyse. Open questions allow the participants to answer freely and so qualitative analysis is needed, which can be more difficult and time consuming, but can also yield more meaningful data.

Ambiguity and bias: Ambiguity must be avoided, as data is of little value if answers cannot be compared, which they can't if different participants have interpreted the question differently. Biased questions must also be avoided as they can lead the witness or provoke reactive answers that are not valid if they are not true.

Attitude scale construction: A Likert scale is the usual way to do this and involves the participant giving self-report ratings on a 5-point scale to indicate their level of agreement/non-agreement with whatever was communicated in the question. For positive statements such as "It is important to get 8 hours' sleep per night", strongly disagree scores 1, through to strongly agree, which scores 5. Whereas for negative statements such as "It is not important to maintain a regular sleep pattern", the scoring is reversed, with strongly disagree scored as 5 and strongly agree scored as 1. This is so that the scores on the questionnaire can be related to each other.

Ethical considerations: Deception, informed consent, protection of participants, right to withdraw, debrief, and confidentiality can all be issues.

Interviews

Structured, semi-structured, or unstructured: A structured interview has a fixed format of questions, which means the same questions are asked in the same order for each participant. Semi-structured also has the same questions, but the order is not fixed, which means they can be selected to suit the flow of the interview and so encourage the participant to be at ease and more forthcoming. Unstructured is participant-led as participants' answers direct the questions. This is the format taken in the clinical interview.

Constructing good questions: This is complex as it is important that the questions are clear and unambiguous because if they communicate different meanings to different participants the answers will not be comparable. Also, they should be free from bias and subjectivity to avoid leading the participant.

Ethical considerations: Ethical issues include abuse of power, particularly in clinical interviews. Privacy is a key issue and so this falls within protection of participants. Confidentiality is another issue.

The "Factors Associated with Research Design" questions

> **?** Identify the IV or DV. **1 MARK OR 2 MARKS**

Experimental: The IV is the variable manipulated or controlled by the experimenter or naturally occurring (e.g. age, gender, culture). The DV is the variable that is measured to show the effect of the IV.

> **EXAM HINT**
> You are unlikely to be asked to describe what an IV or DV is as I have done here—although you never know! Instead, use this information to help you identify the variables from the question stimulus. NOTE: another way to get it the right way round is to see the IV as the cause and the DV as the effect, and it's I before D, because the cause comes before the effect.

> **EXAM HINT**
> It does not matter which of the co-variables is V1 and which is V2, so just identify the two co-variables that are associated in any order.

Correlational: V1 and V2.

Operationalisation of the IV/DV

> **?** Identify two ways in which you could operationalise the behaviour identified in the stimulus . . . **2 MARKS**
>
> How were the variables in the stimulus material operationalised—either IV and DV or V1 and V2? **2 + 2 MARKS**

> **EXAM HINT**
> How were the variables measured? Check the question for mention of a rating scale, score (if so check it says the maximum score so you can give this), time, and or some other way in which the variables were measured, e.g. the dependent variable was the number of letters recalled from a maximum of 30 letters.

Conducting pilot studies

> **?** What is a pilot study? **2 MARKS**
>
> Why should a pilot study be conducted? **2 MARKS**
>
> How can you carry out a pilot study? **2 MARKS**

The pilot study allows for a trial run of the materials so questions or procedures can be checked for clarity, ambiguity, and "workability". This means that adjustments can be made if there are problems before the main study. This saves time and money, as findings would be valueless if there had been ambiguity. The pilot study is also used to check procedures for design errors and timings. This also ascertains whether it is replicable, which is essential for testing reliability. This means the pilot study can identify any flaws or areas for improvement that can then be corrected before the main study.

> **EXAM HINT**
> To answer HOW depends on what behaviour is identified in the stimulus but you can answer this by describing how a small-scale version of the real study could be conducted.

Controlling extraneous variables

> **?** **What two factors might have affected the validity of the data being collected?** **2 + 2 MARKS**

> **EXAM HINT**
> If the question asks you to identify factors that affect validity then consider extraneous variables. Ask yourself what other variables could have affected the DV other than the IV.
>
> For example:
>
> **Participant variables**: Give an example of an individual difference that is relevant to the study described in the question, e.g. age, ability, past experience
>
> **Situational variables**: Give an example of an environmental difference that is relevant to the study described in the question, e.g. time of day, weather conditions, distraction, noise.

> **?** **Explain how the factor identified as affecting validity might be controlled.** **2 MARKS**

Standardisation controls for factors that affect validity (confounding variables) as this ensures the research conditions are the same for all participants. For example, standardised instructions control what is said/given to the participants and the standardised procedure ensures uniformity of experience for the participants. This means that the conditions are comparable. This avoids some participants being treated more favourably than others, or some participants being given more demand characteristics than others, or some participants experiencing more distraction and confusion than others. So standardisation controls for confounding variables, researcher effects, and participant reactivity.

Assessing and improving reliability

> **?** **What is reliability?** **2 MARKS**
>
> **Explain how you can test for reliability and how you would put this into practice.** **3 MARKS**

Reliability refers to the CONSISTENCY of the research. There are two forms of reliability: internal reliability refers to the consistency within the research, whereas external reliability refers to consistency outside the research, which is usually over time. For example, research would have reliability if the same findings are obtained each time the same thing is measured. For example, if a ruler is used to measure 1 cm this would be reliable as the length does not change. If the same research measures the same thing differently, e.g. score on a questionnaire, then it lacks reliability.

Internal reliability: Inter-rater reliability is used to test the accuracy of the observations. Two or more observers are usually used to control for subjectivity, i.e. personal bias in the observations. If the same behaviour is rated the same by two different observers then the observations are reliable. Observers must be well trained and have precise, clear observation criteria. A number of measures are taken and correlated to test for reliability. Consistency in the two observers' measures indicates reliability.

External reliability: Test–retest reliability involves testing once and then again at a later date, i.e. replication of the original research. Meta-analyses draw on this when they compare the findings from different studies that have tested the same hypothesis, e.g. Milgram's study of obedience. The findings are compared for consistency using statistical analysis as consistency is an indicator of reliability.

Internal and external validity

EXAM HINT
Many things affect validity although it is possibly easiest to identify two confounding variables specific to the research in the stimulus.

> **?** **What is validity?** **2 MARKS**
>
> **How can you test for validity? And explain how you would put this into practice.** **3 MARKS** OR

> **What two factors might have affected the validity of the data being collected?** **2 + 2 MARKS**

Validity is used to refer to two things in research: internal validity refers to the extent to which the experiment measured what it set out to, i.e. is the observed effect in the DV a result of the manipulation of the IV? Thus, internal validity refers to whether the research has TRUTH or whether it "worked". External validity refers to the validity of the research outside the research situation itself—the extent to which the findings are generalisable to other situations, especially "everyday" situations.

Construct validity: Findings have construct validity if the measures generalise to other measures of the same variable, e.g. does a new stress questionnaire measure stress at the same level as a measure that is already established as reliable and valid? So a way of checking the construct validity of a measure is to see how it compares to an already existing measure.

Meta-analysis: A meta-analysis involves the comparison of findings from many studies that have investigated the same hypothesis, and so checks for external validity. If findings are consistent (reliable) across populations, locations, and periods in time then this indicates validity, e.g. Van IJzendoorn and Kroonenberg's (1988) meta-analysis of the cross-cultural Strange Situation studies. Thus, if it has validity it is likely to replicate, and reliability in the meta-analysis is used as an indicator of validity.

Ethical issues

> **?** **Identify one (or two) ethical issues that might have arisen in this investigation.** **2 OR 2 + 2 MARKS**

EXAM HINT
In most cases deception and/or protection will be relevant but other issues may also have arisen.

Protection of participants: Any distress to the participants raises this issue. Participants should experience no more stress during the study than they would in everyday life and should leave in the same psychological state as they arrived for the study.

Deception: If the participants are deliberately deceived or any information is withheld (usually the hypothesis) then this is an issue related to respecting participants.

Informed consent: If the participants have been deceived then they cannot have given informed consent because they will not know the true nature and purpose of the research.

Right to withdraw: If the participants have not been told they can leave at any point at the beginning of the study and have their data destroyed then this is an issue.

Confidentiality: If individual information has been published, if individual participants are identifiable in the findings, or if the nature of the study is likely to elicit more information than the participant is comfortable with, e.g. case study, interview, questionnaire, then this is an issue.

EXAM HINT

Note that confidentiality as an ethical issue can be used as a weakness of any of the methods so you could use this instead of the weaknesses given in "the Method question" section.

EXAM HINT

Be careful not to state that you need to get informed consent at the start of the study as a way of dealing with an issue when the hypothesis has been deliberately withheld and the study would completely lack validity if it were revealed. Think about what is appropriate to the study. In most cases deception and/ or protection will be relevant.

? **Explain how the researcher might have dealt with the ethical issue(s) raised in the study.** **2 OR 2 + 2 MARKS**

Deception: CONTEXTUALISE, i.e. link to research and explain that the debrief deals with this, as it is when the true nature and purpose of the research can be explained to the participants, and to cover the fact that they took part without full knowledge. They can be given the opportunity to withdraw their data if they are unhappy about this.

Protection of participants: CONTEXTUALISE, i.e. link to research and explain that participants should be advised at the beginning that they have the right to withdraw if distressed in any way during the research. Confidentiality must be assured as this may control for the fact that they may feel embarrassed about the data they provide and reassure them that they are not personally identifiable. The debrief can be used to assure participants that their behaviour is normal and to address any distress caused by the research.

The Selection of Participants question

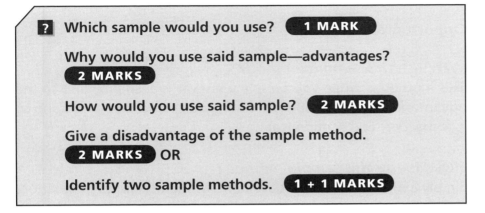

? Which sample would you use? **1 MARK**

Why would you use said sample—advantages?
2 MARKS

How would you use said sample? **2 MARKS**

Give a disadvantage of the sample method.
2 MARKS OR

Identify two sample methods. **1 + 1 MARKS**

Random sampling

WHY use this sample method?
This method is used because every participant in the target population has an equal chance of being chosen. Therefore there is no researcher bias in the selection of participants and so it is considered more representative of the target population than other methods of sampling.

HOW to use this sample method?
Use random number tables, a computer that generates random numbers, or names out of a hat to achieve a random sample. The names of all members of the target population would have to be put into a hat and then drawn out, which means all have an equal chance of being chosen. Or each member of the target population would have to be given a number and then these would be inputted into a computer program that generates random numbers. The participants with the numbers generated would be those selected for the study.

A disadvantage of this sample method
It is difficult to achieve a random sampling in practice because you need knowledge of everybody in the target population, and even if you have this it might not be possible to contact all of the participants drawn for the sample. Or they may not be

available or may not choose to take part. The selection of further participants, should this happen, means that the sample is not truly random.

Opportunity sampling

WHY use this sample method?
This method is when you sample whoever is available, and so the advantage of this method is that it is quick and easy to do and so it is practical and economical.

HOW to use this sample method?
Simply approach whoever is available within the target population.

A disadvantage of this sample method
The fact that it is the researcher's discretion to approach whoever is available leaves room for bias as the researcher may sample people because they find them attractive or who they think look approachable, and so sample bias is a key weakness.

Volunteer or self-selected sampling

WHY use this sample method?
This method involves participants who volunteer to take part in a research study and so the advantage of it is that it is relatively quick and easy to do.

HOW to use this sample method?
Use an advertisement.

A disadvantage of this sample method
Some researchers believe that people who volunteer may be different from non-volunteers, for instance in personality, as they may be more highly motivated, and so may not be a truly representative sample. This makes generalising the findings to the non-volunteering population questionable.

The Relationship Between Researchers and Participants question

Participant reactivity and demand characteristics

> **?** How might participant reactivity threaten the validity of the study? **2 MARKS** OR
>
> What is meant by participant reactivity? **2 MARKS**

EXAM HINT
You could also use this answer if asked to explain why the researcher should not be seen by the participants during the observation.

This occurs when participants respond to the demand characteristics, which are cues in the research situation or given away by the researcher, that might reveal the research hypothesis. Participant reactivity includes the co-operative participants who try to guess the research hypothesis in order to comply with it, or the negativistic participants who try to guess the research hypothesis in order to work against it. If participants' behaviour is influenced in this way then we cannot be sure that the effect (change in the DV) is due to the IV, so the research has not measured what it set out to and internal validity is reduced.

Investigator effects

> **?** How can investigator effects threaten the validity of the study? **2 MARKS**
>
> How can this be overcome? **2 MARKS**
>
> What is meant by investigator/researcher effects? **2 MARKS**

Experimenter expectancy can lead to the investigator giving away cues about the research hypothesis to the participants. If participants pick up on such demand characteristics they may alter their behaviour to meet experimenter expectations and help them achieve the desired results. If participants' behaviour is influenced in this way then it is not genuine behaviour and we cannot be sure that the effect (change in the DV) is due to the IV, so the research has not measured what it set out to and internal validity is reduced.

How to control investigator effects/participant reactivity

> **?** Explain one way to overcome investigator effects OR participant reactivity. **2 MARKS PER QUESTION**

Single-blind procedure controls for participant reactivity, as this is where the hypothesis is withheld from the participants and so they are not aware which condition they are in. This reduces demand characteristics as they are less likely to guess the demand characteristics if they do not know which condition they are in, e.g. CONTEXTUALISE.

Double blind procedure controls for researcher expectancy as this involves a research assistant who collects the data without any knowledge of the research hypothesis. Thus, neither the researcher nor the participants know the research hypothesis and so the expectancy effect is controlled.

DATA ANALYSIS

The Data Analysis question

> **?** What is an appropriate method for analysing the data AND why is it an appropriate method AND how do you carry out this descriptive analysis? **2 + 2 + 2 MARKS** OR
>
> What does the mean/mode/median/range/standard deviation tell us about the data? **2 MARKS PER QUESTION**

> **EXAM HINT**
>
> Quantitative analysis—know which measure of central tendency (mean, median, mode) should be used, which depends on the level of data (nominal, ordinal, interval, ratio).
>
> Know how to interpret the average (there should be a clear difference between the averages of each condition/group) and the spread (this shows the variability of the scores) of the score distribution.
>
> Know the advantages and disadvantages of each measure.

Level of data

Mode and variation ratio are most appropriate for nominal level of data.

Median (good if outliers/anomalies) and range are most appropriate for ordinal level of data.

Mean and standard deviation are most appropriate for interval/ratio level of data.

Strengths and weaknesses

Median: A strength is that it is not distorted by outliers/anomalies/rogue scores, i.e. data that are very different from the rest of the score distribution because they are very high or low, as it only uses the middle datum in the score distribution. This means it can be used when you are unsure about the reliability of the extreme values and when you have skewed distributions. But a weakness is that it is less precise because it does not use all of the data.

Mean: A strength is that it is precise and the most sophisticated measure of central tendency because it uses all of the data, whereas a weakness is that it is easily distorted or skewed by outliers as a result of using all of the data. This means it is fine when the data form a normal distribution (the bell-shaped curve) but when there are extreme outlying values (anomalies) the mean value is easily distorted and so the median should be used instead.

Range: Strengths are that it is easy to calculate and it does not make use of all the data in the score distribution. However, the range may not be very representative because the two most extreme values are used to calculate it and if these are outlying the calculated range will not be representative of the distribution.

Standard deviation: The standard deviation uses all the scores in a set of data and measures dispersion in terms of deviation from the mean. Consequently, it is more precise than the range and so is the best measure of dispersion to use. We can make inferences based on the relationship between the standard deviation and a normal distribution curve. The main weakness is that because interval or ratio levels of measurement are needed, and the data must be approximately normally distributed, then it is not always possible to use this more sophisticated measure.

Discourse analysis: Written transcripts are made and then the researcher looks closely at the words people use and the meanings behind them. It is highly subjective and the researcher needs to have excellent interpretative skills. The researcher will look for

EXAM HINT
Qualitative analysis—the stimulus study may be investigating meanings and so a qualitative analysis is more appropriate. Make sure you know the principles of qualitative analysis, as listed below, and you can describe how to carry it out.

recurrent themes and patterns in the data, which may or may not fit with previously constructed categories of what they expect to find. CONTEXTUALISE.

Content analysis: The researcher may quantify the data by counting the number of items that fall into each category. This is done to summarise the qualitative data and usually accompanies, rather than replaces, the more in-depth qualitative analysis. CONTEXTUALISE.

The Graphs and Charts question

> **?** Which graph would be most appropriate to illustrate the data in Table 1 and why is this an appropriate descriptive method? **1 + 1 MARKS** OR
>
> Give a full title or label both axes for the graph/table. **2 MARKS**

Make sure you can select graphs and charts appropriately, e.g. a scattergraph for correlated data or a bar chart for discontinuous experimental data (nominal/ordinal level do not form a continuous scale) and histogram or frequency polygon for continuous data (interval/ratio level—because equal intervals do form a continuous scale). If you are asked to give a title to a graph or table make sure both variables have been included and are clearly communicated: IV and DV if experimental and V1 and V2 if correlational, e.g. a bar chart to show the gender difference in self-report ratings of the importance of physical attractiveness in mate selection. If asked to label axes, state the variable and include the scale in brackets if it has been given in the question.

The Data Response question

> **?** What was found in the study? **2 OR 4 MARKS** OR
>
> State one or two findings/conclusions that can be drawn from the data in Figure 1/Table 1 and use this data to explain your answer. **2 OR 4 MARKS**

Practise summarising results and conclusions and interpreting graphs and tables. If findings are asked for state what is shown in the graph/table BUT if conclusions are asked for DO NOT state the findings as you must move beyond this and make a JUDGEMENT about what the findings show.

The Quantitative vs Qualitative Approach question

 Give advantages and disadvantages of the quantitative/ qualitative approach. **2 + 2 MARKS PER QUESTION**

Give advantages and disadvantages of each. For example, the quantitative approach is replicable (can be repeated) and so it has high reliability, however, the artificiality of the approach may act as a source of bias and so limit the internal validity (truth) of the research. For example, an artificial experimental set-up that gives away cues to the hypothesis may result in demand characteristics, and so the results might be due to this rather than the IV, and so would lack internal validity. Also, the artificiality of the research and consequent lack of mundane realism may limit the generalisability of the research to other settings (external validity). Qualitative gathers in-depth data, which is high in internal validity (truth) as this tends to make it meaningful and highly representative but is difficult to replicate and so lacks reliability. Also, because the qualitative approach tends to investigate individuals or small groups then the research tends to lack generalisability (external validity).

? **Explain how to obtain quantitative/qualitative data about the participants' behaviour.** **2 + 2 MARKS PER QUESTION**

Quantitative
Quantitative = numbers. This is where you should look at the question stimulus and think about how the behaviour can be recorded as a number, e.g. frequency, self-report rating, time. Closed questions provide quantitative data, e.g. frequency answering yes/no,

or a self-report scale where participants are asked to rate their behaviour, because both the frequencies and rating scores are numerical data.

Qualitative

Qualitative = words. Again you need to look at the question stimulus and think about how themes and patterns of behaviour could be analysed; it is difficult to give examples as these need to be in context. Open questions provide qualitative data because participants answer freely in these questions and so data is in the form of words.

BIOLOGICAL PSYCHOLOGY
Stress

STRESS AS A BODILY RESPONSE

Definition question

The body's response to stress

> **?** **Explain what is meant by the term stress.** **3 MARKS**

AO ADVICE

This is an "explain WHAT" question because it requires you to outline the body's responses to stress, and so this is an AO1 question.

Stress: Stress is a state of psychological and physical tension produced, according to the transactional model, when there is a mismatch between the perceived demands of a situation (the stressor[s]) and the individual's perceived ability to cope. The consequent state of tension can be adaptive (eustress) or maladaptive (distress).

EXAM HINT

This definition of stress is known as the "mismatch" definition. Remember this to help you remember the definition.

Explanation questions

> **?** **What are the two ways the body responds to stress?**
> **3 + 3 MARKS**

EXAM HINT

Try making up an acrostic to help you remember the order of the SAM and the HPA.

1) The sympathetic adrenal medullary axis (SAM) is known as the shock response because it is the body's first response to stress and happens within the first 30 seconds. The stress is detected by the cortex, which transmits messages to the

HYPOTHALAMUS, which activates the SYMPATHETIC BRANCH of the autonomic nervous system. The sympathetic branch causes the ADRENAL MEDULLA to release ADRENALINE AND NORADRENALINE. These stress hormones increase arousal and so provide the energy needed for the "fight-or-flight" response. Other effects of the hormones are increased heart beat, blood pressure, breathing rate, and temperature, increased blood flow to the muscles, and inhibited digestion.

2) The hypothalamic–pituitary–adrenocortical axis (HPA) is known as the countershock response because it happens after the shock response. In this response the HYPOTHALAMUS activates the PITUITARY GLAND, which causes ACTH to be released, which acts on the ADRENAL CORTEX, which releases CORTICOSTEROIDS such as cortisol. These stress hormones increase glucose release and suppress the immune system.

EXAM HINT

Do make sure you know the parasympathetic response. This is a less common question but an important one to know just in case.

? **Explain what happens in the body after the stress has ended.** **3 MARKS**

If the stress disappears, the symptoms of sympathetic arousal will begin to subside, thus, heart rate, temperature, and breathing rate will gradually return to normal levels. This is due to the increased activity of the parasympathetic branch of the autonomic nervous system, which is responsible for relaxation of the body, and decreased activity of the sympathetic branch. The body returns to a normal state of arousal, blood flow will be redirected back from the muscles to the major organs, and digestive processing will normalise.

Essay question

? **Outline and evaluate the body's response to stress.** **8, 10, OR 12 MARKS**

EXAM HINT

Outline the SAM and the HPA for paragraph 1 and to evaluate you will find lots to write about if you focus on the problems of just taking a physiological approach to stress.

> 10-mark question: Leave out the last sentence of paragraph 1 to decrease AO1 and do the same in paragraph 2 to decrease AO2.
>
> 8-mark question: Leave out the last sentence of paragraph 1 and reduce the number of effects of sympathetic arousal, e.g. temperature, increased blood flow, to decrease AO1. Leave out the last two sentences in paragraph 2 to decrease AO2.

Paragraph 1 AO1

The body's initial response to stress, the sympathetic adrenal medullary axis (SAM), is known as the shock response and happens within the first 30 seconds. The stress is detected by the cortex, which transmits messages to the hypothalamus. The hypothalamus activates the sympathetic branch of the autonomic nervous system (ANS). The sympathetic branch causes the adrenal medulla to release adrenaline and noradrenaline. These stress hormones increase the arousal of the sympathetic nervous system. This high physiological arousal creates the energy needed for the "fight-or-flight" response and also leads to increased heart beat, blood pressure, breathing rate, and temperature, increased blood flow to the muscles, and inhibited digestion. The hypothalamic–pituitary–adrenocortical axis (HPA) is known as the countershock response because it happens after the shock response. In this response the hypothalamus activates the pituitary gland causing ACTH to be released, which acts on the adrenal cortex and causes corticosteroids such as cortisol to be released. These stress hormones increase glucose release for the energy needed for the stress response and decrease white blood cell production, so suppressing the immune system.

Paragraph 2 AO2

Research on the body's response to stress has had positive implications in terms of our understanding of stress and illness. However, evidence against the usefulness of this research is that psychological factors that are involved are ignored, e.g. self-perception. Also, individual differences modify the effects of stress and so show that it is not solely a physiological response, e.g. individual differences in self-perception, gender, personality, culture, and stress management could all modify the effects of stress and so there is not an entirely common physiological response as the SAM and HPA suggest. The effects of stress on the body can be measured objectively as these are biological measures that are not open to bias from researcher and participant effects, and so in this sense the research is scientific. Conclusive findings are difficult as in real life many variables are involved in such a complex response and only biological factors have been considered. This is reductionist (oversimplified) because the physiological approach only accounts for nature not nurture. This is only one level of the stress experience: behavioural, cognitive, unconscious, and emotional levels have been ignored.

Recognition questions

EXAM HINT

If you are unsure, go back to the question above on the two ways the body responds to stress and make an acrostic or a visual image. You must learn this scientific bit so try to make it easier for yourself by using what you know about memory improvement!

AO ADVICE

This question requires you to recognise and organise content and so assesses AO1.

? Use the phrases below to complete the diagram, so that it shows the dual-body response to stress.

Stimulates the sympathetic branch of the ANS

Stimulates the adrenal cortex

Releases adrenaline and noradrenaline

Stimulates the adrenal medulla

Releases corticosteroids

Stimulates the pituitary gland to release ACTH

6 MARKS

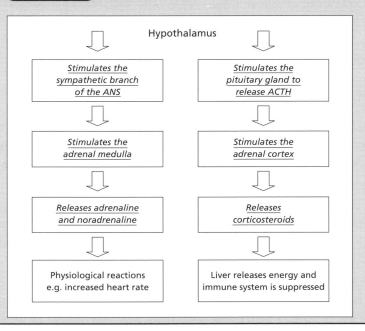

The following are features of the dual response to stress: the hypothalamic–pituitary–adrenocortical axis and the sympathetic adrenal medullary axis.

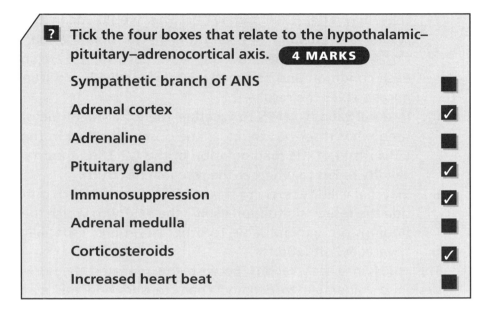

? Tick the four boxes that relate to the hypothalamic–pituitary–adrenocortical axis. **4 MARKS**

Sympathetic branch of ANS ■

Adrenal cortex ✓

Adrenaline ■

Pituitary gland ✓

Immunosuppression ✓

Adrenal medulla ■

Corticosteroids ✓

Increased heart beat ■

How Science Works question

? In an experiment into stress researchers tested the effect of stress on heart beat. The participants' heart rates were first tested at resting and then tested again after experiencing mild stress, during which they spent 20 minutes trying to solve unsolvable anagrams.

(a) (i) Which experimental design is this? **1 MARK**

(ii) Give one advantage and one weakness of this design. **2 + 2 MARKS**

(b) (i) What is internal validity in the context of psychological research? **2 MARKS**

(ii) What is external validity in the context of psychological research? **2 MARKS**

(c) Discuss the validity of this study. **5 MARKS**

EXAM HINT

Note for (a) participants do BOTH conditions. Defining validity is hopefully not too much of a problem; applying it to this study takes more thought. Think about the design and how being in both conditions is more likely to lead to demand characteristics, and also consider what is good about the validity of the study.

(a) (i) Repeated measures.
(ii) Demand characteristics are an order effect, which means because the participants experience two conditions they are more likely to guess the purpose of the study and so they may alter their behaviour. This would mean the results are not valid. A strength is that it minimises participant variables because the same participants are in each condition and so there are fewer individual differences to bias the results.

(b) (i) Internal validity refers to whether the experiment measured what it set out to, i.e. is the observed effect in the DV a result of the manipulation of the IV? Thus, internal validity refers to whether the research has truth.
(ii) External validity refers to the validity of the research outside the research situation itself—the extent to which the findings are generalisable to other situations, especially "everyday" situations.

(c) The study may lack validity because the repeated measures design is vulnerable to demand characteristics and this may mean the participants' behaviour is not genuine. On the other hand, it is not that easy to manipulate one's bodily response and so the fact that a physiological measure is being taken increases validity because it is less affected by participant bias. It is also less affected by researcher bias because the quantitative measure of the heart beat is objective—it is not open to interpretation. There may be a sample bias, which means the participants may all be less stressed by the unsolvable anagrams than the general population, which means the findings would not be representative and so would lack population validity. A further issue is that unsolvable anagrams are not like real-life stress and so lack mundane realism, which means the findings lack generalisability to everyday stressors and this limits external validity.

Stress-related illness and the immune system

Explanation question

> **?** **What are the effects of stress on the immune system?** **6 MARKS**

Stress decreases the number of white blood cells, a process known as immunosuppression. Stress leads to suppression of the immune system due to the action of the corticosteroids (released as part of the HPA axis) because they stop the production of the white blood cells, B and T, the natural killer cells. With fewer white blood cells there are fewer antibodies to fight invading antigens. This makes the body much more vulnerable to the effects of foreign bodies. Short-term suppression is not dangerous as the body can recover, but long-term stress can leave the body vulnerable to infection and disease, e.g. bacterial and viral infections. Immunosuppression has also been linked to cancer as stress reduces the ability of the immune system to fight a range of diseases.

Research questions

AO ADVICE

The research questions require you to outline research and so these are AO1 questions.

EXAM HINT

Kiecolt-Glaser et al. have conducted two key studies into stress and the immune system. In these answers the study of wound healing in caregivers has been used.

? **(a) (i) Outline the procedures of one study into the effects of stress on the immune system. OR Explain how the effects of stress on the immune system have been studied.** **6 MARKS**

Kiecolt-Glaser et al. (1995) studied the effect of stress on wound healing. There were two groups: (1) 13 caregivers who were women looking after a relative with Alzheimer's disease; and (2) 13 control participants who were women matched in age and family income with the caregivers. The caregivers (who had on average been looking after a relative for almost 8 years) scored much higher on a perceived stress scale than did the controls. The functioning of the immune system was studied by creating a small wound on the forearm close to the elbow; this is known technically as a punch biopsy. The time taken for the wound to heal was assessed by photographing the wound regularly and by observing the response to hydrogen peroxide (an absence of foaming indicated healing).

A small amount of blood was obtained for analysis before the punch biopsy took place.

> **?** **(ii) Outline the findings of one or more study(ies) into the effects of stress on the immune system.**
>
> **6 MARKS**

The key finding in Kiecolt-Glaser et al.'s (1995) study into the effect of stress on wound healing was that the time taken for the wound to heal was significantly longer for the caregivers than for the controls. The healing time averaged 48.7 days for the caregivers and 39.3 for the controls, so on average the caregivers took 9 days longer. In addition, the caregivers had a larger average wound size than the controls, especially during the first few days after the wound had been created. Analysis of the blood collected from the participants revealed that the caregivers produced significantly less interleukin-1β than controls under certain conditions. This may be important because interleukin-1β seems to play a role in speeding up wound healing. The caregivers also reported more stress than the controls in a self-report measure of stress.

> **?** **(iii) Give two criticisms of the research into the effects of stress on the immune system.** **3 + 3 MARKS**

(1) The groups of caregivers and controls may have differed in ways other than the level of psychological stress; for example, more caregivers were on medication, and this may have affected their immune system. This means we cannot be sure of the validity of the findings because we cannot be sure that stress was the cause of the immunosuppression.

(2) Sample bias is an issue because it was a small and preliminary study with only 13 participants in each group, and so the study needs to be repeated with a larger sample. The findings of such a small sample lack generalisability to a wider population and so external validity is limited.

Essay question

> **?** **Critically consider the relationship between stress and the immune system.** **8, 10, OR 12 MARKS**

AO ADVICE

The injunction "critically consider" requires both AO1 and AO2 so as usual make sure your answer is evenly balanced in terms of both components.

EXAM HINT

If the question is the shorter 8 or 10 marks then reduce the content on Kiecolt-Glaser et al.'s research by leaving out the procedures. In paragraph 2 leave out the first criticism about individual differences and condense the natural experiment criticism if you need to.

10-mark question: Leave out the last sentence of paragraph 1 to decrease AO1. Leave out the last point about the same wound to decrease AO2.

8-mark question: Leave out the last two sentences of paragraph 1 to decrease AO1. Leave out the last point about the same wound and reduce the point about the caregivers and controls differing in other ways to decrease AO2.

Paragraph 1 AO1

Biological evidence for a link between stress and illness is that stress leads to suppression of the immune system due to the action of the corticosteroids (released as part of the HPA axis) because they reduce the production of the white blood cells, B and T, the natural killer cells. Thus, the number of white blood cells is reduced and so there are fewer antibodies to fight infections and disease. Research by Kiecolt-Glaser et al. (1995) shows the link between stress and illness. They studied caregivers and a control group and assessed the functioning of the immune system by creating a small wound on the forearm close to the elbow (a punch biopsy). The time taken for the wound to heal was assessed by photographing the wound regularly and by observing the response to hydrogen peroxide (an absence of foaming indicated healing). A small amount of blood was obtained for analysis before the punch biopsy took place. The key finding was that the time taken for the wound to heal was significantly longer, 9 days, for the caregivers than for the controls. In addition, the caregivers had a larger average wound size than the controls, especially during the first few days after the wound had been created. Analysis of the blood collected from the participants revealed that the caregivers produced significantly less interleukin-1β than controls under certain conditions. This may be important because interleukin-1β seems to play a role in speeding up wound healing.

Paragraph 2 AO2

However, the research evidence into the relationship between stress and illness has a number of criticisms. The individual differences that characterise humans are largely ignored, e.g. gender, personality, individual differences in physiological reactivity, coping ability, resilience. The research into stress and illness seems to suggest that there is a universal response to stress, i.e. the SAM and HPA, but individual differences may modify the effects of stress. This means that potential vulnerability to stress-related illness is also highly variable. This limits the generalisability of the research, which is already limited due to sample bias as the sample was ethnocentric (only one culture was sampled) and estrocentric (as only females were sampled). The sample was also small (only 13 in each condition), which questions the generalisability of the findings. A further limitation is the natural experimental method. It is a natural experiment because the IV, whether participants were caregivers or not, cannot be controlled. As a consequence, cause and effect cannot be established, because cause can only be concluded when an IV has been directly manipulated. It cannot be said that stress caused the slower wound healing and reduced immune functioning, and so conclusions are limited as association only can be inferred. The groups of caregivers and controls may have differed in ways other than the level of psychological stress; for example, more caregivers were on medication, and this may have affected their immune system. On a positive note, the fact that Kiecolt-Glaser et al. created the same wound in all of the participants means they could observe the effects of stress on the immune system in a controlled way.

Application of knowledge questions

> **?** John has visited his doctor complaining of reoccurring colds. He also feels very tired, but despite this sometimes has trouble sleeping. He explained to the doctor that he is under pressure at work and he often feels irritable, which leads to arguments with his wife.

> Use your knowledge of the effects of stress on the body and the immune system to explain John's experiences. **4 MARKS**

EXAM HINT

Use your knowledge of the dual-stress response and how this affects the body and the immune system. Do make sure you relate your answer to John, otherwise your mark will be limited. You can use both theory (e.g. dual-stress response) and research (e.g. Kiecolt-Glaser et al.'s) in your answer. If you detail the theory you will not need the research as the question is only worth 4 marks.

John is experiencing a number of stressors and this will be affecting his body due to the prolonging of the body's response to stress. The stress hormones released by the SAM axis will be causing a high level of arousal and this explains why he is having trouble sleeping, and high arousal plus tiredness is likely to make him argumentative. Stress also suppresses the immune system. The activation of the HPA axis causes immunosuppression due to the release of corticosteroids. These stop the production of the white blood cells, B and T, and the natural killer cells. With fewer white blood cells there are fewer antibodies to fight infections and disease. This explains why John has recurring colds because his suppressed immune system will leave him unable to fight off the cold virus.

> **?** A teacher has fallen ill with a cold by the third week of September. She found the start of term very busy and tiring. Use your knowledge of the immune system to explain why the teacher may have fallen ill.
> **4 MARKS**

EXAM HINT

In this question detail the HPA axis briefly so that you do have time to use research evidence as well.

Starting back at school after a long holiday is a busy time and this may have placed the teacher under stress if she doubts her ability to cope. Stress can reduce the effectiveness of the immune system because the activation of the HPA axis causes immunosuppression due to the release of corticosteroids. These stop the production of white blood cells, B and T, and the natural killer cells. With fewer white blood cells there are fewer antibodies to fight infections and disease. Kiecolt-Glaser et al. (1984) found that the immune systems of students during the stress of exams were suppressed and this is what has happened to the teacher. Stress has suppressed the teacher's immune system and so made her more likely to become ill.

How Science Works question

EXAM HINT
Consider sample bias and extraneous variables in your answer.

> **?** Explain why research into stress and the immune system can be criticised as lacking validity. **4 MARKS**

Kiecolt-Glaser et al.'s (1995) research is limited by sample bias. The sample was ethnocentric (only one culture was sampled) and estrocentric (as only females were sampled). The sample was also small, with only 13 in each condition, which questions the generalisability and so population validity of the findings. The groups of caregivers and controls may have differed in ways other than the level of psychological stress; for example, more caregivers were on medication, and this extraneous variable may have affected their immune systems. If this is the case then the study has not measured what it set out to and so the research lacks internal validity.

STRESS IN EVERYDAY LIFE

Workplace stress

Definition question

EXAM HINT
Make sure you can explain both these terms but don't worry about learning them word for word; just be able to say what they mean in your own words.

> **?** Explain what is meant by the term . . . **3 MARKS**

Stressor: A stressor is an event that triggers the stress response because it throws the body out of balance and forces it to respond, for example, life changes (e.g. divorce, bereavement), daily hassles (e.g. traffic, lost keys), workplace stressors (e.g. role strain, lack of control), and environmental stressors (e.g. noise, temperature, overcrowding). Stressors are not objective in that they do not produce the same response in all people as this depends on the individual's perception of the stressor. Thus, nothing is a stressor unless it is thought to be so!

Workplace stress: This is stress related to the workplace, and refers to factors in the work environment or aspects of the job that cause stress. For example, overcrowding, noise, and temperature are factors in the environment. Lack of control, interpersonal relationships, role ambiguity, and work overload are all examples of work pressures that cause stress.

Explanation question

> **?** **Outline two sources of stress in the workplace.**
>
> **2 + 2 MARKS**

AO ADVICE

This is an outline question and so requires knowledge and understanding. You should aim to write about 35 words for each source of stress.

(i)   One aspect of the workplace is job control. Lack of control of deadlines or the pace of one's work, e.g. if it is machine paced, can be very stressful because the person is unable to determine how much work they do.

(ii) Another aspect of the workplace is work load—either too much or too little work can cause stress. Too much can leave the person feeling overwhelmed by the volume of work and too little can lead to boredom or frustration.

Research questions

> **?** **(a) (i) Outline the procedures of one study into workplace stress. OR Explain how workplace stress has been studied.** **6 MARKS**

EXAM HINT

Marmot et al.'s research into the civil service is a key study looking at the factor of job control. Remember the second question is asking for the same as the first, i.e. the procedures of a study into workplace stress.

Marmot et al. (1997) studied workplace stress using a sample of 10,308 civil servants aged 35–55 (6895 men—67%, and 3413 women—33%). They were investigated in a longitudinal study over three years. Research methods included questionnaires and observation. Job control and work load (both aspects of workplace stress) were measured through both a self-report survey and by independent assessments of the work environment by personnel managers. Job control and work overload were assessed on two occasions, three years apart. Records were also kept of stress-related illness. Correlational analyses were carried out to test the associations between job control and stress-related illness, and work overload and stress-related illness.

> **?** **(ii) Outline the findings of one or more study(ies) into workplace stress.** **6 MARKS**

In Marmot et al.'s (1997) study, participants with low job control were FOUR times more likely to die of a heart attack than those with high job control. They were also more likely to suffer from other stress-related disorders such as cancers, strokes, and gastro-intestinal disorders. These findings were consistent on both occasions that job control was measured and the association was still significant after other factors, such as employment grade, negative attitude to employment, job demands, social support, and risk factors for coronary heart disease (CHD), had been accounted for. No relationship was found between work load and illness.

> **?** **(iii) Give two criticisms of the research into workplace stress.** **3 + 3 MARKS**

(i) Marmot et al.'s (1997) research is correlational and so there is no control over the variable job control. This makes interpretation difficult because cause and effect can't be established. Thus, we can't say that low job control causes stress-related illness. It is possible that workers whose health is poor are less likely than healthy workers to achieve career success and to have jobs offering good control.

(ii) The jobs performed by those high and low in job control differed in several ways other than simply control. For example, those having high levels of job control generally earn more money, have more interesting jobs, and have more opportunity for interpersonal contact, and so on, than those having low levels of job control. So we don't know which of these various factors is most closely associated with heart disease.

Essay question

> **?** **Discuss the extent to which the workplace is a source of stress.** **8, 10, OR 12 MARKS**

> **EXAM HINT**
> After outlining the factors, do outline some research evidence as well to ensure you have written enough for 6 marks' worth of AO1. Note correlational criticisms and individual differences are both key sources of AO2.
>
> 10-mark question: Reduce the content on Johansson et al., so give a brief summary of the methods and findings to reduce AO1. Leave out the last sentence of paragraph 2 to reduce AO2.
>
> 8-mark question: Reduce the content on Johansson et al., so give a brief summary of the findings to reduce AO1. Leave out the last two sentences of paragraph 2 to reduce AO2.

> **AO ADVICE**
> The injunction "discuss" requires both AO1 and AO2 in equal proportion.

Paragraph 1 AO1

Workplace stress has a number of sources as both factors in the work environment and aspects of the job can be sources of stress. For example, overcrowding, noise, temperature, lack of control, job insecurity, interpersonal relationships, role ambiguity, work overload, and shift work are all examples of work pressures that cause stress. Marmot et al.'s (1997) study found that participants with low job control were four times more likely to die of a heart attack than those with high job control. They were also more likely to suffer from other stress-related disorders such as cancers, strokes, and gastrointestinal disorders. These findings suggest that low job control is associated with high stress and so the variables are negatively correlated. Johansson et al. (1978) studied workplace stress in a Swedish saw mill. They compared two groups of workers. One group, the finishers, was high risk because their job was repetitive, machine paced, required continuous attention, and allowed little time to socialise. They were also responsible for the final output of the factory, and so everybody else's wages. In contrast, the cleaners were the low-risk group because their work was more flexible and allowed them time to socialise. This shows that work overload is a key source of stress.

Paragraph 2 AO2

However, this research evidence has a number of methodological weaknesses. The self-report method used by Marmot is vulnerable to investigator effects and participant reactivity bias. The questions may give cues as to the aim of the research and so create an expectancy effect, which may also have affected the observations made by the personnel managers. Generalisability is an issue because of the ethnocentric samples (Marmot's all-British workers, Johansson's all-Swedish workers) involved in the research, which means the research is not representative of other cultures and so lacks external validity. Methodology is a key weakness as much of the research is correlational and so cause and effect cannot be established because job control and work load cannot be manipulated as an IV, and such control is needed to establish causation. Thus, it cannot be said that low/high job control causes stress-related illness, only that an association can be inferred. The same is true of most workplace pressures as these cannot ethically be manipulated. A correlation predicts a one-directional linear relationship but in fact the direction of effect is not clear, as Marmot et al.'s (1997) research suggests that those with high job control are less stressed but it is also likely to be the case that those who are less stressed achieve positions with higher job control. The lack of control over the variable (workplace stress) means that other factors (e.g. individual differences, personality, gender, self-perception of the stressor, coping skills) may be involved in the correlation. Furthermore, we need to consider that there may be factors in the work environment that affect stress other than those identified as work pressures. Those who earn more money, have more interesting jobs, or have more opportunity for interpersonal contact, and so on, may be better protected than those who lack these "buffers".

Application of knowledge question

> **?** A psychologist has been called in to assess the workplace stress in a media company. Staff absenteeism and turnover are high and so the board of directors wants to find out if there are any particular stressors within their workplace. Using your knowledge of workplace stress, identify three stressors the psychologist might find. **2 +2 + 2 MARKS**

EXAM HINT
This is really the same as the question above that asks you to outline two sources of stress.

The psychologist might find job control and work load are factors because:

(i) Low job control means lack of control of deadlines or the pace of one's work, e.g. if the workers have no say over the amount of time that they have to work on different projects.
(ii) Too much or too little work can cause stress. Too much can leave the person feeling overwhelmed by the volume of work and too little can lead to boredom or frustration.
(iii) Effort–reward imbalance is when the rewards provided at work (e.g. salary, social approval, career opportunities) are very low considering the work efforts that are required. Smith et al. (2005) have linked the effort–reward imbalance with cardiovascular disease.

How Science Works question

> **?** A psychologist decides to investigate the stress experienced by children and teenagers and see how this changes over time. He plans to interview the children aged 6, 12, and 18 years of age.
>
> (a) Give one advantage and one disadvantage of researching stress using interviews. **3 + 3 MARKS**
>
> (b) Give one weakness of a longitudinal study. **3 MARKS**

> **EXAM HINT**
> Another "evaluate the method" question. This should be telling you how important it is to know advantages and weaknesses of each method. Note that 3 marks have been allocated, so you do have to be selective, as some candidates choose relevant evaluation points but the ones they choose are difficult to elaborate for the third mark.

(a) One advantage: A strength of using an interview is that more in-depth data can be obtained from the participant because the interviewer can build up a relationship with the participant and so encourage them to open up more about their experience of stress, which they may not do in a written questionnaire. This means the data would be more meaningful because it would be more true of the participant's experience and so have high internal validity.

One disadvantage: One weakness of the interview method is interviewer bias. Because the questions asked are subjective, the researcher may ask leading questions that encourage the participants to answer how the researcher expects them to. Data analysis is vulnerable to misinterpretation, either deliberately or unconsciously. The researcher may be drawn to data that corroborates the research hypothesis and may disregard data that doesn't, and so internal validity will be reduced because the participant's answers will lack truth.

(b) A weakness of the longitudinal study is that sample drop-off often occurs because not all participants agree to continue to be studied over time. This limits the generalisability, and so external validity, of the findings because the sample that is left of participants who haven't dropped out is no longer as representative as the original sample would have been. The participants who stayed in the study may be more motivated or they may not reflect the full range of results.

Life changes and daily hassles

Definition question

> **?** Explain what is meant by the term life changes.
> **3 MARKS**

Life changes require some degree of social readjustment or alteration in the individual's current life patterns (life change), which is the response to a significant life event. For example, death, divorce, a change of job, marriage, vacation, or Christmas. Each life event is assigned a life change unit (LCU) based on how much readjustment the change would necessitate. The adaptation needed to cope with the life change absorbs energy, and so depletes the body's resources, and thus life changes are a source of stress.

EXAM HINT

Try to refer to social readjustment and LCU in your answer.

Explanation question

? **Outline life changes as a source of stress.** **6 MARKS**

EXAM HINT

Note how this can also be used as paragraph 1 of an essay question.

Life changes refer to major life events. These decrease energy and so weaken the individual's ability to fight illness. Life changes are measured on the Social Readjustment Rating Scale (SRRS), which was based on 5000 patients' medical records. Holmes and Rahe (1967) identified 43 life events that had preceded illness and then asked a group of participants to rate them based on how much readjustment they would involve. Each event was consequently assigned a life change unit (LCU). Of the 43 events, death of a spouse was rated the highest (100) and minor violations of the law was rated the lowest (11). The LCUs for each event experienced are added up and the higher the score the more likely a person is to suffer illness. The evidence from numerous studies is that a LCU of over 100 is correlated with minor illness and a LCU of 300 is correlated with major illness.

Research questions

EXAM HINT

Rahe et al.'s study (1970) of the US naval men offers more content for a procedures question, but you would need to add in Holmes and Rahe's (1967) initial findings to provide enough content on a findings question.

? **(a) (i)** **Outline the procedures of one study into life changes. OR Explain how life changes have been studied.** **6 MARKS**

Rahe et al. (1970) studied 2500 male US naval men over a period of 6 months. A self-report questionnaire measured the number of life events, which was based on the Social Readjustment Rating Scale (SRRS) constructed by Holmes and Rahe (1967). This consisted of 43 life events, defined as positive or negative events that disrupt normal routines and so require social readjustment. Each life event had assigned to it a value (or life change unit, LCU) based on how much readjustment the event required. Participants were asked to indicate how many of the life events they had experienced in the past 6 months. A total life change unit score (stress score) was calculated for each participant by adding up the LCUs of each life event. A health record was also kept of each participant during the 6 month tour of duty. A correlational analysis was carried out to test the association between total LCUs and incidence of illness.

> **?** **(ii) Outline the findings of one or more study(ies) into life changes as a source of stress.** **6 MARKS**

A significant positive correlation of +0.118 was found between the total LCU score and illness (as total LCUs increased so did incidence of illness) in Rahe et al.'s (1970) study. The direction of the correlation was positive and the strength of the relationship was weak. The association was small but significant. Holmes and Rahe (1967), in their original research of patients' records, found that a number of life events preceded illness. They created the Social Readjustment Rating Scale to measure the stress of these life events by giving a life change unit (LCU) score. Evidence from numerous studies is that a LCU of over 100 is correlated with minor illness and a LCU of over 300 is correlated with major illness.

> **?** **(iii) Give two criticisms of the research into life changes.**
> **3 + 3 MARKS**

(i) A weakness of the research is that the evidence is correlational, which means that cause and effect cannot be established because the variables are not under the control of the researcher (causation can only be inferred when an independent variable has been directly manipulated). So it cannot be said that life changes cause coronary heart disease, only an association can be concluded, and so conclusions are limited.

(ii) The research into life changes does not account for self-perception because the values for each life event are assigned and this reduces its value because the amount of stress assigned to each life event is not the same for everyone. For example, marital separation may be less stressful for someone who has already established a relationship with another person.

Essay question

> **?** **Outline and evaluate life changes as a source of stress.**
>
> **8, 10, OR 12 MARKS**

EXAM HINT

Include an explanation of how the life changes scale was developed and a description of the evidence to make sure you access the AO1 marks.

10-mark question: Leave out the point about the participants rating each life event to reduce AO1 and leave out the point about direction of effect to decrease AO2.

8-mark question: Leave out the point about the 5000 patients' medical records and the participants rating each life event to reduce AO1. Leave out the point about direction of effect to decrease AO2 and reduce the commentary on individual differences.

Paragraph 1

Life changes refer to major life events. These decrease energy and so weaken the individual's ability to fight illness. Life changes are measured on the Social Readjustment Rating Scale (SRRS), which was based on 5000 patients' medical records. Holmes and Rahe (1967) identified 43 life events that had preceded illness and then asked a group of participants to rate them based on how much readjustment they would involve. Each event was consequently assigned a life change unit (LCU). Of the 43 events, death of a spouse was rated the highest (100) and minor violations of the law was rated the lowest (11). The LCUs for each event experienced are added up and the higher the score the more likely a person is to suffer illness. The evidence from numerous studies is that a LCU of over 300 is correlated with illness. A weak correlation of +0.118 was found in Rahe et al.'s study, in which they studied American naval men and correlated the number of life events they had experienced and amount of illness during a 6-month tour of duty.

Paragraph 2

A weakness of the research is that the evidence is correlational, which means that cause and effect cannot be established because the variables are not under the control of the researcher (causation can only be inferred when an independent variable has been directly manipulated). Also, other factors are likely to be involved in the association, as these are not controlled for in a correlation. For example, life events may lead to unhealthy behaviours, which are another factor in the relationship between life events and illness. The direction of effect can be questioned: is it that life events lead to stress or does stress lead to life events, such as a relationship breaking down? Also, the correlations found tend to be weak. The research uses a self-report scale, the SRRS, to measure life changes. However, this scale can be criticised because it fails to consider individual differences and these can modify experience of stressful life events, e.g. some people may react badly to a life event because they have a stressful personality type. Other differences include past experience, coping skills, gender, and culture, and these may explain the weak correlations. There are also individual differences in perception of the event, which are not taken into account by the SRRS because the values for each event are assigned and this reduces its value because the amount of stress assigned to each life event is not the same for everyone. For example, marital separation may be less stressful for someone who has already established a relationship with another person. The SRRS does not distinguish between desirable and undesirable life events. DeLongis et al. (1982) argue that daily hassles are more relevant to stress than life changes because life events are rare and only weak correlations have been found between them and illness. However, on the other hand, it should be noted that the research made an enormous contribution to our understanding of stress and illness by showing how stressful life changes can affect health.

Application of knowledge question

> **?** Hannah has been having a very stressful time. She has started a new job, broken up with her husband, and now has two children to look after.
>
> What does research into life changes predict about Hannah's future health? **5 MARKS**

Hannah has experienced significant life changes and, according to Holmes and Rahe, this can lead to ill health because stressful life changes suppress the immune system and so weaken the individual's ability to fight illness. Life changes are measured on the Social Readjustment Rating Scale (SRRS), which was based on 5000 patients' medical records. Holmes and Rahe (1967) identified 43 life events that had preceded illness and then asked a group of participants to rate them based on how much readjustment they would involve. Each event was consequently assigned a life change unit (LCU). The LCUs for each event experienced are added up and the higher the score the more likely a person is to suffer illness. Hannah would have a relatively high score due to the number of events she has experienced recently such as the new job, divorce, etc. The evidence from numerous studies is that a LCU of over 100 is correlated with minor illness and an LCU over 300 is correlated with major illness. So we would need to know Hannah's total LCU score to fully predict the effect of the life changes on her future health.

How Science Works question

> **?** In a study into stress, scores for life changes were calculated using the Holmes and Rahe *Social Readjustment Rating Scale* for 15 people in full-time employment. These were correlated with the number of days the individuals had taken off sick and the data was plotted on the graph below.

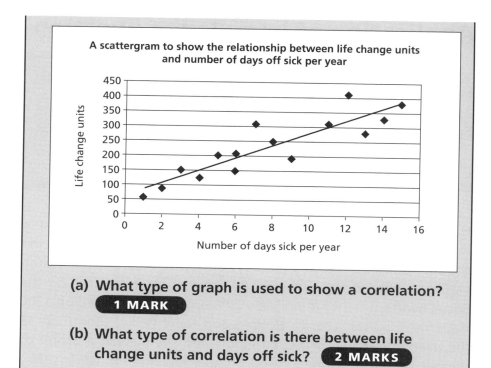

(a) **What type of graph is used to show a correlation?**
1 MARK

(b) **What type of correlation is there between life change units and days off sick?** **2 MARKS**

(c) **Explain the difficulties in concluding that the stress of life changes may result in people taking time off work.** **6 MARKS**

EXAM HINT

Most of the research into stress is correlational so if you can answer these questions, especially part (c), you have a very useful evaluation that you can use in most essays. So that should make it easier for you to get AO2 marks!

(a) Scattergram.

(b) A positive and moderate correlation because the variables rise and fall together but do not form a straight line and so the correlation is moderate rather than strong.

(c) We cannot conclude that the stress of life changes causes people to take time off work because the research is only correlational and so cause and effect cannot be established because the variables are not directly manipulated. We can only conclude that the stress of life changes and illness are related and so conclusions are limited. A further issue is that only two variables are investigated, but other factors may be involved that were not known of or were not accounted for in the research; many factors cause stress, not just life changes, and so the illness could be due to these. This means the inferred association would lack validity. Conclusions are also limited because we cannot be sure of the direction of effect of the correlation: is it that life events lead to stress or does stress lead to life events, such as a relationship breaking down?

Explanation question

> **?** Outline research into daily hassles. **6 MARKS**

The daily hassles and uplifts scale was devised by DeLongis et al. to measure daily hassles and uplifts such as issues to do with parents, children, work, sex difficulties, finances, housing, etc., each of which can be both a hassle and an uplift. Almeida (2005) categorised the daily hassles and found that 37% involved danger (e.g. potential for future loss), 30% involved some kind of loss (e.g. of money), and 27% were frustrations or events outside the individual's control. DeLongis et al. (1982) used a life events scale and their own hassles scale to see which was the better predictor of later health problems. DeLongis et al. (1982) found that the hassles scale correlated with illness, but the daily uplifts and life events had no relationship with illness. This suggests that uplifts do not actually compensate for the hassles, at least not in terms of their effect on health. Daily hassles may cause ill-health because they are associated with increased levels of cortisol, a stress-related hormone which suppresses the immune system (Sher, 2004).

EXAM HINT
To achieve the marks here four pieces of research have been used. It is a 6-mark question so it is only reasonable to include a fair amount of detail. Without research the answer would be basic and achieve half marks or under, which is not going to achieve a C grade or above.

Essay question

> **?** Outline and evaluate research into daily hassles. **8, 10, OR 12 MARKS**

EXAM HINT
You may wish to compare the daily hassles to the life changes scale as part of your commentary but make sure you keep this focused on daily hassles.

> 10-mark question: Condense Sher's research to reduce AO1 and reduce the commentary on individual differences in paragraph 2 to reduce AO2.
>
> 8-mark question: Leave out Sher's research to reduce AO1 and leave out the commentary on individual differences in paragraph 2 to reduce AO2.

Paragraph 1

The daily hassles and uplifts scale was devised by DeLongis et al. to measure daily hassles and uplifts such as issues to do with parents, children, work, sex difficulties, finances, housing, etc., each of which can be both a hassle and uplift. Almeida (2005) categorized the daily hassles and found that 37% involved danger (e.g. potential for future loss), 30% involved some kind of loss (e.g. of money), and 27% were frustrations or events outside the individual's control. DeLongis et al. (1982) used a life events scale and their own hassles scale to see which one was the better predictor of later health problems. DeLongis et al. (1982) found that the hassles scale correlated with illness, but the daily uplifts and life events had no relationship with illness. This suggests that uplifts do not actually compensate for the hassles, at least not in terms of their effect on health. Daily hassles may cause ill-health because they are associated with increased levels of cortisol, a stress-related hormone which suppresses the immune system (Sher, 2004).

Paragraph 2

In real life daily hassles interact with life events and so it is too simplistic to consider them as completely separate. For example, a life event such as loss of a job will lead to daily hassles such as financial concerns and possibly conflict with family. Similarly, daily hassles such as petty arguments with a partner could lead to a life event such as divorce. So it's too simplistic to say daily hassles link more to ill-health than life changes. A key weakness is that the evidence is correlational, which means that cause and effect cannot be established because the variables are not under the control of the researcher (causation can only be inferred when an independent variable has been directly manipulated). Also, other factors are likely to be involved in the association, as these are not controlled for in a correlation. For example, daily hassles may lead to unhealthy behaviours, which are another factor in the relationship between daily hassles and illness. The direction of effect can be questioned:

is it that daily hassles lead to stress or does stress cause daily hassles? For example, people may be more irritated by parents or children when stressed, or they may find work more of a hassle. There are also issues to do with individual differences in the meaning or significance of hassles. For example, a traffic jam may sometimes give you time to relax, whereas at other times it seems highly stressful. A further concern is that there has been much confusion about the distinction between daily hassles and chronic or long-lasting stressors (e.g. poor housing; strains of family life; unsatisfying work). When participants were asked to categorise items as either hassles or chronic stresses, many of the items allegedly measuring daily hassles were categorised as chronic stressors and vice versa, suggesting that the distinction is unclear, which means the validity of the research in these areas is questionable.

Application of knowledge question

> **?** Sarah has experienced a number of big changes in her life: she has moved house, moved job, and became a mother all in the space of 12 months. Hardeep's life has been more settled but she is frustrated by many things on a day-to-day basis: her commute to work, her colleagues at work, who all seem to be more successful than she is, and her children, who always seems to fight with each other.
>
> (a) (i) What is the name for Sarah's stress-related experiences?
>
>   (ii) What is the name for Hardeep's stress-related experiences?
>
> (b) Discuss which of these stressful experiences is more likely to lead to illness.   **4 MARKS**

EXAM HINT
In (b) do provide research evidence such as Holmes and Rahe (1967) and DeLongis et al. (1982).

(a) (i)   Life changes.
   (ii)   Daily hassles.

(b) Holmes and Rahe (1967), in their original research of patients' records, found that a number of life events preceded illness. They created the Social Readjustment Rating Scale to measure the stress of 43 life events, by giving each a life change unit (LCU) score based on how much readjustment the event would involve. Evidence from numerous studies is that a LCU of over 100 is correlated with minor illness and a LCU of over 300 is correlated with major illness. DeLongis et al. (1982) found that the hassles scale correlated with illness, but that life events had no relationship with illness. DeLongis et al. say that daily hassles are more relevant to stress because it is these that are experienced on a day-to-day basis, and so are always ongoing, whereas the life changes are less common experiences. So DeLongis et al. (1982) would say that the daily hassles are more likely to lead to illness than the life changes.

Essay question

> **?** **"Psychological research has provided evidence to show that stress can be caused by life changes and daily hassles. It has also provided evidence of individual differences in response to sources of stress."**
>
> **Critically consider the view that stress is environmentally determined.** **10 MARKS**

AO ADVICE

The injunction "critically consider" in this question is AO1 and AO2 in equal proportion.

EXAM HINT

This question asks you to consider life changes and daily hassles. So you can provide evidence for, but do not just agree with, the question. You also need to give evidence against, which is of course that stress is not just environmentally determined as it depends on the individual's perception of the stressor.

10-mark question: Reduce, the examples of hassles in the last section of paragraph 1 to reduce AO1 and reduce the point about the SRRS not assessing self-perception to reduce AO2.

8-mark question: Condense the Rahe et al. evidence and the examples of hassles in paragraph 1, reduce the point about the SRRS not assessing self-perception, and leave out the example of how the traffic jam can be perceived in different ways.

Paragraph 1

There is evidence that stress is environmentally determined. Holmes and Rahe (1967) provide evidence that stress can be caused by life changes. The number of events experienced when totalled generates a life event score (the total number of LCUs), and incidence of illness is also recorded to test for a positive correlation. The evidence from numerous studies is that a LCU of over 100 is correlated with minor illness and a LCU of over 300 is correlated with major illness. Rahe et al. found a weak correlation of +0.118 in their study of American naval men and correlated the number of life events they had experienced and amount of illness during a 6-month tour of duty. DeLongis et al. (1982) found evidence that daily hassles correlated with illness. These hassles include parents, children, work, sex difficulties, finances, housing, etc. This shows that a number of environmental factors can cause stress.

Paragraph 2

However, the problem with this evidence is that it does not account for individual differences, e.g. some people may react badly to a life event because they have a stressful personality type. Other differences include past experience, coping skills, gender, and culture, and these may explain the weak correlation. One of the strongest criticisms is that the SRRS doesn't assess self-perception because the values for each event are assigned, and this reduces its value because the amount of stress assigned to each life event is not the same for everyone. For example, marital separation may be less stressful for someone who has already established a relationship with another person. There are also issues to do with individual differences in the meaning or significance of hassles. For example, a traffic jam may sometimes give you time to relax, whereas at other times it seems highly stressful. A Type A person may cope better with these minor stressors than a Type B and so stress is not just environmentally determined. Stress is not just something external that happens to you, it is just as much internal and how the stress is perceived.

How Science Works questions

? A study using the daily hassles and uplifts scale correlated the amount of uplifts against the amount of stress to test if the uplifts did in fact lower stress. This was completed on an opportunity sample of mothers of young children.

(a) What sort of correlation was being tested? **1 MARKS**

(b) (i) Give one advantage and one weakness of the opportunity sample. **2 + 2 MARKS**

(ii) Which alternative method of sampling could be used and how is this carried out? **2 MARKS**

(a) A negative correlation.

(b) (i) An advantage of the opportunity sample is that sampling whoever is available is faster and easier and so more economical than other sample methods. However, the fact that it is up to the researcher's discretion to approach whoever is available leaves room for bias as the researcher may sample people he or she thinks are attractive or approachable, and so sample bias is a key weakness.

(ii) Random sampling could be used. This means every participant in the target population has an equal chance of being chosen. Random number tables, a computer that generates random numbers, or names out of a hat can be used to achieve a random sample.

? A psychologist decided to study daily hassles in teenagers. She decided to carry out a pilot study in which she listed the 10 most common hassles she felt were experienced by the age group. She also included an open question asking the participants to list up to three further hassles they felt had been missed out.

> **(a) (i) What is a pilot study?** `1 MARKS`
>
> **(ii) Why was it a good idea for the psychologist to conduct a pilot study?** `3 MARKS`

(a) (i) A pilot study is a small-scale trial run of the method and materials to be used in the real study to check that they work. So the timings of the procedure, how the researcher approaches the participants, and the clarity and appropriateness of the materials can be checked.

(ii) The daily hassles and uplifts scale is based on adults, and the participants in this study are teenagers, so it was a good idea to conduct a pilot study to test the relevance of the daily hassles to the age group of the participants. The pilot study allows the psychologist to check if the 10 hassles she has identified are correct and, if not, modify the list before the main study. Drawing on the ideas of participants from the same age group as will be used in the main study reduces researcher bias and is likely to make the list of hassles more relevant. This will mean the main study is better designed, and so the results should have greater validity.

> **?** **What are the weaknesses of using the hassles and uplifts scale to predict health and well being?** `4 MARKS`

EXAM HINT
Don't make the mistake of describing the hassles and uplifts scale; you simply have to take it that the examiner knows what it is and begin with the criticisms, which is what the question asks for.

A key weakness is that the evidence is correlational, which means that cause and effect cannot be established because the variables are not under the control of the researcher (causation can only be inferred when an independent variable has been directly manipulated). We can only conclude that the stresses of daily hassles and illness are related, and so conclusions are limited, which means we cannot really predict illness from the hassles and uplifts scale. A further issue is that only two variables are investigated, but other factors may be involved that were not known of or were not accounted for in the research; many factors cause stress—diet, lifestyle, life changes— not just daily hassles, and so the illness could be due to these. So this further limits any predictions that can be made from the scale.

Personality factors

Definition question

> ❓ **Explain what is meant by . . .** **2 MARKS**

EXAM HINT

Type A is more likely to be asked but do be ready to explain type B also.

AO ADVICE

If you get asked to explain a term, i.e. give AO1 content for 2 marks, to make sure you get the second mark give examples of characteristics of the personality type.

Type A behaviour: Type A personality was identified by Friedman and Rosenman (1974) as more stressed than other personality types due to three key characteristics (or traits): hostility, competition, and time pressure, which translate into many different characteristics such as ambition, impatience, competitiveness, workaholism, and intense and fast speech and movements.

Type B behaviour: Type B was identified by Friedman and Rosenman (1974) as the opposite of the stressful personality type A. So Type B is a low-stress personality type: less competitive, less hostile, more patient, slower speech, more easygoing, and slower movements.

Hardy personality: The hardy personality is characterised by the "three Cs". *Commitment*: "Hardy" individuals show greater involvement in their work and personal relationships. *Challenge*: Stressful situations are perceived as a challenge rather than a threat. *Control*: "Hardy" individuals feel that they are in control of their lives and this decreases stress because a lack of control is stressful. This personality type is thought to increase immunity to stress-related illnesses.

Explanation question

EXAM HINT

Use the words of the question to make sure you are clearly focused on the question.

> ❓ **Give two ways in which personality modifies the effects of stress.** **3 + 3 MARKS**

Personality Types A/B were researched by Friedman and Rosenman (1959) who had noticed consistent characteristics of the men referred to their clinic with coronary heart problems. Based on this they identified personality Type As as more stressed than other personality types. Type As have personality characteristics that modify the effects of stress and make them more susceptible to the ill effects of stress, such as being more likely to develop coronary heart disease (CHD) due to their increased hostility and competitiveness, and time-pressure leading to behaviours such as excessive ambition, impatience, workaholism, and a lowering of their immune function. Kobasa (1979) showed that other individuals described as hardy resist the ill effects of stress and consequent health problems such as CHD. Hardy individuals are better able to cope with stress because of certain characteristics. These people are committed to their personal and work roles, perceive stressful situations as a challenge rather than a threat, and feel that they are in control of their lives, all of which reduce the effects of stress on them. This personality type is thought to increase immunity to stress-related illnesses.

Research questions

> **?** **(a) (i) Outline the procedures of one study into personality factors in stress. OR Explain how personality factors have been studied.** **6 MARKS**

EXAM HINT
Friedman and Rosenman's study on personality and heart disease is the key study to consider here because it gives so much to write about on procedures, findings, and criticisms.

(i) Friedman and Rosenman (1974) studied the role of Type A/B personality in coronary heart disease (CHD). A volunteer sample of nearly 3200 Californian men aged between 39 and 59 years was used. This was a prospective, longitudinal study as the participants were healthy at the outset in 1960 and were assessed over a period of 8½ years. Part one of the study included a structured interview and observation, which assessed personality type and current health status. Personality type was determined by the amount of impatience, competitiveness, and hostility reported and observed during the structured interview. Participants were also observed to see how they reacted to conditions designed to stress them, such as being interrupted. For example, tapping of fingers on the table during the interview was seen as an indicator of impatience and so Type A. On the basis of the structured interview, participants were classified as A1 (Type A), A2 (not fully Type A), X (equal amounts of Type A and Type B), or B (fully Type B). Part two of the study was the follow-up 8 years later when incidence of CHD was recorded. A correlational analysis was carried out to test the association between Type A/B personality and CHD.

> **?** (ii) Outline the findings of one or more study(ies) into personality factors in stress. **6 MARKS**

Of the original sample of 3200, 257 participants had developed coronary heart disease (CHD) during the 8½ years, 70% of whom had been classified as Type A. CHD was twice as likely in men with Type A personalities than Type B, even when other factors (e.g. blood pressure, smoking, obesity) known to be associated with heart disease were taken into account. Compared to Type Bs, Type As were found to have higher levels of adrenaline and noradrenaline (both associated with stress) and cholesterol. A significant but moderate correlation was found between personality type and coronary heart disease. Matthews et al. (1977) re-analysed the data and found that the hostility component of Type A correlated higher with CHD than any of the other characteristics.

> **?** (iii) Give two criticisms of the research into personality factors in stress. **3 + 3 MARKS**

(1) Type A behaviour pattern consists of a number of characteristics and so it is not clear which characteristics of the personality type are most associated with coronary heart disease (CHD). This means the personality type is too broad to be useful and the research lacks internal validity, because it has not measured what it set out to, i.e. which characteristics increase vulnerability to CHD.

(2) Weaknesses of the correlational method mean that there is no control over Type A/B personality as a variable, which makes interpretations difficult. Cause and effect cannot be established because the variables are not under the control of the researcher (causation can only be inferred when an independent variable has been directly manipulated). So it cannot be said that Type A causes coronary heart disease,

only an association can be concluded, and so conclusions are limited.

Essay question

> ? Outline and evaluate research into personality factors in stress. Discuss psychological evidence that personality can modify our experience of stress.
>
> **8, 10, OR 12 MARKS**

EXAM HINT

Although these questions are worded differently, the same answer can be given so don't be thrown by the wording of the question.

10-mark question: If the shorter question is asked, reduce the content on the procedures in paragraph 1 and the direction of effect point in paragraph 2.

8-mark question: If the shorter question is asked, leave out the content on the procedures in paragraph 1 and the direction of effect point in paragraph 2.

Paragraph 1

Research into personality factors includes Friedman and Rosenman's (1974) research of personality Types A/B, based on their observation of consistent characteristics in the men referred to their clinic with coronory heart problems. Based on this they identified personality Type As as more stressed than other personality types due to three key components: hostility, competition, and time pressure, which translate into many different characteristics such as ambition, impatience, competitiveness, workaholism, etc. This personality type is considered more at risk for coronary heart disease (CHD), which is well supported by research evidence. However, later research has identified the hostility component as being the main risk factor as opposed to the personality type as a whole. Type B personalities are the opposite of Type A and so are usually more relaxed. Friedman and Rosenman tested this on a self-selected sample of nearly 3200 Californian men aged between 39 and 59 years. They were assessed over a period of 8½ years. Methods included a structured interview and observation, which assessed personality type and current health status. Personality type was determined by the amount of impatience, competitiveness, and hostility reported and observed during the structured interview and from their answers to questions under conditions designed to stress the participants, such as being interrupted. For example, tapping fingers on the table during the interview was seen as an indicator of impatience and so Type A. Friedman and Rosenman found that, of the 3200 participants, 257 developed coronary heart disease (CHD) during the 8½ years, 70% of whom had been classified as Type A. This was nearly twice as many as were Type B, even when other factors (e.g. blood pressure, smoking, obesity) known to be associated with heart disease were taken into account.

Paragraph 2

A weakness of the research is that Type A personality consists of a number of characteristics, and so the variable Type A lacks precision: does it make much sense to assign everyone in the world to only four categories? It is too broad to be useful, because it is not clear *which* aspect of Type A is most strongly associated with coronary heart disease (CHD). Consequently, the research lacked internal validity, as it did not precisely measure what it set out to. Later research by Matthews et al. (1977), who re-analysed the data, found that the hostility component of Type A correlated highest with CHD. Thus, hostility, rather than Type A in general, may explain the findings. Further issues, which include the weaknesses of the correlational method, mean that there is no control over Type A/B personality as a variable, and this makes interpretations difficult. For example, rather than causing physiological reactivity, the Type A personality may be a response to heightened physiological reactivity in some individuals. Thus, the direction of effect can be questioned: does Type A result in increased physiological reactivity or is Type A a result of high levels of physiological reactivity, which may be genetically determined? Most importantly, cause and effect cannot be inferred, as the variables are not under the control of the researcher (causation can only be inferred when an independent variable has been directly manipulated). Thus, it cannot be said that Type A personality *causes* coronary heart disease and so conclusions on the role of personality in stress are limited to associations.

Application of knowledge question

> **?** A mother thinks about her two daughters and how they have responded to going to school. Olivia always seems to be able to cope, with making new friends, with the amount of homework, and with the pressures of exams. Daisy is a lot more sensitive and worries about everything, including whether her friends will fall out with her. She spends hours making sure her homework is perfect, and really panics about her exams.
>
> Using your knowledge of stress, explain which factors could account for these different responses. **6 MARKS**

EXAM HINT

Although it hasn't explicitly mentioned them, this question is really asking about personality factors in stress. Remember, don't describe the personality factors in general; relate your answer to Olivia and Daisy.

The different responses of Olivia and Daisy can be explained by personality factors. Daisy finds things a lot more stressful and so she may have what Friedman and Rosenman (1974) identified as a Type A personality. Type As are more stressed than other personality types due to three key components: hostility, competition, and time pressure, which translate into many different characteristics such as ambition, impatience, workaholism, etc. This accounts for Daisy spending so long on her homework and getting so worried by her exams. Because she is competitive it will be important to her to do well. Olivia, on the other hand, is more laid back and so she may be a Type B personality, which is basically the opposite of A, so less competitive and less hostile, which explains why Daisy may be less affected by the stress of school and exams. This type is also characterized as more laid back, which may explain why Daisy has little trouble making friends. Another possibility is that Daisy copes well with stress because she has a hardy personality. This is supposed to make you more resilient to stress because of the characteristics of control, commitment, and challenge.

Explanation questions

Problem-focused and emotion-focused approaches to coping with stress

> **?** Outline the problem-focused approach to coping. **3 MARKS**

EXAM HINT

Remember this is an active approach that deals directly with the problem.

Problem-focused coping refers to strategies to reduce the stressor by changing the way the stressor is dealt with, for example, by seeking information about what to do to address the problem and seeking ways to control the stress such as through psychological methods of stress management to change the way the stressor is perceived. If the stress was work–life balance, the problem-focused approach would be to find ways of completing work faster, or reducing hours of work to solve the problem. Thus it is an active approach that attempts to deal directly with the problem and so the cause of the stress.

EXAM HINT

Make sure you focus on two strategies, don't give an account of the problem-focused approach in general.

? **Identify and explain two strategies used as part of the problem-focused approach to stress management.**

2 + 2 MARKS

(i) One problem-focused approach is seeking information; this can be from other people or other sources because this can help the person deal with the cause of the stress.

(ii) Another problem-focused approach is to use psychological methods of stress management to change how you think. This may solve the cause of stress if, for example, pessimism or other forms of cognitive bias were the cause of the stress.

Essay question

? **Critically consider the problem-focused approach to coping with stress.** **8, 10, OR 12 MARKS**

EXAM HINT

Just because the question is on problem-focused does not mean that you shouldn't include emotion-focused. Comparing the approaches is a great source of AO2 marks.

10-mark question: Reduce the last example in paragraph 1 and reduce the self-report criticisms in paragraph 2.

8-mark question: Leave out the last example in paragraph 1 and in paragraph 2 leave out the point about the social desirability effect.

Paragraph 1

Problem-focused coping refers to strategies to reduce the stressor by changing the way the stressor is dealt with, for example, by seeking information about what to do and seeking ways to control the stress such as through psychological methods of stress management. If the stress was work–life balance, the problem-focused approach would be to find ways of completing work faster, or reducing hours of work to solve the problem. This might include strategies such as making decisions, planning, and direct or indirect action. Thus it is an active approach that attempts to deal directly with the problem and so the cause of the stress. Folkman et al. (1986) suggest problem-focused coping is better. This may be because problem-focused is more likely to deal with the cause of the stress in comparison to emotion-focused coping, which just deals with the symptoms and so is less useful in reducing stress in the long term. Another example is a young mother stressed by family life using the problem-focused approach. She may introduce stress management techniques to her daily routines, which reduce her stress and so solve the problem.

Paragraph 2

However, this is not always the case, as problem-focused coping can only work if the stressor is to some extent controllable and so emotion-focused works best for uncontrollable stressors, according to the goodness-of-fit hypothesis. Thus, the best coping strategy may need to change to fit the situation. For example, Folkman and Lazarus (1985) found students faced by a stressful examination sought information (i.e. problem-focused coping) before the examination. Afterwards, while waiting to hear the results, the students typically made use of emotion-focused coping (e.g. forgetting all about the examination). However, an issue is that the goodness-of-fit hypothesis suggests the coping methods are completely separate approaches when they are not. Many forms of coping are both problem-focused and emotion-focused. For example, making a plan not only guides problem solving but also calms emotion. Another issue is that coping strategies are typically assessed by self-report questionnaires. What people report about general stress on a questionnaire may not be how they cope in real life and may not relate to specific stressors. They may exaggerate the effect of any coping strategy due to the social desirability effect (wanting to appear to cope well). This means the results may not be true, and so would lack validity, and so it is difficult to assess how effective the problem-focused approach is.

Explanation questions

EXAM HINT
There is a lot to write about emotion-focused so do think about what you would leave out for a 3-mark or 4-mark version.

? **Outline the emotion-focused approach to coping.**

6 MARKS

Emotion-focused refers to strategies to manage emotions by changing the way you feel about the stressor. These tend to manage the stress rather than address it directly because the strategies do not alter the stress but make the person feel better. For example, ego defence mechanisms, such as denial and repression, can help manage emotions by either denying the existence of the stressor or burying the unpleasant feelings caused by the stressor in the unconscious. Other strategies include venting anger on others or crying rather than confronting the source of the stress; or drinking, smoking, wishful thinking, and distraction activities such as comfort eating or escaping reality in some other way, such as watching TV. All of these are ways to manage emotions rather than dealing directly with the stressor, and so it is a passive approach that deals with the symptoms rather than the cause of the stress.

EXAM HINT
Note that the question asks for two strategies, and of course there are many, so pick two that you can easily elaborate for the second mark.

? **Identify and explain two strategies used as part of the emotion-focused approach to stress management.**

2 + 2 MARKS

(i) One emotion-focused approach to coping with stress is to use a defence mechanism such as denial because this helps manage the emotions by pretending the stress does not really exist.

(ii) Distraction activities, such as comfort eating or escaping reality in some other way such as watching TV, are ways to manage emotions and feel better rather than dealing directly with the stressor.

> **?** **Explain the difference between problem-focused and emotion-focused approaches to coping.** **6 MARKS**

Problem-focused takes a more direct approach to the stressor than emotion-focused because problem-focused involves using strategies to try to deal with the problem, the stressor, e.g. confronting somebody who is causing you stress, whereas emotion-focused is less direct than this because rather than confronting the stressor it involves reducing the way you feel about the stressor. This leads to the conclusion that the approaches differ because problem-focused is more likely to deal with the cause of the stress, whereas emotion-focused doesn't end the stressor, it provides a way to tolerate it and deal with the symptoms. Problem-focused is active because it addresses the cause, whereas emotion-focused is passive because it just deals with the effects of stress. Problem-focused can only work if the stressor is controllable and so emotion-focused works best for uncontrollable stressors.

EXAM HINT
Make sure you keep contrasting the approaches as the answer does, rather than desribing them separately, because that of course is not a comparison, but it is what some candidates do so make sure you avoid this common mistake. Note the use of whereas!

Essay question

> **?** **Critically consider the emotion-focused approach to coping with stress.** **8, 10, OR 12 MARKS**

EXAM HINT
Bring problem-focused in to gain extra marks through a comparison of the effectiveness of the two techniques in paragraph 2, so that you can use much of the same commentary in both essays, which leaves you less to learn!

10-mark question: Leave out the last example in paragraph 1 and reduce the self-report criticisms in paragraph 2.

8-mark question: Leave out the two examples in paragraph 1, and in paragraph 2 leave out the point about the social desirability effect.

Paragraph 1

The emotion-focused approach refers to strategies to manage emotions by changing the way you feel about the stressor. These tend to manage the stress, not remove it, because the strategies do not alter the stress but make the person feel better and therefore cope better. For example, ego defence mechanisms such as denial and repression can help manage emotions by either denying the existence of the stress or burying in the unconscious the unpleasant feelings caused by the stress. Other strategies include venting anger on others or crying rather than confronting the source of the stress; drinking, smoking, wishful thinking, and distraction activities such as comfort eating or escaping reality in some other way such as watching TV. All of these are ways to manage negative emotions rather than dealing directly with the stressor, and so it is a passive approach that deals with the symptoms rather than the cause of the stress. For example, a stressed-out manager may cope by venting and shouting at his staff as a way of expressing his negative emotions. Or a person may deal with their feelings of sadness by doing things that make them feel happier to try to manage their emotions.

Paragraph 2

The effectiveness of the emotion-focused approach has been questioned because Folkman et al. (1986) suggest problem-focused coping is better. This is because problem-focused tries to deal with the cause of the stress, whereas emotion-focused just deals with the negative symptoms. Emotion-focused coping strategies can even be dangerous, e.g. if the person is in denial that they have a serious illness, or if drugs or alcohol are used to numb emotions, their personal situation could get worse, or not improve. However, the emotion-focused approach can work better than the problem-focused approach if the stressor is uncontrollable because problem-focused only works for controllable stressors, and of course many stressors are difficult to control so emotion-focused may have more real-life validity because it may be used more in real life than problem-focused. Thus, the best coping strategy may need to change to fit the situation, according to the goodness-of-fit hypothesis. For example, Folkman and Lazarus (1985) found students typically made use of emotion-focused coping (e.g. forgetting all about the examination) while waiting to hear the results but sought information (i.e. problem-focused coping) before the examination. Another issue is that coping strategies are typically assessed by self-report questionnaires. What people report about general stress on a questionnaire may not be how they cope in real life and may not relate to specific stressors. They may exaggerate the effect of any coping strategy due to the social desirability effect (wanting to appear to cope well). This means the results would not be true and so would lack validity, and so it is difficult to assess how effective the emotion-focused approach is.

Application of knowledge question

? **Two managers of a large hotel take very different approaches to coping with the stressful situations that arise in the hotel. Robert is admired by all the staff for the calm way he analyses the situation, which allows him to identify the right strategy for dealing with the issue. David is not so well thought of as he tends to shout a lot when things go wrong, and this has alienated many of his colleagues. He realises this and frequently seeks comfort through alcohol.**

Using your knowledge of the approaches to coping with stress, explain the approach being favoured by each of the managers. **3 + 3 MARKS**

EXAM HINT

I'm sure you've picked up the fact that Robert is dealing with the problem, whereas David is just dealing with his emotions.

AO ADVICE

This question requires you to apply your knowledge of coping strategies so that you're able to explain why particular ones are favoured and so this "explaining WHY" makes this an AO2 question.

Robert: Robert takes a problem-focused approach to stress. This is clear from the question because it explains that he takes a solution-orientated approach to stress, in which he seeks to solve the problem by analysing the situation so that he can identify the right strategy to deal with it. He takes the active problem-focused approach because he uses strategies to tackle the cause of stress.

David: David is taking an emotion-focused approach because he copes by doing things to manage his emotions. This is clear from the fact that he vents his emotions by shouting at colleagues and by the way he tries to seek comfort through alcohol to divert him from, or temporarily forget, the stressors. Emotion-focused coping is all about managing one's emotions, and so the symptoms of stress, which is what David is doing. It is a passive approach because it does not solve the cause of the stress.

How Science Works question

EXAM HINT
Draw from the last part of the essays and the problem of using self-report to assess effectiveness of the approaches.

> **?** **Explain why research into problem-focused and emotion-focused coping may lack validity.** **3 MARKS**

An issue that affects validity is that coping strategies are typically assessed by self-report questionnaires. What people report about general stress on a questionnaire may not be how they cope in real life and may not relate to specific stressors. They may exaggerate the effect of any coping strategy due to the social desirability effect (wanting to appear to cope well). This would mean the results would not be true and so would lack validity.

Physiological and psychological methods of stress management

Definition question

> **?** **Explain what is meant by the term . . .** **3 MARKS**

EXAM HINT
You may be asked to explain stress management in general or the question may specify one of the approaches.

Stress management: Stress management is the attempt to cope with stress through reduction of the stress response. This may be aimed at the physiological effects of stress (e.g. anti-anxiety drugs or biofeedback) and the psychological effects of stress (e.g. stress inoculation training or hardiness training). Stress management can be problem- or emotion-focused and is often based on changing the person's perception of the stressor and/or increasing the individual's perception of control.

Physiological methods of stress management: These are techniques that try to control the body's response to stress by reducing physiological reactivity. For example, anti-anxiety drugs decrease the "fight-or-flight" response such as high blood pressure, increased heart rate, etc. Biofeedback is another technique, which works by training the participant to recognise their heightened physiological reactivity and reduce it through relaxation exercises.

Explanation questions

> **?** Outline one physiological method of stress management. **6 MARKS**

Anti-anxiety drugs reduce the "fight-or-flight" response of the SAM and HPA axes. Beta blockers act directly on the body, in particular the sympathetic nervous branch of the ANS, by blocking adrenaline receptors. This reduces the arousal of the SAM response and so beta-blockers lower heart rate and blood pressure by widening the arteries. They act on the body not the brain. Benzodiazepines, e.g. Valium, act on the central nervous system, i.e. the brain. Benzodiazepines increase the activity of the neurotransmitter GABA by binding to the GABA receptor sites. This neurotransmitter is the body's natural form of anxiety relief because GABA decreases serotonin activity. Serotonin is linked to arousal of the neurons and so lowering serotonin activity reduces arousal and so decreases anxiety. GABA may also slow down nerve cell activity by allowing chloride ions into the neurons. This slows their activity and so reduces excitation.

> **?** Give a strength and a weakness of one physiological method of stress management. **3 + 3 MARKS**

(i)   A strength of anti-anxiety drugs such as benzodiazepines is that they are effective because they are fast acting. They have a rapid onset of action as they act directly on the brain, which means that very high levels of stress and anxiety can be reduced in a short period of time.

(ii) A weakness of anti-anxiety drugs is that because they just deal with the effects of stress in the body they treat symptoms not causes. They are treatment not cure, which means the stress is being managed rather than being dealt with. Thus, the treatment is emotion-focused, as it deals with the associated anxiety, rather than problem-focused (where the problem is tackled).

Essay question

> **?** **Outline and assess the physiological approach to stress management in terms of strengths and weaknesses.**
>
> **8, 10, OR 12 MARKS**

> **EXAM HINT**
> Think about what you will leave out for the shorter versions of this question.
>
> 10-mark question: Leave out the last sentence of paragraph 1 to reduce AO1 and leave out the last point about a placebo effect.
>
> 8-mark question: Condense the description of the effect of GABA to reduce AO1 and leave out the last point about a placebo effect and condense the point about the approach being emotion-focused.

Paragraph 1

This approach targets the body and brain to reduce the effects of stressors. Anti-anxiety drugs reduce the "fight-or-flight" response of the SAM and HPA axes. Beta blockers act directly on the body, in particular the sympathetic nervous branch of the ANS, by blocking adrenaline receptors. This reduces the arousal of the SAM response and so beta blockers lower heart rate and blood pressure by widening the arteries. They act on the body not the brain. Benzodiazepines, e.g. Valium, act on the central nervous system, i.e. the brain. Benzodiazepines increase the activity of the neurotransmitter GABA by binding to the GABA receptor sites. This neurotransmitter is the body's natural form of anxiety relief because GABA decreases serotonin activity. Serotonin is linked to arousal of the neurons and so lowering serotonin activity reduces arousal and so decreases anxiety. GABA may also slow down nerve cell activity by allowing chloride ions into the neurons. This slows their activity and so reduces excitation.

Paragraph 2

However, there are issues of dependence, both physical and psychological. Physical dependence is dangerous, e.g. if benzodiazepines are taken over long periods the person can become addicted and so find it hard to stop taking the drugs because they experience withdrawal symptoms when they try to stop. Also, side-effects can be very unpleasant. On the other hand, drugs are effective in relieving the unpleasant physiological effects of stress, particularly because they are fast acting and so can reduce stress and anxiety quickly. Another positive is that drugs are accessible because they are easy for the patient to use as they require little commitment. This makes them easier to use than psychological techniques. The physiological approach alone is oversimplistic because it only works at one level, the physiological level, when a complex response like stress must be dealt with at the cognitive, emotional, and behavioural levels also. This means stress management requires a multi-perspective approach. A weakness of the anti-anxiety drugs is that because they just deal with the effects of stress in the body, they treat symptoms not causes. They are treatment not cure, which means the stress is being managed rather than being dealt with. Thus, the treatment is emotion-focused, as it deals with the associated anxiety, rather than problem-focused (where the problem is tackled). There may even be a placebo effect, that is the drugs work because the patients expect them to and so it is very difficult to know the true effectiveness of the drugs.

Definition question

> **?** **Explain what is meant by the term psychological methods of stress management.** **3 MARKS**

EXAM HINT
Remember the key focus of psychologcial techniques is to change the way we think about stress.

Psychological methods of stress management: Psychological techniques try to change the way we think about stress because this can affect the way we behave and feel. They attempt to address some underlying causes of stress, such as faulty thinking and disproportionate emotional responses (over-reactions and under-reactions). Cognitive-behavioural techniques such as stress inoculation take a psychological approach.

Explanation questions

> **?** **Outline one psychological method of stress management.** **5 MARKS**

EXAM HINT

Stress inoculation has been used in these answers but you could use increasing hardiness or biofeedback (as long as you focus on the psychological aspects) if you choose.

Stress inoculation training (Meichenbaum, 1977, 1985) is a cognitive-behavioural method because it tries to change both cognition and maladaptive behaviour. It involves three stages: the first stage is assessment, and in this stage the therapist asks the patient to identify problem(s) and asks for their perception on how it can be treated. Patient and client work together to agree on the assessment. In the second stage, stress reduction techniques such as relaxation techniques and self-instruction are practiced. Relaxation techniques include deep breathing and muscle relaxation. Self-instruction involves reinforcing and coping self-statements (e.g. "If I keep calm I can cope"), which are intended to replace negative perceptions with positive. In the final stage, application and follow-through are involved. Individuals imagine using the stress-reduction techniques in stressful situations, then role-play using them with their therapist so that they are ready to apply them to real-life situations. The therapist will set homework that increases in difficulty as a way to practise the techniques in real life.

EXAM HINT

Note 1 mark would be awarded for explaining the strength or weakness and 2 more marks for elaboration of this point.

> **?** **Give a strength and a weakness of one psychological method of stress management.** **3 + 3 MARKS**

(i) A key strength is that stress inoculation training (SIT) is effective because it may treat the causes better than physiological techniques. The underlying cognitions treated by SIT may well be the root causes of stress and so the cognitive-behavioural approach may deal better with the causes of stress than physiological techniques that just deal with the symptoms.

(ii) A weakness is that SIT is less effective in highly stressful situations because the individual can only be moderately stressed as they need to be able to sit down and analyse their problems if the technique is to work, and they may lack such self-insight when highly stressed. Thus, when stress is extreme, physiological methods may be needed as an interim measure to reduce stress so that the individual can use SIT. It has the potential to be very effective but it is also one of the most difficult techniques to use, which detracts from its usefulness.

> ### ❓ Explain differences between physiological and psychological approaches to stress management.
> **6 MARKS**

EXAM HINT

Make sure you do draw the comparison—don't make the mistake of just describing the two approaches.

The physiological approach treats the body, e.g. by using drugs, whereas the psychological approach does not treat the physical; instead it treats the mind and/or behaviour, e.g. stress-inoculation therapy (SIT) is a cognitive-behavioural treatment. Physiological methods deal with the effects of stress in the body and so can be criticised as just treating the symptoms of stress not the causes. Whereas the underlying cognitions treated by SIT may well be the root causes of stress and so the psychological approach may deal better with the causes of stress than the physiological approach. The physiological approach is often invasive. For example, drugs can have many unpleasant side effects, whereas the psychological approach taken by SIT is less invasive because it does not have physical effects. The physiological approach is often easier for the patient to use than the psychological, e.g. drugs are easy to take and fast acting, whereas the psychological approach taken by SIT requires commitment and time to learn the technique. It can also be difficult for some to use, e.g. if there is a lack of belief in the therapy. Also, the effects may not be felt for some time and so require perseverance and patience.

Essay question

> ### ❓ Outline and assess the psychological approach to stress management in terms of strengths and weaknesses.
> **8, 10, OR 12 MARKS**

EXAM HINT
There is more than enough content if you just focus on one psychological technique, so don't feel that you have to write about more than stress inoculation training.

> 10-mark question: To reduce content, condense the descriptions of each of the stages to reduce AO1 and leave out the point about the placebo effect to reduce AO2.
>
> 8-mark question: To reduce content, condense the descriptions of each of the stages to reduce AO1 and leave out the point about the placebo effect to reduce AO2 and condense the point about the general effects of therapy.

Paragraph 1

The psychological approach to stress management involves techniques that try to control the cognitive, social, and emotional responses to stress. They attempt to address the underlying causes of stress, such as faulty thinking and disproportionate emotional responses (over-reactions and under-reactions). For example, a technique that takes a cognitive-behavioural approach to stress management is stress inoculation training (SIT; Meichenbaum, 1977, 1985). SIT involves three phases: the first stage is assessment, and in this stage the therapist asks the patient to identify problem(s) and asks for their perception on how it can be treated. Patient and client work together to agree on the assessment. In the second stage, stress reduction techniques such as relaxation techniques and self-instruction are practiced. Relaxation techniques include deep breathing and muscle relaxation. Self-instruction involves reinforcing and coping self-statements (e.g. "If I keep calm I can cope"), which are intended to replace negative perceptions with positive. In the final stage, application and follow-through, the individuals imagine using the stress-reduction techniques in stressful situations, then role-play using them with their therapist so that they are ready to apply them to real-life situations. The therapist will set homework that increases in difficulty as a way to practise the techniques in real life. Meichenbaum (1977) found that the technique generalises to similar situations and so can be effective in reducing more than the original problem.

Paragraph 2

A weakness of SIT is that it is less effective in highly stressful situations because patients need to be able to sit down and analyse their problems if the technique is to work and they may struggle to do this when highly stressed. A strength is that it is less invasive than physiological techniques because it does not have the physical effects that physiological treatments have on the body. For example, drowsiness and depression are effects of some anti-anxiety drugs, and so in this sense SIT compares favourably because it is less invasive and does not have such alarming side-effects. A further strength of SIT is that it is considered to address the causes of stress more than the physiological approach, which just treats the symptoms. The key strength of the psychological approach is that it takes a multi-dimensional approach as it combines cognitive and behavioural approaches. However, it is unclear whether the cognitive changes or behavioural changes are more important in benefiting stressed individuals. The effectiveness of the psychological approach is subject to individual differences as the psychological techniques may work better for some than others as assessment requires the patient to have a high level of self-insight. Also, SIT requires commitment and a belief in the approach and so failure rates may be due to a lack of motivation or belief in the technique. For example, some may feel uncomfortable using the self-coping statements. The effects may not be felt for some time and so require perseverance and patience. A further issue is that any beneficial effects may be due to the general effects of therapy (e.g. therapist warmth; sympathetic relationship) rather than SIT. There may even be a placebo effect; that is, it works because patients expect it to and so it is very difficult to know the true effectiveness of the technique.

Application of knowledge question

> **?** Catherine is suffering with stress. She has a demanding job as a solicitor and a busy family life with three young children to care for. She knows she must do something about her stress and so needs some advice on which approach, physical or psychological, she should use.
>
> Using your knowledge of stress management, give Catherine advice on the two approaches. **6 MARKS**

EXAM HINT
This question is allocated 6 marks so do make sure you make enough comparisons to achieve the marks.

Physiological methods deal with the effects of stress and so can be criticised as just treating the symptoms of stress, not the causes. Whereas stress inoculation therapy (SIT) may well treat the root causes of stress and so the psychological approach may be better for Catherine. She would also have to consider that the physiological approach is often invasive. For example, drugs can have many unpleasant side effects, whereas the psychological approach taken by SIT is less invasive because it does not have physical effects. So again this suggests the psychological approach would be better for Catherine as she needs to be fit and well to cope with the demands of work and small children. On the other hand, the physiological approach is often easier for the patient to use than the psychological, e.g. drugs are easy to take and fast acting whereas the psychological approach taken by SIT requires commitment and time to learn the technique. So SIT may be a difficult technique for Catherine to find time for, given she works and has children. She will need to weigh-up whether she has time for the psychological approach.

SOCIAL PSYCHOLOGY
Social Influence

Definition question

Conformity

> ❓ **Explain what is meant by the term . . .**　**3 MARKS**

Social influence: The influence of a group (majority influence) or individual (minority influence or obedience) to modify the thinking, attitudes, and/or behaviour of others. For example, fashion trends are a consequence of conformity or majority influence; and complying with the demands of an authority figure, such as an employer, is an example of obedience.

Conformity/majority influence: Conformity is when members of a group change their behaviour, views, and attitudes to fit the views of the group. In this sense they publicly yield to group pressure (compliance), although in some cases they yield privately (internalisation). The majority is able to influence because of other people's desire to be accepted (normative) or their desire to be right (informational).

> **EXAM HINT**
> You may be asked to define a key term. You do not have to write out the definition word for word; just make sure you clearly communicate what the term means.

Research questions

> **EXAM HINT**
> Majority influence, or conformity, has been studied by Asch (1951) and Zimbardo (1973) so both studies have been included here. If you do choose to use Zimbardo don't get so caught up in describing the many details of the study that you lose focus on the question, which is of course majority influence/conformity.

> **?** **Outline the procedures of one study into majority influence/conformity. OR Explain how research into majority influence/conformity has been studied.**
>
> **6 MARKS**

Asch (1951) tested conformity using the Asch paradigm, which is a situation in which seven people all sat looking at a display. In turn, they had to say out loud which one of the three lines A, B, or C was the same length as a given stimulus line, X (see illustration below). All but one of the participants were confederates of the experimenter, and on some "critical" trials the confederates were instructed unanimously to give the same wrong answer. The one genuine participant was the last (or the last but one) to offer his opinion on each trial. The performance of participants exposed to such group pressure was compared to performance in a control condition in which there were no confederates. In total, 123 American male participants were sampled.

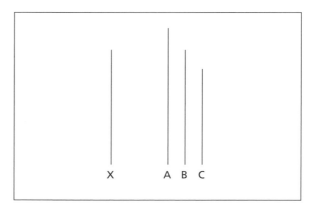

> **?** **Outline the findings of one or more study(ies) into majority influence/conformity.** **6 MARKS**

Asch (1951) found, on the critical trials in which the confederates gave the same wrong answer, that the genuine participants also gave the wrong answer on approximately 37% of these trials. This should be compared against an error rate of only 0.7% in the control condition (75% conformed at least once). Many of the participants who gave wrong responses indicated that they had yielded to majority influence because they didn't want to stand out. Individuals who gave only correct answers said either that they were confident in the accuracy of their own judgement or focused on doing the task as directed (i.e. being accurate and correct).

? **Give two criticisms of the research into majority influence/conformity.** **3 + 3 MARKS**

1) Asch's results may be explained as zeitgeist in terms of the fact that the study took place in America in the 1950s, a time when conformity was high and "doing your own thing" was less socially acceptable, because the communist "witch-hunt" trials punished those who did not conform to the American ideal. However, Asch's basic findings have been repeated several times more recently in various cultures.

2) The research raises important ethical issues. Asch's participants were deceived and so didn't provide fully informed consent, because they were misled about key aspects of the experimental procedures (e.g. presence of confederates). In addition, they were placed in a difficult and embarrassing position and so this raises the issue of protection of participants from psychological harm, such as raised stress levels.

? **Outline the procedures of one study into majority influence/conformity. OR Explain how research into majority influence/conformity has been studied.** **6 MARKS**

Zimbardo (1973) studied 24 male American undergraduate volunteers who formed a self-selected sample. They were randomly allocated to either the role of prisoner or guard. This was a controlled observation study, which was made as realistic as possible. For example, "prisoners" were arrested at their homes and taken to a police station before transfer to the "prison". Once at the mock prison they were deloused, and issued with a prison uniform and an ID number (they were then addressed by this instead of their name). The guards were also issued with uniforms and 16 rules, which they were asked to enforce to maintain a "reasonable degree of order". The interaction between prisoners and guards, mood state, self-perception, and coping behaviour were observed as indicators of conformity. Data was collected via videotape, audiotape, direct observation, questionnaires, and interviews.

> **?** **Outline the findings of one or more study(ies) into majority influence/conformity.** **6 MARKS**

Zimbardo found an extremely high level of conformity to perceived social roles in both the guards and the prisoners. The "guards" conformed by taking on an authoritative role, e.g. they readily issued punishments for prisoner misbehaviour. At first, punishment took the form of loss of privileges. However, later, highly unpleasant punishments included food and sleep deprivation, solitary confinement, and humiliation, e.g. cleaning toilets with bare hands. The guards' aggression was out of proportion to the threat to prison order posed by the prisoners who, after some initial resistance, became passive, excessively obedient, showed flattened mood, and distorted perception of self. Some prisoners conformed to their role by becoming "sick", and five prisoners had to be released early because of extreme emotional disturbance. Further evidence of prisoner conformity was that five experienced a parole board! The study was stopped on the sixth day instead of running for 2 weeks as planned as a result of the extreme pathological behaviour.

> **?** **Give two criticisms of the research into majority influence/conformity.** **3 + 3 MARKS**

1) The artificial set-up and consequent demand characteristics resulted in participant reactivity bias. The guards and prisoners were play-acting rather than genuinely conforming to their roles. The guards reported afterwards that they were influenced by the film *Cool Hand Luke*, which stereotyped prison guards as tough and aggressive. Thus, the research may lack validity as the conformity to roles may not have been a genuine effect and if so the research did not measure what it set out to.

2) The findings have been positively applied to real-life prisons as the insights revealed have been incorporated into guards' training. This means the research is useful because it has been instrumental in improving the American prison system. However, the current prison system is increasingly impersonal and brutal and so we can question how useful the study has been.

Explanation questions

? **Outline two explanations of conformity.** **3 + 3 MARKS**

EXAM HINT
Make sure you can clearly distinguish between the two types of explanation. Don't make a common mistake and mix up the two explanations by identifying informative as an explanation!

Deutsch and Gerard (1955) proposed two explanations for conformity:

(i) Normative influence: This is when conformity occurs because the individual wants to be liked and fit in with other members of the group (the majority). Behaviour and the opinion underlying it change publicly but not privately. Compliance is the type of conformity that results from this influence as the individual does not necessarily agree with the majority. Compliance disappears in the absence of group pressure and so this is called "public conformity".

(ii) Informational influence: This is when conformity occurs because the individual wants to be right and so relies on the superior knowledge of others. Internalisation is the type of conformity that is most likely to result from this influence as opinion changes publicly and privately because the individual already sympathises with the opinion he or she is conforming to. This is sometimes called "true conformity" because the change is genuine, and usually permanent, and so continues even in the absence of group pressure.

? **Outline two types of conformity.** **4 MARKS**

EXAM HINT
Make sure you include whether behaviour and/or mind change.

(i) Compliance is when you change your behaviour but not your mind. Opinion changes publicly, but not privately, as the individual does not necessarily agree with the majority.

Compliance disappears in the absence of group pressure and so this is called "public conformity".

(ii) Internalisation is when you change your mind and behaviour. Opinion changes publicly and privately because the individual already sympathises with the opinion they are conforming to. This is sometimes called "true conformity" because the change is genuine, and usually permanent, and so continues even in the absence of group pressure.

EXAM HINT

Don't describe the types of conformity separately, you must contrast them to answer the question.

> **?** **Explain the difference between compliance and internalisation.** **4 MARKS**

Compliance (or group acceptance) is only superficial, and stops when there are no group pressures to conform. Of crucial importance, compliance typically involves conformity at a public (behaviour) level but not at a private level—the individual's behaviour shows conformity but their private beliefs haven't changed—whereas internalisation, often known as true conformity, involves a genuine acceptance of group norms and so there is conformity at a public and private level because the person is really in agreement with their views and so they change their behaviour and their private views.

Essay question

> **?** **Outline and evaluate research into conformity (majority influence).** **8, 10, OR 12 MARKS**

EXAM HINT

Zimbardo has been used in this answer but you could of course use Asch. Do make sure you focus on conformity when describing Zimbardo's research as a common mistake is that candidates get caught up describing the procedures and forget what the question is about—conformity!

10-mark question: Condense the description of the procedures of Zimbardo's study to decrease AO1, and to reduce AO2 leave out the last sentence of paragraph 2.

8-mark question: To reduce AO1 condense the description of the procedures of Zimbardo's study and leave out the description of Asch's research. To reduce AO2 leave out the commentary about Asch and leave out the last sentence of paragraph 2.

Paragraph 1 AO1

Zimbardo aimed to investigate conformity by seeing how far prisoners or guards conformed to these roles. Twenty-four male American undergraduate student volunteers formed a self-selected sample. They were randomly allocated to either the role of prisoner or guard. Attempts were made to make the study as realistic as possible, for example, the "prisoners" were arrested at their homes and taken to a police station before transfer to the "prison". The interactions between prisoners and guards, mood state, self-perception, and coping behaviour were observed as indicators of conformity. Data was collected via videotape, audiotape, direct observation, questionnaires, and interviews. An extremely high level of conformity to social roles was observed in both the guards and the prisoners. The "guards" conformed to a sadistic role, e.g. they readily issued punishments for prisoner misbehaviour. At first punishment took the form of loss of privileges, however, later punishments included food and sleep deprivation, solitary confinement, and humiliation, e.g. cleaning toilets with bare hands. Some prisoners conformed to a passive, "sick" role, and five prisoners had to be released early because of extreme emotional disturbance. Further evidence of prisoner conformity was that five experienced a parole board! Asch asked male students to assess which of three straight lines was the same length as a stimulus line. Each participant did not know that the others in the assessment group were confederates who sometimes all gave the wrong answer. The real participants also gave the wrong answer in about 37% of trials, and 75% of participants conformed at least once.

Paragraph 2 AO2

Asch's study has been criticised as being more a study of independence, as on 63% of the trials participants did not conform. The mundane realism and external validity of the study is also questionable given the task was so unusual, so far from normal everyday tasks. Zimbardo's research shows the strength of conformity as a form of social influence. However, the study can be criticised as lacking mundane realism because the prison was artificial and consequently demand characteristics may have resulted in participant effects. The guards and prisoners may have been play-acting rather than genuinely conforming to their roles. The guards reported afterwards that they were influenced by the film *Cool Hand Luke*, which stereotyped prison guards as tough and aggressive. Thus, the research may lack validity as the conformity to roles may not be a genuine effect and so the research did not measure what it set out to. Ethical issues are a further weakness as the prisoners especially experienced real suffering during the study, for example, the prisoners responded with crying, screaming, and showed depression; five prisoners had to be released early because of extreme emotional disturbance. Perhaps more significantly, the guards may have experienced long-term effects as they may have suffered a loss of self-esteem as a result of their sadistic behaviour. The issue is that participants should have been protected from this psychological harm, and so we can question whether the findings can justify the distress experienced by the participants. However, it must be remembered before this study it was thought that prisons were bad places because of the people in them and so Zimbardo provided a valuable insight by showing how the situation can cause normal people to conform to sadistic roles. Thus, the findings have revealed important insights into conformity and have been positively applied to real-life prisons as the insights revealed have been incorporated into guards' training. However, the validity of the research may not extend into other everyday behaviours as the situation was so unusual. We can also question how much knowledge of the research acts as prevention because the abuse of prisoners by American soldiers at the Abu Ghraib prison in Iraq shows that sadistic behaviour continues despite what the study has revealed about the conditions in which such behaviour may flourish.

Research questions

EXAM HINT
Use Asch's (1951) study.

? **Outline one study into conformity that demonstrates normative social influence OR compliance.** **4 MARKS**

Asch's (1951) test of conformity was deliberately based on a non-ambiguous task, the line test. This was to see if participants would conform to a majority that gave the wrong answer even when the right answer was obvious. He found that 75% conformed at least once, which shows that participants conformed even though they knew the answer was wrong. This is compliance because the conformity is public; the participants change their behaviour by giving the wrong answer but they don't privately accept the wrong answers as right. The participants conformed even though they could clearly see the right answer and so this is explained by normative influence because the participants conform to "fit in" with the group.

> **?** **Outline one study into conformity that demonstrates informational social influence OR internalisation.**
>
> **4 MARKS**

EXAM HINT
You can use Sherif's (1935) study or Jenness' (1932) beans study.

Sherif's (1935) study of conformity using the autokinetic effect used a visual illusion, where if we look at a small spot of light in a darkened room, small movements of the eyes make the stationary light appear to move. Sherif first asked participants individually to estimate how much the light moved and a variety of estimates were given. When the participants were put into groups of three a group norm emerged. This conformity is internalisation and is an example of informational influence. Because the test was a visual illusion the participants had no way of knowing the "right" answer and so were unsure of how much the light moved, so when in the group they relied on the knowledge of others and accepted their estimate as right. The change in their estimate after being in a group could show they have changed their mind (private acceptance) and behaviour (public acceptance) and this would be internalisation.

Explanation questions

> **?** **What is meant by *compliance* in the context of conformity research? Give a real-life example of compliance.** **3 MARKS**

EXAM HINT
A straightforward definition but you also need to give a real example.

AO ADVICE
This is an "explain WHAT" question because it requires you to outline compliance and give an example and so this is AO1.

Compliance is when you change your behaviour but not your mind. Opinion changes publicly, but not privately, as the individual does not necessarily agree with the majority. Compliance disappears in the absence of group pressure. So an individual might go along with the majority and laugh at a joke but privately they think it is rubbish and do not find it funny.

EXAM HINT

Think carefully about a real-life example as it has to involve public and private change.

? **What is meant by *internalisation* in the context of conformity research? Give a real-life example of internalisation.** **3 MARKS**

Internalisation is when you change your mind and behaviour. Opinion changes publicly and privately because the individual already sympathises with the opinion they are conforming to. This is sometimes called "true conformity" because the change is genuine, and usually permanent, and so continues even in the absence of group pressure. For example, somebody with a majority political opinion may convert to one of the minority parties if they become convinced by their policies and so accept them as right—they have internalised the minority view.

Recognition question

EXAM HINT

Be careful with this question as you need to distinguish between the explanations of conformity and the types of conformity. So focus on types not explanations.

? **The following statements are all related to conformity:**

A **Going along with the group in order to be liked.**

B **Going along with the group because we think they are right.**

C **Going along with the group, even if we do not really agree with what they are doing.**

D **Going along with the group because we accept their beliefs and attitudes into our own cognitions.**

In the table below, write the statement label A, B, C, or D to describe each type of conformity.

Type of conformity	Statements
Internalisation	<u>D</u>
Compliance	<u>C</u>

Application of knowledge questions

? Ashley has begun to attend football practice. He notices all of the other boys wear a certain make of football boots and so asks his mother if he can get the same. He is particularly impressed by one boy, Joe, who has the top goal-scoring record and so he copies the way he approaches and controls the ball.

(a) From the description of Ashley's behaviour above, identify one example of normative social influence. Explain why you think this is an example of normative social influence. **3 MARKS**

(b) From the description of Ashley's behaviour above, identify one example of informational social influence. Explain why you think this is an example of informational social influence. **3 MARKS**

EXAM HINT
Remember there is often more than one possible reason for someone conforming. Normative is when you conform to be liked and informational is when you conform to be right. Make sure you clearly link these to the question by saying how they are demonstrated in Ashley's behaviour.

AO ADVICE
This is an application of knowledge question and so this is an AO2 question.

(a) Normative influence is when the individual conforms to be liked and to "fit in" and so Ashley wants to wear a certain make of football boots because he has noticed so many of the other boys wearing the make of football boots, and so has identified this as a group norm. He wants to conform to the norm to "fit in" and gain approval of the group.

(b) Informational influence is when the individual conforms to be right and so relies on the superior knowledge of others. Ashley's copying of the way Joe approaches and controls the ball is an example of informational influence. Ashley is doing this because Joe is well respected as a good player and so Ashley believes his technique is superior and that his own technique will improve by copying him, and so he is looking to Joe as a source of knowledge.

EXAM HINT

Why do you want to achieve internalisation rather than just compliance? Note you can use informational influence and the social impact theory here.

? A school aims to develop their students' knowledge of the environment by teaching them about the importance of recycling, for example using paper recycling bins at school and encouraging them to recycle within the home. Using your knowledge of conformity, how can they encourage their students to engage in the recycling programme? **6 MARKS**

If the school wants the students to fully engage in the recycling programme they really need the students to show internalisation rather than compliance. This is because compliance is just changing behaviour publicly but not privately and so they may not bother to recycle when they are on their own. Whereas internalisation is public and private acceptance and so if this true conformity is achieved the students would be fully committed to the recycling effort and would do so when in groups and when on their own. To achieve internalisation, informational influence needs to be used, which means the students need to be persuaded that recycling is right. So statistics and information showing the importance of recycling could be given to persuade students that recycling is the right thing to do. Also, according to social impact theory (SIT), a message has more persuasion when the message has strength. This can be in terms of the number of people supporting it and the status of the people supporting the message. So there could be a message and photo board showing that the majority of students are committed to the project. To bring status to the project they could ask a local celebrity to endorse the campaign. SIT also identifies immediacy as a factor, meaning that a message has more impact when it is given in person, so this means it would be best if the local celebrity could visit the school or could record a video message rather than just send a letter of support.

? Chloe has just moved to a new school. She quickly makes friends with one group of girls and begins conforming to their style of dress and behaviour to make sure she fits in and is liked by the group. Explain Chloe's behaviour in terms of compliance. **2 MARKS**

Chloe is showing compliance because she has changed her behaviour publicly by changing her style of dress and behaviour, but she may not have changed her mind privately and so this may be public rather than true conformity, and so she may reverse the changes if group pressure disappears.

How Science Works questions

? Research studies investigating conformity have often used laboratory-based experiments.

(a) **Explain two limitations of laboratory-based experiments into conformity.** **2 + 2 MARKS**

(b) **Suggest an appropriate way to overcome one of the limitations identified in (a).** **2 MARKS**

(a) 1. The laboratory is an artificial environment and consequently the research lacks mundane realism, i.e. it is not like real life. This means the findings may not generalise to settings other than the laboratory and so the research lacks external validity as it may not represent real-life conformity.

2. The artificiality of the situation may have created demand characteristics where participants guessed they were expected to conform, and so did so, which means this was not their true behaviour and so results may not be valid.

(b) A field instead of a laboratory experiment could be done whereby the variables can still be manipulated but in a natural setting where participants do not realise they are in a study and so cannot guess the demand characteristics.

> **?** A psychologist plans to conduct an experiment to see if males or females are more affected by conformity.
>
> (a) Suggest a suitable procedure for this experiment.
>
> **4 MARKS**
>
> (b) Identify one potential ethical issue and suggest how the psychologist might deal with this.
>
> **3 MARKS**

EXAM HINT

Part (a) is really asking for a description of Asch's procedure. You have a choice of ethical issues you can use in (b) because there is the issue of deception, which means there is also an issue of informed consent, and of course the embarrassment caused to the participants also raises the issue of protection of participants. However, your choice of which issue to go with should be based on which one you can resolve as the question also asks you to explain how the psychologist might deal with the issue.

(a) The psychologists could test for a gender difference in conformity using the Asch paradigm. This is a situation in which seven people all sat looking at a display. In turn, they had to say out loud which one of the three lines A, B, or C was the same length as a given stimulus line X. All but one of the participants were confederates of the experimenter, and on some "critical" trials the confederates were instructed unanimously to give the same wrong answer. The one genuine participant was the last (or the last but one) to offer his/her opinion on each trial. The performance of 10 males and 10 females when exposed to such group pressure would show if there was a gender difference.

(b) An ethical issue is deception because the psychologist would have to conceal that the real purpose of the test was conformity. So the line test could be introduced as a test of perception instead, which deliberately misleads the participant so that they do not guess what the test is really about. This could be dealt with by giving a debrief after the test that would explain the true nature and purpose of the study, and give the participants the opportunity to withdraw their data if they so wished.

Definition question

Obedience

> **?** **Explain what is meant by the term . . .** **3 MARKS**

Obedience: Obedience is behaving as instructed, usually in response to individual rather than group pressure. This usually takes place in a hierarchy where the person issuing the order is of higher status than the person obeying the order. Obedience occurs because the individual feels they have little choice; they cannot resist or refuse to obey. It is unlikely to involve a change in private opinion.

EXAM HINT
Remember you don't need to learn these terms word for word, just be able to give the gist of what it means, so long as you are clear and accurate in what you say.

Research questions

> **?** **(i) Outline the procedures of one study into obedience. OR Explain how research into obedience has been studied.** **6 MARKS**

EXAM HINT
Milgram's "electric shock" study is the first and perhaps most memorable study of obedience. That is not to say you have to use this study as other studies of obedience are just as appropriate. You will need to describe the later replications of Milgram's research OR some of the field studies such as Hofling's and Bickman's to access all of the marks on the findings question.

In Milgram's (1963) study of obedience to authority, 40 male volunteers responded to a newspaper advert (a self-selected sample). They took part in a controlled observation and were deceived because they were told the study was a test of the effect of punishment on learning, which concealed that it was really a test of obedience. The participant was always assigned the role of "teacher" and a middle-aged confederate, Mr Wallace, played the role of "learner". Mr Wallace was said to have a heart condition. A word association test was the learning task, and the participant was instructed to deliver an electric shock to the learner for each wrong answer. The "learner" deliberately gave wrong answers to test how far the real participants would go on the electric shock scale. The measure of obedience was the strength of the maximum electric shock administered by the participants, which was on a scale of 15 to 450 volts with 15-volt increments for each wrong answer. The teacher and learner were in separate rooms with no voice contact; the only sound made by the "learner" was banging on the wall at 300 and then 315 volts. After this all went silent and the "learner" gave no further answers. The participants understood that the highest levels of shock might be fatal, especially to a man with a heart condition! The participants did not know until the end of the experiment that the shocks were not real. They were encouraged to continue when they objected by an experimenter who said, "You must go on" and, "It is essential that you go on".

? (ii) Outline the findings of one or more study(ies) into obedience. 6 MARKS

In the original version of Milgram's study all participants gave shocks up to the 300-volt level (i.e. 100%), and 65% of participants continued to the highest level, 450 volts, which was past the range of shocks marked on the machine as "Danger: severe shock". The marking for 435 and 450 was simply "XXX". This completely contradicted the predicted results that 3% or fewer would reach 450 volts. The participants showed signs of extreme tension. For example, they trembled, sweated, stuttered, groaned, dug their fingernails into their flesh, and three had uncontrollable seizures. In the later replications of the study Milgram began with a version in which the confederate shouted out about being in pain and about his heart condition. Milgram found this reduced the obedience only slightly as 62% went up to the 450 volts. Changing the location from Yale University to a run-down office also reduced obedience as 48% went to 450 volts, and so there was nearly 20% less obedience. Obedience also dropped when the orders were given by telephone (20.5%) and when a disobedient role model was present (10%).

? (iii) Give two criticisms of the research into obedience. 3 + 3 MARKS

1) Orne and Holland (1968) claimed the experimental set-up was simply not believable (so lacks experimental realism) as electric shocks were not proportionate to a wrong answer and so participants would have guessed that they were not real and

just played along with the experimenter, which means that their behaviour was not genuine, it was due to demand characteristics. This would mean the research did not measure what it set out to and so lacks internal validity. However, the participants' stress reactions contradict this.

2) Milgram's research raises numerous ethical issues: he tried to prevent the participants from leaving the experiment (so preventing their right to withdraw) and they were placed in a very stressful situation, where three even had seizures because of the stress, which raises the issue of lack of protection of participants from psychological harm. It would be very difficult (or impossible) to carry out such a study nowadays in many countries. A key reason for this is that Milgram totally failed to obtain informed consent from his participants—they simply didn't know what was in store for them.

Explanation questions

> **?** **Outline two explanations of obedience.**
>
> **4 + 4 MARKS**

> **EXAM HINT**
> The answer here takes a dispositional and a situational explanation. If you are not familiar with the authoritarian personality use another situational explanation such as the power of the authority figure. Use examples from the research, such as the power of the experimenter as represented by his white coat in Milgram's research and the effect of the police-style uniform in Bickman's research, to illustrate the effect of authority.

(i) The agentic state is a situational explanation, as according to this the individual becomes the agent of the authority figure and so believes the authority figure is responsible for the consequences of their actions. This was evident in Milgram's study because participants sought reassurance by checking if the experimenter was responsible for the wellbeing of the learner. According to Milgram, they shifted (agentic shift) from an autonomous state, in which the individual takes responsibility for their own actions, into the agentic state, in which they no longer feel responsible for the consequences of their behaviour. The individual becomes the "instrument" of an authority figure and so, because the authority figure is ultimately responsible, this makes it easier to obey.

(ii) The authoritarian personality is a dispositional explanation because Adorno et al. (1950) felt that personality explained obedience. According to Adorno et al., people with an authoritarian personality experience a strict upbringing whereby they are punished for disobedience, and this leads to rigid thinking, which includes high respect for authority. Characteristics include rigid beliefs in conventional values, general hostility towards other groups, intolerance of ambiguity, submissive attitudes towards authority figures, and dismissive attitudes towards those considered beneath them. This focus on hierarchy explains why those with this personality type are more obedient.

EXAM HINT

Note three differences are needed for the first question but only two for the second question.

AO ADVICE

This question asks you to outline differences and so this is an AO1 question.

> **?** **Outline three differences between conformity and obedience.** `2 + 2 + 2 MARKS` OR
>
> **Two forms of social influence are obedience and conformity. Explain how these two forms of social influence are different.** `4 MARKS`

(i) Obedience occurs within a hierarchy as the person in authority demands obedience from subordinates. Thus, power is the emphasis. Whereas conformity is an influence felt within a peer group, i.e. usually by people of fairly equal status. Acceptance is the emphasis.

(ii) An order to obey is direct and clear, i.e. it is overt and explicit, whereas group norms are not always clear, i.e. they are often ambiguous because they are the unspoken and unwritten rules that must be conformed to for group acceptance and so are implicit.

(iii) Participants embrace obedience as an explanation of their behaviour. It can be used to justify undesirable behaviour as it can be used to reject responsibility, which occurs in the agentic state, whereas participants deny conformity as an explanation of their behaviour. People in individualistic cultures are encouraged to see themselves as autonomous (i.e. independent) and so do not perceive themselves as conformists.

> ❓ **Discuss what research has to tell us about why people display obedience.** **8, 10, OR 12 MARKS**

EXAM HINT

There are many explanations of obedience. However, describing these only accesses half of the marks so you need to make sure you access AO2 by referring to the research as evidence to back-up the explanation. So this essay does not follow the usual structure of all AO1 in paragraph 1 and AO2 in paragraph 2. It makes more sense to describe and then evidence and evaluate each explanation in turn. Just make sure you do keep to 50:50 AO1 to A02.

10-mark question: To reduce AO1 condense the description of the agentic state, and to reduce AO2 leave out the point about dropping bombs as evidence of a buffer effect.

8-mark question: To reduce AO1 condense the description of the agentic state and leave out the references to Bickman and Hofling. To reduce AO2 leave out the content about the role of buffers.

Paragraph 1 AO1/AO2

The status of the authority figure is perhaps the most obvious explanation of obedience. In Milgram's (1963) study the laboratory coat gave the experimenter the authority of a scientist, and the fact it took place at Yale, a prestigious university, added to the status of the experimenter and that of the research. Bickman's (1974) study demonstrated the power of a uniform and Hofling et al.'s (1966) the authority of a doctor over nurses and so these provide further support that we obey an authority figure because of the figure's legitimate authority. This has real-life explanatory power because we do obey authority figures in real life, such as police officers and teachers. The authority figure links to another explanation, the agentic state, in which the individual becomes the agent of the authority figure and so believes the authority figure is responsible for the consequences of their actions. This was evident in Milgram's study because participants sought reassurance by checking if the experimenter was responsible for the wellbeing of the learner. According to Milgram, they shifted (agentic shift) from an autonomous state, in which the individual takes responsibility for their own actions, into the agentic state, in which they no longer feel responsible for the consequences of their behaviour, and so are more likely to obey because they do not feel responsible.

Paragraph 2 AO1/AO2

The agency theory has been criticised because the fact that the participants were so distressed suggests they did feel responsible and so the explanation has questionable validity. The generalisability of the explanation has also been questioned. Milgram attempted to explain the Holocaust using his agency theory because many of the Nazi war criminals used the obedience alibi that they were only following orders. This is a negative implication of the explanation because it attempts to justify inhumane behaviour. Furthermore, critics argue the agentic shift doesn't explain the Nazis' behaviour. It is too simplistic as an explanation and it is not clear when such a change in thinking would occur. The Nazis had years to reflect on their actions, whereas Milgram's participants did not, and so lack of time to think may explain the obedience of Milgram's participants but not that of the Nazis. The murder of millions of Jews is not comparable to electric shocks and neither relates to real-life, everyday behaviour and so the lack of mundane realism limits validity. Interlinking with the agentic state is the role of buffers in explaining the obedience. In Milgram's study the wall acted as a buffer because it was easier to deliver shocks when the learner could not be seen; this made it easier for the participant to shift into the agentic state. However, many Nazi soldiers killed Jews in cold blood with no buffers, and so again this has limited external validity. On the other hand, some have argued buffers explain how it is easier to drop a bomb far away from one's own country than fight on one's doorstep, and perhaps this is true of the wars in the Middle East and the bombing of Hiroshima in World War II, so supporting external validity. The "obedience alibi" these situational explanations provide should not be accepted uncritically as Milgram provides no independent evidence for the validity of the agentic state other than participants' own statements, which of course could be biased by demand characteristics.

Application of knowledge question

> ❓ A psychologist tests the effect of authority by asking participants in the street to do random things such as change the hand they are holding a bag in or jump up and down on the pavement. The psychologist finds that the participants are much more likely to obey when he is dressed in a uniform than in ordinary clothes.
>
> Use your knowledge of obedience to explain these findings. **4 MARKS**

EXAM HINT
Use research such as Milgram's (1963) and Bickman's (1974) to explain how a uniform supports the legitimate power of an authority figure and how this would explain the findings.

The findings that people in the street are more likely to obey a man when he is in uniform than when he is not is explained by research such as Milgram's (1963), where the laboratory coat gave the experimenter the authority of a scientist and the fact it took place at Yale, a prestigious university, added to the status of the research and the experimenter, and this would have affected how obedient the participants were. Bickman's (1974) study of uniform is closest to the study in the question as he found that participants were more likely to obey the experimenter dressed as a guard (which resembled a police uniform) than when he was dressed as a milkman or in civilian clothes. These studies reveal that we obey an authority figure because of the figure's legitimate authority and the uniform adds to the sense they have a rightful authority and so should be obeyed.

How Science Works questions

> ❓ Explain what is meant by the term internal validity and illustrate your answer with reference to one social influence study. **3 + 3 MARKS**

AO ADVICE
The following questions ask you to examine validity, so they are methodology questions and count as AO3.

EXAM HINT
Remember internal validity is about the truth of the research; it lacks this if the experimenter did not measure what they set out to. This is easy to illustrate using Milgram's (1963) research because it has been suggested demand characteristics rather than genuine behaviour explain the obedience.

(i)   Internal validity refers to the extent to which the experiment measured what it set out to, i.e. is the observed effect in the dependent variable a result of the manipulation of the independent variable? Thus, internal valdity refers to whether the research has *truth* or whether it "worked". Any threats to internal validity reduce the meaningfulness of the findings, as they lack truth.

(ii) Orne and Holland (1968) have questioned the internal validity of Milgram's (1963) study of obedience because they claim it was not a true measure of obedience. They give two reasons for this: 1) that the study lacked experimental realism, and 2) that the obedience was due to demand characteristics. Orne and Holland claimed the experimental set-up was simply not believable (so lacks experimental realism) as electric shocks were not proportionate to a wrong answer and so participants would have guessed that they were not real and just played along with the experimenter, which means that their behaviour was not genuine, it was due to demand characteristics instead. This would mean the research did not measure what it set out to and so lacks internal validity.

EXAM HINT

Remember external validity is about generalisability, which again can easily be linked to Milgram's study because it took place in the artificial conditions of the laboratory.

> ❓ **Explain what is meant by the term external validity and illustrate your answer with reference to one social influence study.** **3 + 3 MARKS**

(i)   External validity refers to the validity of the research outside the research situation itself—the extent to which the findings are generalisable to other situations, especially "everyday" situations. The question is whether you would get the same findings in a different setting or whether they are limited to the original research context. If the latter is true then there is a lack of external validity.

(ii) Orne and Holland (1968) have questioned the external validity of Milgram's (1963) study of obedience because they claim Milgram's study bears no resemblance to obedience in real life and so has low mundane realism because the research set-up is artificial. This means external validity can be questioned because if it is not like real life then the research may lack generalisability to other settings. Orne and Holland claim that

Milgram's findings are context-bound, i.e. they are a product of the research setting at Yale, and so the findings would not be the same elsewhere.

> **?** **Assess the validity of research into obedience.**
>
> **6 MARKS**
>
> "Milgram's research is of no value because it was conducted in a laboratory."
>
> Explain the methodological difficulties faced by social psychologists conducting their research in a laboratory.
>
> **5 MARKS**

EXAM HINT
Combine the part (ii) answers to the last two questions.

EXAM HINT
You can use the above content on both internal and external validity as both can be linked to the laboratory set-up.

One of the problems of conducting research in the laboratory is that the artificial conditions can cue participants as to what the research is about. Participants may change their behaviour as a result of these cues or demand characteristics and so their behaviour would not be genuine. This would mean the research did not measure what it set out to and so lacks internal validity. Another issue is that often the laboratory bears no resemblance to real-life settings and so the research has low mundane realism because the research set-up is artificial. The findings may be context-bound, i.e. they are a product of the laboratory setting and so the findings would not be the same elsewhere. This is particularly true of research into social psychology because of course it's easy for our behaviour to be inhibited or altered by an unfamiliar setting. This questions external validity because if the laboratory research is not like real life then the research may lack generalisability to other settings.

Essay questions

> **?** **Discuss the internal validity of obedience research.**
>
> **8, 10, OR 12 MARKS**

Paragraph 1 AO1

Orne and Holland (1968) have questioned the internal validity of Milgram's (1963) study of obedience. Internal validity refers to the extent to which the experiment measured what it set out to and so refers to whether the research has truth or whether it "worked". Orne and Holland claim Milgram's study lacks internal validity because it was not a true measure of obedience. They criticise Milgram's research as lacking internal validity on two counts: 1) that the study lacked experimental realism and 2) that the obedience was due to demand characteristics. Orne and Holland claimed the experimental set-up was simply not believable (so lacks experimental realism) as electric shocks were not proportionate to a wrong answer and so participants would have guessed that they were not real and just played along with the experimenter, which means that their behaviour was not genuine, it was due to demand characteristics instead. This would mean the research did not measure what it set out to and so lacks internal validity.

Paragraph 2 AO2

Milgram defended the internal validity of his study. He claimed it had experimental realism because the participants' behavioural reactions (sweating, stuttering, digging finger nails into palms) showed that they did really think they were delivering electric shocks. He claimed the video tapes provided evidence that the participants showed real concern for the learner, distress at giving the shocks, and that many wished to leave the experiment, all of which support experimental realism. Milgram also claimed that the careful construction of the set-up increased experimental realism: for example the participants signed a contract as they arrived; it was at Yale University, which provided credibility; the status of the experimenter, which was emphasised with his laboratory coat; and the use of deception, for example in the rigged allocation to roles, all helped make the experiment believable. Milgram provided further evidence that it was believed as 70% of the participants when questioned said they thought the shocks were real and rated them as 14/15 on a pain scale. However, self-report criticisms weaken the validity of this evidence. Orne and Holland also claim that obedience is a demand characteristic of any experiment and so not due to Milgram's experimental-set up. This further questions internal validity, as if the obedience is not a result of the experimental set-up then the research has again not measured what it set out to. However, the carefully constructed set-up challenges this criticism as it supports the fact that the obedience was due to the specific nature of Milgram's experimental set-up.

> **?** **Discuss the external validity of obedience research.**
>
> **8, 10, OR 12 MARKS**

EXAM HINT

Consider how generalisability is limited by the artificiality, and so lack of mundance realism, of the research.

Paragraph 1 AO1

Orne and Holland (1968) have questioned the external validity of Milgram's (1963) study of obedience because they claim Milgram's study bears no resemblance to obedience in real life and so has low mundane realism because the research set-up is artificial. For example, the giving of electric shocks for getting an answer wrong on a memory test is so far from what would happen in real life. Orne and Holland believe the lack of realism of the electric shocks may have acted as a demand characteristic. Also, the obedience shown to a fake experimenter may not be the same as that shown to real-life authority figures. Orne and Holland claim that Milgram's findings are context-bound, i.e. they are a product of the research setting at Yale and so the findings would not be the same elsewhere because Yale's world-class reputation led the participants to assume any research would be worthy/worthwhile, whereas this would not be true in a different setting. This is particularly true of research into social psychology, such as Milgram's obedience research, because of course it's easy for our behaviour to be inhibited or altered by an unfamiliar setting. This questions external validity because if the laboratory research is not like real life then the research may lack generalisability to real-life settings.

Paragraph 2 AO2

Milgram concedes that the study lacked mundane realism but he uses his replications of the research to defend the external validity as these are evidence of similar findings in different settings, e.g. the replication in the run-down office in New Haven where a 48% obedience rate was found as compared to 65% in the original study shows that the study is generalisable beyond the research setting, though clearly not to the same degree. Milgram argues that this replication shows the findings were not solely due to the prestige of Yale University. Although certainly the latter is likely to have had some effect given that obedience was higher there. The cross-cultural replications also support external validity as Smith and Bond (1993) found that obedience was 80% or higher in replications of Milgram's experiment in Italy, Spain, Germany, Holland, and Austria. These findings suggest that high levels of obedience exist across cultures just like the high level found in Milgram's original study and so suggest the findings are generalisable. However, there was a lack of standardisation in the replications, which weakens this evidence for external validity. The fact that an androcentric (all male) and ethnocentric (culture-biased) sample was used means the sample is biased and so the research lacks population validity. This is another form of external validity and it means the research lacks generalisability to other populations. Another concern is temporal validity (external validity over time) because the relevance of Milgram's findings in today's society is questionable, given that today authority figures tend to be challenged rather than blindly obeyed, because social norms have changed and it is much more acceptable to challenge those in authority. Thus, the status of the experimenter would be reduced automatically. Furthermore, we are less naive and have greater awareness of psychological research and so are probably less likely to believe in the experimental set-up. This means the research may be era-dependent, and so whilst it had external validity at the time it is likely to be lower now. On the other hand, we can argue that the findings still have relevance today because in 2006 British psychological illusionist Derren Brown showed in a Channel 4 television programme *The Heist* that participants do still obey in the Milgram test.

How Science Works questions

> **?** **Explain ethical issues raised by research into social influence.** **6 MARKS**

Deception is an ethical issue that has arisen in various social influence studies. This is particularly true of Milgram's (1963) study as participants were deceived in many ways. They were told the experiment was a test of memory and learning when it was actually a test of obedience; they were led to believe the electric shocks were real when they were not, and that they were painful, particularly in the voice feedback condition in which they thought the cries were real; they were told Mr Wallace was a real participant like themselves when he was a confederate; they were deceived into thinking they had an equal chance of ending up as the "teacher" or the "learner" when in fact the drawing of lots was rigged so that the real participant was always the teacher. Protection of participants is an ethical issue that arises when participants are distressed by the research. For example, in Milgram's study the participants suffered, e.g. sweating, trembling, and three had uncontrollable seizures. In Zimbardo's study the prisoners responded with crying, screaming, and showing depression; five prisoners had to be released early because of extreme emotional disturbance. The issue is that participants should have been protected from this psychological harm, and so we can question whether the findings can justify the distress experienced by the participants.

> **?** **Outline ways in which psychologists deal with the ethical issues that arise in psychological research.** **6 MARKS**

In the UK, since the mid 1970s, the British Psychological Society (BPS) ethical guidelines have imposed limitations and set standards on *how* research should be conducted. The written code of conduct is designed to aid psychologists when designing and running their research. The code focuses on the need to treat participants with respect and to not cause them harm or distress. The setting of such standards aims to prevent ethical issues arising and to provide guidance on how to deal with ethical issues that do arise. For example, the debrief is used to resolve issues such as deception or lack of informed consent that arise when guidelines are not observed. It is given to explain the deception and the true nature of the research and it may be an opportunity to gain retrospective consent. The right to withdraw and confidentiality are used to help resolve participant distress, and so support protection of participants. Ethical committees are another safeguard to help deal with and prevent ethical issues arising. They take the decision whether to do the research, and how exactly it is to be done, out of the hands of the individual who is more likely to be biased, and so can make the decision more objective and fair. The cost–benefit analysis is another way of dealing with ethical issues as it requires the researcher to weigh up the costs to the participant (harm to the participants as a consequence of the research, such as distress, ridicule, or loss of self-esteem) against the end result (benefits to society such as the value of research, i.e. usefulness of insights provided and applications). Thus, the cost–benefit analysis allows the researcher to answer the question, "Is the research worth doing, or is it trivial?" and so consider any potential ethical issues at the outset of the research.

EXAM HINT
This is a challenging question. Don't get caught up in describing the safeguards; you must move straight to evaluating them.

> **?** **Evaluate how well psychologists have dealt with the ethical issues that arise in psychological research.**
> **6 MARKS**

The BPS ethical guidelines have no legislative power and so enforcing them is a problem, particularly because detecting whether they have been breached is also an issue. The ethical guidelines lack power because, whilst rogue psychologists found guilty of breaching the BPS code of conduct can be expelled from the BPS and their university, this does not stop them from continuing to do research in the private sector. Another issue is that breaches of the guidelines can be justified and so it is too easy to disregard them. The ethical guidelines differ across cultures and this lack of consistency means that what is acceptable in one culture may be considered unethical in a different culture. This means there are no universal ethical standards, and so the guidelines are country-specific, meaning BPS guideines only apply within the UK. A further criticism of the guidelines is that they provide a "managerial" ethic only and they lack a "social" ethic (Howitt, 1991) because they advise on *how* to manage research but not *what* can be researched and whether it *should* be. This means they only protect the research participants, not the social groups that may be affected by the research, and so do little to resolve the issues of socially sensitive research. On the other hand, it can be argued that the guidelines do provide clear guidance. For example, the debrief is used to resolve issues that arise when guidelines are not observed, and the right to withdraw and confidentiality can be used to help resolve participant distress, so the guidelines do have some success in supporting the ethical treatment of participants.

SOCIAL INFLUENCE IN EVERYDAY LIFE

Explanation questions

Explanations of independent behaviour

> **?** **Outline explanations of independent behaviour.**
> **6 MARKS**

Explanations of independent behaviour include situational and individual differences. The situation can lead to independent behaviour because people are more likely to resist social influence under certain conditions. For example, reducing the influence of the authority figure, as happened in one replication of the Milgram study, when the orders were given by telephone there was a drop of 45% in obedience. The greater the distance between teachers and learner made it easier to resist the authority figure. Similarly, the presence of a disobedient role model challenges the authority figure and also leads to a drop in obedience. Asch (1951, 1956) identified social support as an important factor in decreasing conformity. First, he found that conformity dropped dramatically from 37% to 5% when one confederate gave the correct

EXAM HINT
There are many explanations, so it may help to categorise them into situational and individual explanations.

answer on all trials. As with obedience to authority, the presence of support from someone else makes it much easier to resist social pressure—you're not being left completely isolated. Another factor that reduces conformity is privacy. Asch (1951) found conformity dropped to 12.5% when participants were allowed to answer privately rather than out loud. This happened because there is much less normative social influence when other group members are unaware of your judgements.

EXAM HINT
Three factors have been used: social support, privacy, and culture.

? **Explain factors that increase resistance to conformity.**
5 MARKS

Asch (1951, 1956) identified social support as an important factor in decreasing conformity because he found that conformity dropped dramatically from 37% to 5% when one confederate gave the correct answer on all trials. As with obedience to authority, the presence of support from someone else makes it much easier to resist social pressure—you're not being left completely isolated. Another factor that reduces conformity is privacy. Asch (1951) found conformity dropped to 12.5% when participants were allowed to answer privately rather than out loud. This happened because there is much less normative social influence when other group members are unaware of your judgements, as in these circumstances there is less pressure to "fit in". Culture is another factor that can affect resistance to conformity. Individualistic cultures are much less conformist than collectivistic cultures because individualists emphasise independence whereas collectivists emphasise interdependence and the good of the group. Individualistic cultures would find it easier to resist conformity than collectivist cultures.

? **Outline two reasons why people might resist obedience** **3 + 3 MARKS**

EXAM HINT
The two factors identified were systematically manipulated by Milgram across the later replications and so it makes sense to use these factors and the findings from the replications as evidence.

(i)   Reducing the influence of the experimenter (authority figure) can lead to a resistance to obedience. This was made clear in some of the later variations of the Milgram study, e.g. changing the location from Yale University to a run-down office reduced the status of the research and the experimenter and increased resistance, as the obedience rate dropped from 65% (rate in original study) to 48%, meaning there was nearly 20% less obedience. Obedience also dropped when the orders were given by telephone to 20.5% as this also reduced the influence of the experimenter. The presence of a disobedient role model also led to resistance as the obedience rate was just 10%. The disobedient role model showed the participant that the experimenter could be resisted, and so again the experimenter's influence was reduced.

(ii) Increasing the consequences of the obedience (obviousness of the learner's distress) can lead to a resistance to obedience. This was made clear in some of the later variations of the Milgram study, e.g. in the voice feedback variation a tape recording of the victim could be heard apparently thumping on the wall and complaining of a heart condition. This increased the obviousness of the learner's distress compared to the remote-victim experiment, when the participant could be neither heard nor seen. This increased resistance slightly as obedience dropped by 3% to 62%. Placing the teacher and learner in close proximity also increased the obviousness of the learner's distress, and consequently resistance increased as obedience dropped by 25% to 40%. The effect of the learner's distress was even greater in the variation in which the teacher had to force the learner's hand down onto the shock plate, and consequently obedience dropped to 30%. This further demonstrates that resistance increases as the obviousness of the learner's distress increases.

Essay question

> **?** **Discuss what research has to tell us about why people display resistance to social influence.**
> **8, 10, OR 12 MARKS**

AO ADVICE

Remember essay questions always involve a 50:50 split of AO1:AO2 marks.

EXAM HINT

Milgram's replications provide key information about why there is resistance to obedience, and the criticisms of his research in terms of validity provide lots of AO2. But as the question is on social influence in general, do include something on conformity as well.

10-mark question: Leave out the last sentence of paragraph 1 to reduce AO1 and the last sentence of paragraph 2 to reduce AO2.

8-mark question: Leave out the last section of paragraph 1 about answering privately, and leave out the last sentence of paragraph 2 to reduce AO2 and condense the commentary about internal locus of control.

Paragraph 1 AO1

Milgram's replications showed that increasing the consequences of the obedience, i.e. learner's distress, or decreasing the status of the authority figure decreases obedience and so increases resistance. For example, when the buffer of the wall was removed in later replication, this led to resistance because the learner's distress was more apparent to the participant. The effect of the learner's distress was even greater in the variation in which the teacher had to force the learner's hand down onto the shock plate, and consequently obedience dropped to 30%, and so further demonstrates that resistance increases as the obviousness of the learner's distress increases. The disobedient role model and giving orders by telephone also increased resistance because both of these decrease the influence of the authority figure. Asch (1951, 1956) identified social support as an important factor in decreasing conformity and increasing resistance because he found that conformity dropped dramatically from 37% to 5% when one confederate gave the correct answer on all trials. Asch (1951) also found that conformity dropped to 12.5% when participants were allowed to answer privately rather than out loud. This happened because there is much less normative social influence when other group members are unaware of your judgements, as in these circumstances there is less pressure to "fit in".

Paragraph 2 AO2

The findings that resistance can be increased have useful social implications because we can train people to resist obedience when they are uncomfortable with the consequences. However, the methodological weaknesses of Milgram's research question the usefulness of the insights because the research findings may lack truth. Orne and Holland's (1968) suggest that demand characteristics limit internal validity, meaning that the participants were just role playing because it was obvious the electric shocks were not real, and so the obedience shown is not genuine, meaning that the findings lack internal validity. Another weakness is that individual differences also play a part and these are ignored by most of the research. For example, people with high self-esteem are more capable of resisting obedience and conformity. And those with an internal locus of control are also more likely to resist obedience and conformity because they have a high sense of personal responsibility and so are less influenced by external factors than those with an external locus of control. In the context of World War II, those with an internal locus of control were more likely to disobey the Nazis and help the Jews because of their sense of personal responsibility, whereas those who didn't help felt helpless to challenge or resist. Then there is the issue of the consequences of resisting—disagreement and losing a fee, as in Milgram's research, does not compare with being killed for disobeying the Nazis or other military figures. But at the other extreme, there are those with a heroic imagination, such as Nelson Mandela who disobeyed an unfair and racist government because of his moral ideology, who show that individual differences are as important as situational explanations.

Application of knowledge question

> ❓ When a teacher tells you to do something, it is usual for you to obey.
>
> (a) Using your knowledge of factors that have been found to affect obedience, explain why you might obey in this situation. **6 MARKS**
>
> (b) In what ways would the situation have to change in order for you to resist the command? **2 MARKS**

EXAM HINT

For (a) draw from the explanations of obedience, such as the legitimate power of the authority figure and the agentic state. For (b) use what Milgram's replications show about decreasing the influence of the authority figure.

(a) The status of the authority figure is perhaps the most obvious explanation of obedience. In Milgram's study the white coat gave the experimenter the authority of a scientist and the fact it took place at Yale, a prestigious university, added to the status of the experimenter as an authority figure. In the same way, a teacher has legitimate authority because of his or her status as a teacher, and so because the teacher has legitimate power he or she is more likely to be obeyed. The students might question the point of disobeying, especially as this could result in sanctions or punishments, and affect any reference the teacher might write. Another factor is the agentic state. Because the teacher is in a position of authority, the students are more likely to experience this state whereby the individual becomes the agent of the authority figure and so believes the authority figure is responsible for the consequences of their actions. According to Milgram, shifting (agentic shift) from an autonomous state, in which the individual takes responsibility for his or her own actions, into the agentic state, in which they no longer feel responsible for the consequences of their behaviour, increases obedience because they do not feel responsible.

(b) Milgram's research showed that decreasing the influence of the authority figure by changing the location or including a disobedient role model significantly decreased obedience and so increased resistance. So if the teacher's status was reduced, perhaps by other students disobeying and seemingly "getting away with it", then other students would be less likely to obey the teacher.

Explanation questions

EXAM HINT
Use the internal/external locus of control.

? **Outline individual differences in independent behaviour.** 6 MARKS

Individual differences in independent behaviour can be explained by Rotter's (1966) locus of control. This is a personality dimension concerned with whether we perceive what happens to us as under our own control (internal locus of control) or whether it is determined mainly by situational factors (external locus of control). So internals are less likely than externals to show blind obedience and conformity because they are less influenced by external factors. Individuals with an internal locus of control would be more likely than those with an external locus of control to show independent behaviour in the Asch and Milgram situations. This is because internals would be less likely to conform because they would trust their own judgement during the Asch task, as they perceive what happens to be under their control, whereas externals would be more likely to conform because they are more influenced by external factors and so would be more easily swayed by the confederates. Similarly, in the Milgram scenario the internals would feel more responsible because they believe what happens is under their control and so they would be less likely to go into the agentic state, in which they become the agent of the authority figure and place all responsibility with the authority figure, whereas externals would be more likely to go into the agentic state as they are less autonomous (self-responsible) in the first place and so are more likely to obey without challenging.

> **?** **Explain what is meant by locus of control.**
> **4 MARKS**

Individual differences and independent behaviour

Locus of control describes where a person thinks main control over him/herself is situated. According to Rotter, individuals with an internal locus of control attribute success and failure to their own efforts and so perceive that they have control over their life and so are less easily influenced by external factors; their locus of control is internal. Whereas individuals with an external locus of control feel less in control of their own lives and perceive their lives as being shaped by external influences such as luck, fate, and other people. So an internal is less likely to show blind obedience and conformity because they are less influenced by situational factors, and, as Milgram's and Asch's research shows, the situation is a powerful influence on obedience and conformity.

EXAM HINT
Explain Rotter's personality dimension. Do link it to social influence.

> **?** **Evaluate research into individual differences in independent behaviour.** **6 MARKS**

EXAM HINT
Try to include both strengths and weaknesses of the Rotter scale.

The locus of control has typically been assessed by the Rotter scale, which provides a very good measure of whether a given individual has an external or internal locus of control. However, it is unlikely that such a general measure would allow us to predict accurately individuals' behaviour in the specific Asch and Milgram situations. Thus, the general nature of the locus of control scale may not generalise well to specific situations. Further weaknesses include the fact that the locus of control is too general a measure and so cannot predict with accuracy how individuals will behave in Milgram and Asch scenarios, not least because there are multiple internal and external factors in these scenarios and so it is too simplistic to say internals will be independent and externals will obey or conform because they may be more influenced by the situational (external) factors. The scale is also oversimplified because individuals are unlikely to be solely internal or external and there are other internal and external factors than just locus of control. The fact that the majority did conform in Asch's study at least once and the majority obeyed in Milgram's study can be used as evidence that situational factors override individual factors when the situational pressures are great.

Essay question

> ? **Discuss research into the influence that individual differences have on independent behaviour.**
>
> **8, 10, OR 12 MARKS**

EXAM HINT

Note how you can combine the two above answers to answer this essay question. Do think about what you would leave out if the shorter 8- or 10-mark question is asked.

10-mark question: Condense the description of internals and externals in the Milgram study to reduce AO1, and to reduce AO2 leave out the contradictory study by Miller.

8-mark question: Condense the description of internals and externals in the Milgram study and leave out the research evidence at the beginning of paragraph 2.

Paragraph 1 AO1

Milgram was sceptical about the importance of individual differences in terms of the results of his study. However, individual differences in independent behaviour can be explained by Rotter's locus of control. This is a personality dimension concerned with whether we perceive what happens to us as under our own control (internal locus of control) or whether it is determined mainly by situational factors (external locus of control). Individuals with internal locus of control would be more likely than those with external locus of control to show independent behaviour in the Asch and Milgram situations. This is because internals would be less likely to conform because they would trust their own judgement during the Asch task, as they perceive what happens to be under their control, whereas externals would be more likely to conform because they are more influenced by external factors and so would be more easily swayed by the confederates. Similarly, in the Milgram scenario the internals would feel more responsible because they believe what happens is under their control and so they would be less likely to go into the agentic state, whereby they become the agent of the authority figure and place all responsibility with the authority figure, whereas externals would be more likely to go into the agentic state as they are less autonomous (self-responsible) in the first place. Furthermore, those who did not obey to 450 volts in the Milgram study displayed individual differences to the majority, and so this highlights that there are individual differences in independent behaviour.

Paragraph 2 AO2

Some studies have found no relationship between locus of control and majority influence (Williams & Warchal, 1981). However, a clear effect of locus of control on obedience was found in a study that involved participants giving themselves electric shocks (Miller, 1975)! There is not a clear link between locus of control and independent behaviour as self-esteem is another key variable. However, the fact that they correlate is predictable, and strengthens the argument that locus of control is a key determinant of independent behaviour. Furthermore, because locus of control cannot be manipulated cause and effect cannot be inferred, so we cannot conclude that the locus of control causes independent behaviour. Further weaknesses include the fact that the locus of control is too general a measure and so cannot predict with accuracy how individuals will behave in Milgram and Asch scenarios, not least because there are multiple internal and external factors in these scenarios and so it is too simplistic to say internals will be independent and externals will obey or conform because they may be more influenced by the situational (external) factors. The fact that the majority did conform in Asch's study at least once and the majority obeyed in Milgram's study can be used as evidence that situational factors override individual factors when the situational pressures are great.

Application of knowledge questions

> **?** **Identify whether each of the statements below represents internal or external locus of control.**
>
> **4 MARKS**
>
> A Children get into trouble because their parents punish them too much.
>
> B People's misfortunes are the result of the mistakes they make.
>
> C In the long run, people get the respect they deserve in this world.
>
> D No matter how hard you try, some people just don't like you.

Locus of control	Statements
Internal	_B C_
External	_A D_

> **?** **A Deputy Headteacher is pleased with the fact that the majority of the students are dressed in suitable uniform. But he struggles to get a significant minority to conform to the dress code.**
>
> **Using your knowledge of individual differences in independent behaviour explain why the minority do not conform to the dress code.** **4 MARKS**

Rotter's locus of control can explain these individual differences in independent behaviour. This is a personality dimension concerned with whether we perceive what happens to us as under our own control (internal locus of control) or whether it is determined mainly by situational factors (external locus of control). Individuals with internal locus of control would be more likely than those with external locus of control to show independent behaviour. This is because internals would be less likely to conform because they would trust their own judgement so they may have more confidence in their own sense of style and so do not conform to the dress code. Internals are also less influenced by external factors and so would not be swayed by the fact the majority conform to the dress code, and would be less influenced by the legitimate authority of the school rules. Internals are less likely to go into the agentic state, whereby they become the agent of the authority figure and place all responsibility with the authority figure, and so internals are less likely to obey the school dress rules because they will stay in an autonomous state (take responsibility for own actions) rather than an agentic state.

Explanation question

Implications for social change

> ❓ **Outline the implications from social influence research for social change.** **6 MARKS**

The implications from social influence research mainly point to the negative consequences of blind conformity and obedience. Thus the implications for social change are how to reduce such social influence, and a number of suggestions come out of the research: 1) Provide social support because individuals are much less likely to obey immoral orders or to be persuaded to conform to the mistaken views of a majority if they have at least some social support. Asch (1956) found that participants who had one supporter conformed on only 5% of trials rather than 37%, as happened when they lacked support; 2) Increase self-esteem. Arndt et al. (2002) argued that people will tend to be independent and less conforming when they focus on one aspect of the self that increases their self-esteem. As predicted, participants told to think of such an aspect of the self were more independent than were controls when rating an abstract painting in

EXAM HINT
Make sure you do focus on implications and don't make the mistake of outlining social influence research. It may seem obvious but this is a common mistake!

the knowledge of the ratings of others; 3) Educate—the actual participants in Milgram and Asch's research provide strong support for this. Many of the participants in the research carried out by Asch and by Milgram reported afterwards that they had learned much from the experience. Of most immediate relevance, they felt that they had learned more about themselves and were determined in future to be very careful not to conform or obey an authority figure in an unthinking way. Thus, we can reduce unthinking obedience to authority and conformity by means of education and learning; 4) Another consideration is that the minority has the potential to influence the majority for the better, and to be effective the minority must be consistent, committed, and not dogmatic in their views.

Essay question

> **?** **Critically consider the implications for social change of research into social influence.**   **8, 10, OR 12 MARKS**

> **EXAM HINT**
>
> The AO1 paragraph draws from the above question. AO2 provides more of a challenge as you need to evaluate the potential implications. AO2 can partly be achieved from using evidence to support the implications, so evaluating the evidence is another source of AO2 marks.
>
> 10-mark question: Reduce the description of Arndt et al. to cut AO1 and leave out the last sentence of paragraph 2 to reduce AO2.
>
> 8-mark question: Reduce the description of Arndt et al. and leave out the findings from the Asch study to cut AO1 and leave out or condense the last two sentences of paragraph 2 to reduce AO2.

Paragraph 1 AO1

The implications from social influence research mainly point to the negative consequences of blind conformity and obedience. Thus the implications for social change are how to reduce such social influence effects and a number of suggestions come out of the research: 1) Providing social support. Individuals are much less likely to obey immoral orders or to be persuaded to conform to the mistaken views of a majority if they have at least some social support. Asch (1956) found that participants who had one supporter conformed on only 5% of trials rather than 37% as happened when they lacked support;

2) Increasing self-esteem. Arndt et al. (2002) argued that people will tend to be independent and less conforming when they focus on one aspect of the self that increases their self-esteem. Participants told to think of such an aspect of the self were more independent than controls when rating an abstract painting in the knowledge of the ratings of others; 3) Education. The actual participants in Milgram's and Asch's research provide strong support for this. Many of the participants in the research carried out by Asch and by Milgram reported afterwards that they had learned much from the experience, they felt that they had learned more about themselves and were determined in future to be very careful not to conform or obey in an unthinking way; 4) Another key implication of the research is that when people have time to think about their actions they are less likely to show obedience and conformity; 5) Another consideration is that the minority has the potential to influence the majority for the better, and to be effective the minority must be consistent, commited, and flexible in their views.

Paragraph 2 AO2 Discuss the implications

Asch's and Milgram's research can be challenged in terms of artificiality because this limits the relevance to real-life behaviour. However, even though the studies are artificial, what they show about the importance of social support seems to have some validity. In real life we often have access to social support and this gives us time to think, which considerably reduces blind obedience and conformity. It should also be considered that reducing conformity and obedience is not entirely a positive thing. Conformity and obedience can be good things and so our understanding of the conditions that increase these can also be used in a positive way; for example, to encourage students to obey the rules in school, or to encourage children to conform to norms on healthy eating. Research into minority influence provides even further evidence of how social influence research can be used to influence change for the better. Moscovici (1985) identified characteristics a minority needed to have to be persuasive, such as consistency, commitment, flexibility, and relevance. If we apply these to minority leaders such as Nelson Mandela we can see how his success in his fight against apartheid can be partly explained by these factors. Although in reality the true situation is much more complex and the unjustness of apartheid and the fact that the White minority held all the power over a Black majority also help explain the success of his campaign for freedom, which shows that trying to explain behaviour using just one factor, minority influence, is reductionist and overstates the effect of social influence.

Application of knowledge question

> **?** **In America one strategy used as part of the civil rights movement was to hold sit-ins where African-American activists would sit-in at places according to the segregation laws they were not permitted to be. The activists were told to leave every other seat free so that the White majority could join in with the protest.**
>
> **How can social influence research be used to explain this example of social change?** **6 MARKS**

Minority influence and resistance to obedience help us understand why African-Americans were driven to rebel against the laws of segregation. First, the laws can be seen as having an unjust authority—the fact that segregation was not equal and the effect of it was to discriminate against Black Americans means that the law was perceived as being wrong and unjust. We are more likely to obey when authority is seen as having legitimate power and so when the opposite is true, as in the case here, then disobedience is more likely. The effectiveness of the civil rights message can be explained by the conditions for conversion identified by Moscovici as needed if a minority is to be successful. Conversion is when the majority are persuaded to accept the position of the minority because they become convinced that the minority position is right. To be persuasive the minority needs to be consistent and this was true of the civil rights movement—they were completely consistent in their call for the end to segregation and inequality and need for the Black vote. The minority message also has to be relevant, and it was, because the lack of freedom for Black Americans was all the more pronounced and seen as unfair because it contrasted with the new freedoms being introduced in the 1960s.

INDIVIDUAL DIFFERENCES
Psychopathology (Abnormality)

DEFINING AND EXPLAINING PSYCHOLOGICAL ABNORMALITY

Definition question

Definitions of abnormality

> **?** **Explain what is meant by the term . . .**   **3 MARKS**

Abnormality: Behaviour that is considered to deviate from the social norm or ideal mental health. It is dysfunctional because it is harmful or causes distress to the individual or others and so is considered to be a failure to function adequately. Abnormality is characterised by the fact that it is an undesirable state that causes severe impairment in the personal and social functioning of the individual, and often causes the person great anguish depending on how much insight they have into their illness.

Deviation from social norms: Behaviour that deviates from the norms and values of society, that is, behaviour that deviates from what is the approved and expected way of behaving in a particular society is considered to be abnormal. There are unwritten or implicit rules of expected behaviour in society; they are implicit because they are not as clear as the law and they have to be learned through experience of the culture. People who ignore the implicit rules have ignored social norms and so are considered abnormal. For example, drug abuse, violent behaviour, or wearing beach clothes to the office and a suit to the beach would be examples of behaviours that deviate from social norms.

EXAM HINT

You may be asked to define any of the following key terms. You do not have to write out the definitions word for word; just make sure you can clearly communicate what the term means.

AO ADVICE

Note "Explain what" is asking you to describe the key terms and so this is AO1 content. The keys to high marks are accuracy and detail. You should be writing approximately 50 words for a 3-mark question.

Deviation from ideal mental health: The deviation from ideal mental health definition of abnormality proposed by Jahoda (1958) suggests that abnormality is a deviation from optimal psychological wellbeing (a state of contentment that we all strive to achieve). This state of wellbeing is known as self-actualisation and means the individual is in a state in which they have fulfilled their potential, as suggested by humanistic psychology. Deviation from ideal mental health is characterised by a lack of the following: positive self-attitudes (e.g. high self-esteem), personal growth (the motivation to be all that one can be and so develop one's capabilities and fulfil one's potential), autonomy (self-responsibility), accurate view of reality (i.e. rational, not too idealistic because this would be unrealistic, nor too pessimistic), environmental mastery (adequacy at work and at play and so able to adjust to new environments), and resistance to stress (ability to cope with stressful situations without becoming overwhelmed); all of these prevent the individual from achieving self-actualisation and so result in abnormality.

Failure to function adequately: A model of abnormality based on an inability to cope with day-to-day life caused by psychological distress or discomfort. Failure to function adequately refers to failure to fulfil individual, social, and occupational roles. Rosenhan and Seligman (1989) suggested seven features of abnormality including suffering, maladaptiveness (behaviour is negative), unpredictability, and observer discomfort. An alcoholic is likely to experience suffering, cause observer discomfort, and show maladaptive behaviour, and therefore would be classed as abnormal. A severely depressed person may struggle to get out of bed and so be unable to function adequately, for example, being unable to maintain a job or have positive relationships.

Criticism questions

EXAM HINT
If you choose to use cultural relativity do make sure you evaluate the definition using this and don't just describe cultural differences. The latter does not evaluate the definition and so would only access the bottom mark band.

? Identify and explain two criticisms of the deviation from social norms definition of abnormality
3 + 3 MARKS

(i) Social norms are culturally relative. For example, in some cultures homosexuality is still socially unacceptable, whereas others have afforded more equal rights than Britain, such as offering the status of marriage (as opposed to civil partnership in Britain). Within any culture there are many sub-cultures that also have different opinions as to what is and isn't deviant. This means that the definition is culturally relative as social norms are culture bound. This means that the norms are ethnocentric (take one cultural perspective); what is the socially accepted way to behave in one culture may differ in another, e.g. South American Indians participate in a sun dance, which can involve their flesh being torn as part of the dance, and this would be seen as abnormal by other cultures as it is a form of self-abuse. This means the definition does not provide a universal account of abnormality and so lacks generalisability.

(ii) Value judgements underpin this definition since what is deviant is a subjective decision (a decision based on opinion rather than objective measures) made by society, which can change over time. This means that the definition is era-dependent. For example, in the Middle Ages some women were burned as witches because they were considered to be evil, whereas now it is believed that they may have suffered from mental illness, or were proficient healers. A second memorable example is homosexuality. This was considered a mental abnormality in the USA until 1973 when it was removed as a disorder from the DSM classifications (not appearing in the 1980 edition of DSM). This highlights the issue that social norms are era-dependent, which means that this definition does not reliably define abnormality because there is no consistency over time.

? **Give/outline two criticisms of the deviation from ideal mental health definition of abnormality.**

3 + 3 MARKS

EXAM HINT

Try to link at least one of the criticisms to specific elements of optimal living, such as autonomy.

(i)   Cultural relativism is a weakness of the ideal mental health definition as not all of the elements of optimal living generalise to collectivist cultures. For example, autonomy would not be seen as essential to mental health in collectivist cultures as this criterion encourages independence, which is discouraged in collectivist cultures where the common good is more important than the individual's needs. The definition is culturally relative to individualistic cultures and so is culture bound. This means that the definition is ethnocentric (based on one cultural perspective). The elements of optimal living are not universal and so the definition lacks generalisability.

(ii) The humanistic perspective, which the ideal health definition is based upon, is very idealistic. This is a weakness of the ideal mental health definition as the elements are too challenging; we cannot all achieve the criteria all of the time, and a failure to do so does not make us abnormal. We all experience stress at times and so may be lacking resistance to stress or have low self-esteem. It has been suggested that self-actualisation cannot be realised by everybody and that it is more accessible for higher socio-economic groups. This means the population validity (generalisability) of the ideal mental health definition is limited by its idealism.

> **EXAM HINT**
> Note how culture bias is a criticism of all definitions. To ensure you access the marks, explain why the definition is culture biased—don't just describe cultural differences.

> **?** **Give/outline two criticisms of the failure to function definition of abnormality.** **3 + 3 MARKS**

(i)   Culture bias is a weakness of the failure to function definition as judgements will be influenced by cultural norms, such as what is classed as unconventional behaviour, and so we are more likely to judge other cultures as abnormal compared with our own culture. Each criterion will involve to some extent a value judgement of whether behaviour is undesirable/unacceptable, e.g. hallucinations would be considered abnormal in our culture, but are desirable in some other cultures, in which they confer high status because the hallucinating person is thought to be in touch with the gods. This means the definition lacks generalisability.

(ii) Deciding whether somebody meets the criteria for a failure to function involves a value judgement and so is subjective (a decision based on opinion rather than objective measures). Judgements may be ethnocentric (based on one cultural perspective) and so apply more to one culture than another. This means reliability (consistency) and validity (truth) of judgements about abnormality are issues that limit the usefulness of the failure to function definition as it lacks generalisability.

EXAM HINT

Note how many of the examples and the criticisms can be used across all three questions. A good way to cut down revision!

Essay questions

? **Outline and evaluate the deviation from social norms definiton of abnormality.** **8, 10, OR 12 MARKS**

EXAM HINT

The exam question could be worth 8, 10, or 12 marks so note how the answer can be condensed for the shorter questions.

10-mark question: Condense the AO1 by leaving out the third example about anorexia. Reduce the AO2 by leaving out the point about witches in the Middle Ages.

8-mark question: Condense AO1 by leaving out the examples about OCD and anorexia. Reduce the AO2 by leaving out the point about witches in the Middle Ages and reduce the evidence of norms being ethnocentric by leaving out the point about the Dani culture.

Paragraph 1 AO1

According to the deviation from social norms definition, behaviour that deviates from the norms and values of society (i.e. behaviour which deviates from what is the approved and expected ways of behaving in a particular society) is considered to be abnormal. There are unwritten or implicit rules of expected behaviour in society; they are implicit because they are not as clear as the law and they have to be learned through experience of the culture. People who ignore the implicit rules have flouted social norms and so are considered abnormal. For example, drug abuse, violent behaviour, or wearing beach clothes to the office and a suit to the beach would be examples of behaviours that deviate from social norms. A depressed person may struggle to cope with their job and their personal relationships and so does not conform to the norm of holding down a relationship and a job. A person with obsessive-compulsive disorder (OCD) who constantly has to wash their hands and check doors are locked because they think if they don't something bad will happen is deviating from the social norm as this is not an expected way to behave. An anorexic who starves herself on fewer than 500 calories per day would similarly be seen as not conforming to social norms.

Paragraph AO2

The deviation from social norms definion is culturally biased because it is based upon individualistic culture and so is Western-centric. Judgements on whether behaviour fits social norms vary greatly across cultures because judgements are subjective, i.e. open to interpretation. This means that the norms are ethnocentric (based on one's own culture). For example, the sexual practices of the Dani society of New Guinea, who wait two years after marriage before having sex, would be seen as an acceptable social norm in the Dani culture but would deviate from social norms in other cultures. In the Wodaabe culture it is the social norm for the men to wear make-up and compete in some sort of beauty pageant, whereas in most cultures it is the other way round as the social norm is for females to compete based on their beauty. This means the definition does not provide a universal account of abnormality and so lacks generalisability even within a culture as different sub-cultures will also vary in what is classed as a deviation from social norms. Another issue is with the temporal validity as social norms change over time. For example, homosexuality was considered a mental abnormality until 1973 when it was removed as a disorder from the DSM classifications (not appearing in the 1980 edition of DSM). Another example is how in the Middle Ages some women were burned as witches because they were considered to be evil, whereas now it is believed that they may have suffered from mental illness, or were proficient healers. These examples highlight how social norms change dramatically over time and so social norms are era-dependent (limited to one time period). This means the definition does not generalise across time periods and so lacks temporal validity.

> **?** **Discuss the deviation from ideal mental health definition of abnormality.** **12 MARKS**

EXAM HINT

Try to link the examples and the criticisms to the ideal mental health criteria.

10-mark question: To reduce AO1 leave out the last example about OCD. To reduce AO2 leave out the last sentence about many people living in less than optimal conditions.

8-mark question: To reduce AO1 leave out the last example about OCD. To reduce AO2 leave out the last sentence about many people living in less than optimal conditions, just identify the point that the definition is too idealistic, and don't give any elaboration. You will have elaborated earlier points and so this will be enough if you only have 4 minutes for AO2.

AO ADVICE

Remember "discuss" means you have to describe and evaluate in equal proportion.

Paragraph 1 AO1

The deviation from ideal mental health definition of abnormality proposed by Jahoda (1958) suggests that abnormality is when we deviate from optimal psychological wellbeing, otherwise known as self-actualisation, which means to fulfil one's potential, as suggested by humanistic psychology. Deviation from ideal mental health is characterised by a lack of positive self-attitudes (e.g. high self-esteem, self-liking, and strong sense of identity), personal growth (the motivation to be all that one can be and so develop one's capabilities and fulfil one's potential), autonomy (self-responsibility and independence, the ability to make decisions for oneself and so not be reliant on others), accurate view of reality (i.e. rational, not too idealistic because this would be unrealistic, nor too pessimistic), environmental mastery (adequacy at work and at play and so able to adjust to new environments such as a new workplace or social setting without getting too stressed, good interpersonal relationships, good problem-solving), and resistance to stress (ability to cope with stressful situations without becoming overwhelmed); all of which prevent the individual from achieving self-actualisation and so result in abnormality. For example, somebody who lacks a positive self-attitude due to low self-esteem would be classed as abnormal. A depressed person may struggle to cope with their job and their personal relationships and so lacks environmental mastery. A person with OCD who constantly has to wash their hands and check doors are locked because they think if they don't something bad will happen lacks an accurate view of reality.

Paragraph 2 AO2

The ideal mental health definition is culturally biased because it is based upon individualistic culture and so is Westerncentric.

Judgements on whether behaviour fits the elements for optimal living in the ideal mental health definition vary greatly across cultures because judgements are subjective, i.e. open to interpretation. This means that the definition is ethnocentric (based on one culture) as the criteria for optimal living are based on American culture. For example, the sexual practices of the Dani society of New Guinea who wait two years after marriage before having sex would be seen as environmental mastery (adequacy at work and at play) in the Dani culture because this is the right way to begin a marriage in the Dani society, but would not be seen as healthy in other cultures. Another example of culture bias is the criterion autonomy. This would not be seen as essential to mental health in collectivist cultures as this criterion encourages independence, which is discouraged in collectivist cultures where the common good is more important than the individual's needs. This means the definition lacks generalisability and so does not provide a universal account of abnormality. The definition lacks generalisability even within a culture because different sub-cultures will also vary in what is defined as ideal mental health. Another weakness is that the ideal mental health definition is very idealistic because the elements of optimal living are too challenging, we cannot all achieve these, and a failure to do so does not make us abnormal. It's not clear how many you must lack to be abnormal. Also, many people live in less than optimal conditions, e.g. a dirty house, and so some may see this as a lack of environmental mastery but it does not necessarily make them abnormal.

> **?** **Outline and evaluate the failure to function adequately definition of abnormality.** **8, 10, OR 12 MARKS**

EXAM HINT

Try to engage with what this definition is about by using examples to illustrate when somebody is failing to function.

10-mark question: To reduce AO1 leave out the last sentence of paragraph 1, and to reduce AO2 leave out the last point about people appearing to function normally.

8-mark question: To reduce AO1 condense the example of how somebody with depression fails to function, and to reduce AO2 leave out the last two sentences of paragraph 2.

Paragraph 1 AO1

The failure to function definition states that abnormality is an inability to cope with day-to-day life, usually because psychological distress is so great that it interferes with normal, everyday behaviour. Failure to function adequately refers to failure to fulfil individual, social, and occupational roles. Rosenhan and Seligman (1989) suggested seven abnormal characteristics, including: suffering—for example an alcoholic may be distressed by their drinking; maladaptiveness—the behaviour is negative, for example, the binge eating and vomiting of the bulimic has a negative effect upon their health. Unconventionality of behaviour, unpredictability and loss of control, irrationality, observer discomfort, and violation of moral and ideal standards are the remaining features. For example, a woman wearing a bikini to work would be classed as displaying unconventional behaviour, and so abnormal, unless she worked at the beach. A depressed person who has a very low sense of self-worth, and so may feel suicidal, meets the criteria of suffering; family and friends may well be concerned by their distressed state and so their behaviour causes observer discomfort. The depressed person may struggle to get out of bed and so be unable to function as they may be unable to maintain a job or have positive relationships.

Paragraph 2 AO2

The failure to function adequately definition is culturally biased because it is based upon individualistic culture and so is Western-centric. Judgements on whether behaviour is functional vary greatly across cultures because judgements are subjective, i.e. open to interpretation. The judgements may be ethnocentric (based on one's own culture). For example, the sexual practices of the Dani society of New Guinea who wait two years after marriage before having sex would be seen as normal functioning, but in other cultures could be seen as sexual dysfunction. This means the definition does not provide a universal account of abnormality and so lacks generalisability even within a culture as the different sub-cultures will also vary in what is classed as a failure to function. Another issue is that the definition is context-bound—running down the street screaming would normally be seen as bizarre and irrational, but not if being followed by a film crew, so interpretations must consider context and this can be hard to do. This is particularly true of eccentrics; their behaviour may seem bizarre to others but this does not necessarily make them abnormal. Another issue is that we may experience the features of abnormality without being abnormal; everybody suffers some of the time, for example, when a loved one dies, but this does not make them abnormal. Also, people can appear to function normally but be abnormal, for example, Harold Shipman the serial killer was a highly respected doctor. There are alcoholics and even drug addicts in respected jobs.

Application of knowledge questions

EXAM HINT

Do make sure you go beyond just identifying the criteria, you must describe them to access the second mark.

> **?** According to the ideal mental health definition, one must meet certain criteria to be classed as healthy. One such criterion is resistance to stress, which is the ability to cope with stressful situations without becoming overwhelmed.
>
> Using your knowledge of psychology, describe two other criteria that you would expect a person to display if they were psychologically healthy, according to the ideal health definition. **2 + 2 MARKS**

1) Environmental mastery, which means adequacy at work and at play, and so the individual is able to adjust to new environments such as a new work place or social setting without getting too stressed, has good interpersonal relationships, and good problem solving.
2) Personal growth, which is the motivation to be all that one can be and so develop one's capabilities and fulfil one's potential, which is called self-actualisation.

> **?** Sharanpal is struggling to cope with her everyday life. She finds work too stressful, has no energy or

motivation to meet up with friends, and has felt close to tears on a few occasions without there really being a reason. Her family and friends are very concerned about her because her behaviour is out of character, as previously she has coped well with stress and work. Sharanpal meets one of the criteria of failure to function adequately because the fact that she feels tearful meets the criteria of personal distress.

Using your knowledge of the failure to function adequately definition, identify two other criteria used to define abnormality. **2 + 2 MARKS**

EXAM HINT
Note you must explain the criteria for the second mark.

1) Others' distress—the fact that Sharanpal's behaviour is causing her friends and family to be concerned shows she meets the criteria of others' distress.
2) Maladaptive behaviour—the fact that Sharanpal is behaving out of character and is withdrawing from her friends can be seen as meeting the criteria of maladaptive behaviour because her behaviour is negative rather than positive.

? Three of the following statements describe limitations of different definitions of abnormality.

A   This definition is too idealistic; not all people can achieve all of the criteria suggested by this definition.

B   This definition does not tell us which infrequent behaviours are undesirable.

C   This definition suggests people with abnormality cannot cope with everyday life but some very abnormal people do appear to live a normal life.

D   This definition has sometimes been used as a form of social control to punish non-conformists.

In the table below, insert the limitation A, B, C, or D that matches the corresponding definition of abnormality. **3 MARKS**

EXAM HINT

With this question, to ensure that a choice always has to be made, four statements are supplied from which three must be chosen in order to complete the table. So watch out for the statement that is surplus to requirements.

Definitions of abnormality	Limitation of definitions
Deviation from social norms	_D_
Deviation from ideal mental health	_A_
Failure to function adequately	_C_

EXAM HINT

You probably will not get asked to relate all three definitions to the same stimulus but it makes sense for revision to see how all three can be related and so it would just be a case of tweaking your answer to a different scenario.

? John is obsessive about cleanliness. He cleans his hands repeatedly until they are red raw and has very high standards in terms of the cleanliness of his home. He is very obsessive about the arrangement of his belongings and can spend hours checking they are in exactly the right place.

(a) Use the social norms definition of abnormality to explain why John is exhibiting abnormal behaviour. **3 MARKS**

(b) Use the failure to function definition of abnormality to explain why John is exhibiting abnormal behaviour. **3 MARKS**

(c) Use the ideal mental health definition of abnormality to explain why John is exhibiting abnormal behaviour. **3 MARKS**

AO ADVICE

Note that the application of your knowledge to an unfamiliar situation is credited as AO2 because the question requires you to explain WHY John's behaviour would be considered abnormal rather than just describing the definition.

(a) John's behaviour deviates from a number of social norms. First, the amount that one should wash one's hands. The fact that he washes his hands until they are red raw goes beyond an appropriate amount and so breaches social norms. Similarly, his constant checking of the arrangement of his belongings also goes against the unwritten rules of society as the amount of time that he does this is far beyond what would be considered normal in society.

(b) One of the criteria of failure to function is suffering and the fact that John cleans his hands until they are red raw suggests that he is experiencing a certain level of suffering. Another aspect of failure to function is that the individual is unable to cope with everyday life. The fact that he spends so long arranging his belongings suggests that his obsession does interfere with his day-to-day life and so would be considered a failure to function.

(c) John's behaviour could be seen as deviating from ideal mental health as he lacks an accurate view of reality because the cleaning of his hands until they are red raw is not rational and nor is the arranging of his belongings obsessively. John could also be classed as lacking environmental mastery (adequacy at work and at play and so able to adjust to new environments such as a new work place or social setting without getting too stressed). His arranging of his belongings suggests an inability to relax, even in his own home, and so the fact that he cannot deal with his own home environment suggests he will be even less at ease in less familiar environments.

Explanation question

Biological approach to psychopathology

> ❓ **Outline two features of the biological approach to psychopathology in relation to the causes of abnormality.** **3 + 3 MARKS**

According to the biological model, genetic predisposition and biochemical imbalances may be the causes of abnormality:

(i) Genetic factors: This assumption is that there are abnormal genes that are inherited, i.e. passed down from parents to children, from generation to generation, even though they may not be expressed in every generation. Family, twin, and adoption studies are used to establish concordance rates (the extent to which members of the same family share a particular characteristic) to test for genetic predispositions as an explanation of abnormality. Family studies have shown that relatives of schizophrenics are 18 times more likely to develop the disorder (Masterson & Davis, 1985). This suggests that people may be more vulnerable to abnormality because of inherited predispositions. Twin studies show that MZ twins (who have identical genes) have higher concordances than DZ twins (who have approximately 50% of the same genes), which supports a genetic basis.

(ii) Biochemistry: An imbalance of chemical messengers in the brain may explain abnormality. Neurochemicals include hormones,

EXAM HINT
To access all of the marks do include evidence for the biological factors, such as the study on schizophrenia running in families, and the specific detail on whether neurotransmitters are high or low in different disorders.

neurotransmitters, and neuromodulators. For example, the neurotransmitters serotonin, dopamine, and noradrenaline are linked to mental disorders such as depression, schizophrenia, and eating disorders. Serotonin is lower than normal in depression and dopamine is higher than normal in schizophrenia. These biochemicals are needed for transmitting messages in the brain and so imbalances have serious consequences for brain functioning, which may explain abnormality.

How Science Works question

EXAM HINT

This answer focuses on how genetic relatedness has been tested but you could equally choose to write about neurochemicals being tested with blood or urine tests.

> **?** **Explain how the biological model investigates abnormality.** **4 MARKS**

AO ADVICE

This is an AO3 question because it is testing your understanding of how science works by asking you to explain how research is carried out by psychologists who take a biological approach.

The biological model tests the genetic hypothesis, which is that abnormality is inherited, by looking for inherited patterns in families, comparing concordances in family, and twin studies. Concordance is the extent to which members of the same family share a particular characteristic. In the case of abnormality, if both family members have a disorder they are concordant. Family studies have shown that relatives of schizophrenics are 18 times more likely to develop the disorder. In twin studies, MZ twins (identical with 100% of the same genes) are compared to DZ twins (non-identical, approximately 50% of the same genes) because if the disorder is caused by genes then MZ twins should have higher concordances than DZ twins as they share more genes. The concordance rate for MZ twins for anorexia is 56% compared to 7% in DZ twins, which is strong evidence for a genetic basis. These studies are a form of natural experiment because genetic relatedness is a naturally occurring IV and the concordances are the DV.

Essay question

> **?** **Describe and assess the biological approach to psychopathology.** **8, 10, OR 12 MARKS**

EXAM HINT

Note that "assess" requires you to evaluate the model, and so as with ALL essay questions you need an equal proportion of AO1 to AO2.

10-mark question: Reduce the last section of paragraph 1 on biochemical imbalances and to reduce AO2 leave out the point about determinism in paragraph 2.

8-mark question: Leave out the section on biochemical imbalances in paragraph 1 and leave out the points about ethics and determinism in paragraph 2.

Paragraph 1 AO1

The biological model assumes that mental illness is similar to physical illness and proposes that abnormality has physical causes such as genetics, brain dysfunction, and biochemical imbalances. Genes can contribute to abnormality in that some disorders are inherited from parents, or at least a susceptibility to develop those disorders can be inherited. The role of genetic factors in abnormality is supported by family, twin, and adoption studies, which are used to establish concordance rates (i.e. if one family member has it, does the other?) to test for genetic predispositions as an explanation of abnormality. Family studies have shown that relatives of schizophrenics are 18 times more likely to develop the disorder (Masterson & Davis, 1985). Twin studies are particularly useful as MZ (identical genes) are compared with DZ twins (fraternal and so same number of genes in common as any sibling, i.e. approximately 50%) and if concordance rates are higher for MZ than DZ then this suggests a genetic basis as they have more genes in common, e.g. the concordance rate for MZ twins for anorexia is 56%, which is strong evidence for a genetic basis. This suggests that people may be more vulnerable to abnormality because of inherited predispositions. Biochemical imbalance is another cause, according to the biological model, for example, serotonin is lower than normal in depressives and dopamine is higher than normal in schizophrenics. These biochemicals are needed for transmitting messages in the brain and so imbalances have serious consequences for brain functioning, which may explain abnormality.

Paragraph 2 AO2

Strengths of the biological model include that it is scientific because biological measurements, e.g. neurotransmitter levels, concordance percentages, or brain anatomy, are objective and so less open to bias because they are less open to interpretation. The model does help explain mental illnesses such as depression and schizophrenia. Ethics can be seen as a strength because the patient is not blamed for their illness. However, weaknesses include a lack of evidence such as there are no 100% concordance rates in genetic studies so genetics cannot be the only factor. In fact the low concordance rate of MZ twins for bulimia, 23%, means that environmental factors are much more important than genetic ones in accounting for the eating disorder. The model is biologically deterministic as it implies that the individual has no control (free will) over their mental state and that instead they are victims of their genes, biochemical imbalances, etc. The model is also reductionist (oversimplified) because it focuses on only one level of explanation and so ignores other alternative explanations such as the psychological causes of abnormality, e.g. internal factors as covered by the psychodynamic (psyche and unconscious conflicts) and cognitive (faulty thinking), and external factors (the environment) as covered by the behavioural model. Thus, there is an overemphasis on nature and insufficient consideration of nurture. The diathesis–stress model provides a more comprehensive explanation as it considers the interaction of nature, as the "genes load the gun", and nurture, because the "environment pulls the trigger".

Behavioural approach to psychopathology

Explanation question

> ? **Outline the key features of the behavioural approach to explaining psychopathology.** **6 MARKS**

According to the behavioural model, all behaviour is learned, including maladaptive or abnormal behaviour. The emphasis of this approach is that we are a product of learned experience of our environment and the role of biology, and any internal processes are ignored. Classical conditioning (Pavlov, 1927) involves learning an association between two stimuli, e.g. fear and a rabbit in the Watson and Rayner study, in which they conditioned

Little Albert to fear a rabbit by pairing the rabbit (CS) with a loud bang (UCS). Little Albert automatically feared the loud bang and transferred this to the rabbit due to the two stimuli being repeatedly paired together until an association was made. Operant conditioning (Skinner, 1938) involves learning through the consequences of behaviour. The consequence is the reinforcement: positive reinforcement (e.g. receiving rewards), negative reinforcement (e.g. avoiding unpleasant consequences), and punishment (experiencing unpleasant consequences), e.g. depression may be due to a lack of positive reinforcement from social interactions. Anorexia may be maintained by negative reinforcement as the unpleasant consequence of gaining weight is avoided and there may be positive reinforcement, e.g. compliments on weight loss. According to social learning theory, we learn through observation and imitation and so learn abnormal behaviour from seeing others being rewarded for such behaviour (vicarious reinforcement).

EXAM HINT
Don't make the mistake of writing about Pavlov or Skinner. Your answer should be focused on abnormality so you need examples of how abnormality is learned through classical and operant conditioning.

How Science Works question

? **Explain how the behavioural model investigates abnormality.** **4 MARKS**

EXAM HINT
Remember behaviourism takes a scientific approach. Use examples of real research such as Watson and Rayner's study of Little Albert.

The behavioural approach takes a scientific approach to research because, according to this approach, only what is observable and measurable should be researched. This means only behaviour that can be observed and measured is studied. Emotions and cognitions are not studied because they cannot be observed or measured. Research takes place in controlled conditions, for example, the Watson and Rayner study of Little Albert. This was a controlled study in which the researchers used a young child to control any previous learning and then controlled his exposure to a rabbit. His behaviour was observed to see how he learned to fear the rabbit due to the rabbit being associated with a loud bang that he was automatically frightened of, and through repeated pairings the fear transferred to the rabbit.

Comparison question

? Explain how the biological model differs from the behavioural model of psychopathology. **4 MARKS**

The biological and behavioural models take very different approaches to explaining abnormality. The biological model considers nature, that the abnormality is innate and so you are born with it, whereas the behavioural model considers nurture, and so is the opposite, because the individual is not born with abnormality; according to this approach, they are a blank slate, and so it is something they learn from the environment during their life. The biological model suggests internal causes, i.e. physical factors such as genes, neurochemicals, and brain structure as causes of abnormality and these are internal because they are within the individual, whereas the behavioural model suggests external causes, because the abnormality is due to learning from the environment, which is external to the individual.

Essay questions

? Discuss the behavioural model of psychopathology. **8, 10, OR 12 MARKS**

Paragraph 1 AO1

According to the behavioural model, classical and operant conditioning may be the causes of abnormality as it assumes all behaviour is learned. Classical conditioning (Pavlov, 1927) involves learning to associate a neutral stimulus with an automatic stimulus. A stimulus response bond is created, e.g. Watson and Rayner conditioned Little Albert to fear a rabbit by pairing the rabbit (CS) with a loud bang (UCS). Operant conditioning (Skinner, 1938) involves learning through positive reinforcement (e.g. receiving rewards), negative reinforcement (e.g. avoiding unpleasant consequences), and punishment (experiencing unpleasant consequences). For example, the child whose tantrum in the supermarket is followed by the receipt of sweets is likely to misbehave next time they are at the shops because the behaviour has been rewarded or positively reinforced. Abnormality can also be learned through the observation and imitation of role models, according to social learning theory. If the behaviour of a role model is seen to be rewarded (vicarious reinforcement), e.g. the aggressive role models rewarded with sweets in Bandura's study, or a child observes a parent getting their own way by shouting then sulking, then the child is likely to copy the behaviour to receive the same rewards, and so abnormal personality patterns may develop.

Paragraph 2 AO2

The strengths of the model include the fact that behavioural therapies are particularly effective for phobias, and a further strength is that it tends to be non-judgemental of the individual as it is assumed that abnormality is learned from the environment and so the individual is not responsible. Behaviourism takes a scientific approach as only that which is observable and measurable is studied, and so it is supported by well-controlled studies, which means the approach has scientific validity. The controlled nature of research into conditioning makes it artificial and this means external validity can be questioned. For example, the Little Albert case study has been difficult to replicate, which means repetitions of the study have not produced the same findings and so we can question the generalisability of the original findings. Another limitation includes the fact that underlying causes are ignored because the behaviourists refuse to investigate internal processes. They investigate only that which is observable and measurable and so ignore underlying causes such as emotions and cognitions because these are not considered suitable for study. Ignoring cognition is a key weakness as faulty cognition definitely plays a part in abnormality, e.g. the hopeless thinking of depression. As a consequence of only treating behaviour the therapies may treat symptoms not causes and so symptom substitution may occur, which is when another disorder develops because the causes of the initial disorder have not been treated. The behavioural model exaggerates the importance of environmental factors and so is environmentally deterministic because it suggests the environment controls the individual's behaviour, which ignores the individual's free will to control their own behaviour. The approach is also reductionist because it only considers the environment as a cause of abnormality, when in reality there are many more factors, and so the diathesis–stress model may offer a more comprehensive understanding.

Psychodynamic approach to psychopathology

> **?** **Outline two key features of the psychodynamic approach to psychopathology in relation to the causes of abnormality.** **3 + 3 MARKS**

EXAM HINT
In this question you need to select key features that can be elaborated for 3 marks.

According to the psychodynamic model, unresolved childhood conflicts and fixation/regression to earlier stages of psychosexual development may be the causes of abnormality:

(i) Conflict between the id, ego, and superego occurs because these are very different aspects of personality. The id develops first and is based on the "pleasure principle", as it is our innate drive (libido) for physical satisfaction. The ego is the conscious part of the mind based on the "reality principle". The superego operates on the "morality principle" because it is our conscience. They conflict with each other because they work on very different principles. If the conflicts are not resolved abnormality results because there is a lack of ego development, which means either the id or superego is dominant. The ego is the rational part of the mind and so the lack of development results in a loss of contact with reality. The id may dominate instead and, because this is childlike, the behaviour is irrational and pleasure seeking, or if the superego is dominant the individual feels excessive guilt because the superego is the moral conscience.

(ii) Another cause of abnormality is fixation at one of the psychosexual stages. Freud proposed we all develop through psychosexual stages and that excessive or lack of gratification at any of these stages can lead to fixation or regression. If fixated the person has never really left the childhood psychosexual stage. With regression, when problems occur, the adult regresses back to an earlier stage and this may manifest in the nature of the illness, e.g. anal fixation and obsessive-compulsive disorder (OCD). The individual is fixated at the anal stage of development due to trauma at this stage during childhood, which could have been caused by too strict potty training. This leaves the individual feeling unclean and hence the desire to clean obsessively, which characterises many cases of OCD.

> **?** **Explain how the psychodynamic model investigates abnormality.** **4 MARKS**

EXAM HINT

Note that the psychodynamic model draws heavily from Freud's theory of psychoanalysis and so you can use this to explain the methods used by the psychodynamic model.

Freud, the father of psychoanalysis, used the case study method and clinical interview to investigate abnormality. The psychodynamic model is based on Freud's theory of psychoanalysis and so has adopted Freud's methods. The clinical interviews were the therapy sessions Freud had with his sample of middle-class Viennese women. Psychodynamic therapists use a range of techniques first practised by Freud, such as: free association, in which the individual is asked to talk about the first thing that comes into his/her head; dream analysis, in which the psychotherapist looks for hidden conflicts in the symbolic meaning of the dream; and word association, in which the individual is given a word and has to respond with the first word they think of in response to the given word. All of these techniques are used as a means of accessing the unconscious conflicts so that patients can gain insight into their mental disorder. To do this the patient has to access the unconscious. The insight gained from accessing repressed material can extinguish the neurotic symptoms of the abnormality. The psychodynamic therapist keeps case notes of each session with the client, and the success, or lack of success, of the various techniques, and this information is put together to form a case study.

> **?** **Outline and evaluate key features of the psychodynamic explanation of abnormality.**
>
> **8, 10, OR 12 MARKS**

> **EXAM HINT**
>
> Think about which parts you will leave out if the shorter 8- or 10-mark questions are asked.
>
> 10-mark question: Leave out the point about the defence mechanisms to reduce AO1 and leave out reductionism to decrease AO2.
>
> 8-mark question: Leave out the last two sentences of paragraph 1 to reduce AO1, and to reduce AO2 condense the point about researcher bias and leave out reductionism.

Paragraph 1 AO1

The psychodynamic model developed by Freud introduced psychology to abnormality and emphasised the internal dynamics of the mind. The model suggests abnormality is caused by unconscious forces that drive behaviour. The unconscious is shaped in childhood by traumatic experiences. Early childhood trauma leads to unresolved unconscious conflicts and fixation/regression to earlier stages of psychosexual development: conflicts occur between the id, ego, and superego. The id develops first and is based on the "pleasure principle", as it is our innate drive (libido) for physical satisfaction. The ego is the conscious part of the mind and so is based on the "reality principle". The superego operates on the "morality principle", as it is our conscience. They conflict with each other because they work on very different principles and, if the conflicts are not resolved, abnormality may result because the individual may become fixated or regress to earlier psychosexual stages of development. Freud also proposed we all develop through psychosexual stages and that conflict or excessive/lack of gratification at any of these stages can lead to fixation. When problems develop the adult regresses back to the stage they were fixated at during childhood and this may manifest in the nature of the abnormal behaviour, e.g. anal fixation and obsessive-compulsive disorder, or oral fixation and eating disorders. The repressed conflicts cause problems for the individual in their day-to-day life because they will be unaware of the source of conflict. The defence mechanisms, such as repression and denial, can also cause abnormality because they don't solve the problem; they are like a plaster, they just cover it up.

Paragraph 2 AO2

Strengths of the psychodynamic model include the fact that Freud is celebrated because he introduced psychological causes to mental illness. Childhood certainly can play a part in the development of abnormality and so this and the defence mechanisms have face validity as people do show denial if they are unable to cope with disturbing information; there is some evidence for repression in victims of child abuse. However, not enough attention is paid to later adult experience and there is an overemphasis on sexual factors and an underemphasis on social factors. Even supporters of Freud make this criticism and neo-Freudians such as Erikson proposed different psychodynamic explanations with more emphasis on social factors. Methodological weaknesses include researcher bias in Freud's interpretations of his clinical interviews—Freud's theories were based on his own patients and even his analysis of his own neuroses. He has been accused of being highly selective in the examples he drew from the case studies and ignoring alternative explanations and information that didn't support his theories. Sample bias is a further issue as his patients were all middle-class Viennese women who were not representative of the wider population and their neuroses may not be true for other types of abnormality. This means Freud's research lacks generalisability, and so external validity is questionable. The psychodynamic model is reductionist (oversimplified) because only unresolved issues from childhood are considered when other factors such as biological, cognitive, and learning may explain the abnormality. The id, ego, and superego are hypothetical structures and so cannot be tested, which means they cannot be verified or falsified and so the model is not very scientific.

> **?** **Outline two features of the cognitive approach to psychopathology.** **3 + 3 MARKS**

Cognitive approach to psychopathology

According to the cognitive model, faulty thinking and a breakdown in information processing may be the causes of abnormality:

EXAM HINT

Candidates often perform poorly when asked to describe the cognitive model. Make sure you access the marks by giving detailed examples of distorted cognition such as Beck's cognitive triad.

(i) Cognitive dysfunction or faulty/distorted thinking causes abnormality because such thinking causes abnormal emotional reactions and behaviour, which can deeply distress the individual. Beck's cognitive triad explains depression as an example of faulty thinking whereby the individual's thoughts about the self, world, and future can lead to depression. For example, "I'm old and fat, everyone is horrible to me. I will never have a chance of happiness in life or have a boyfriend". The more negative and hopeless the cognition, the greater the risk of depression. Other examples of faulty thinking include "musterbating" or "should statements" where the individual's thinking is very inflexible and negative and is known as all or nothing thinking, e.g. "I must be liked by everybody otherwise I'm unlikeable".

(ii) The computer is used as an analogy because the individual is seen as an information processor and a breakdown in processing leads to irrational thinking. An example of such a breakdown is when the individual fails to distinguish between imagination and reality, leading to psychosis. Elaborating on the computer analogy, according to this, there is a breakdown in the inputs, i.e. the sensory input, and outputs, which are the individual's thought processes. The faulty processing leads to abnormality in emotions and behaviour.

EXAM HINT

This model also favours a scientific approach and so you need to explain how faulty cognitions have been studied using the scientific method.

? **Explain how the cognitive model investigates abnormality.** **4 MARKS**

The cognitive model takes a scientific approach to abnormality and so tries to investigate cognition following the principles of science, i.e. formulating hypotheses and testing them by measuring the faulty cognitions. For example, patients' faulty cognitions of body size can be measured by asking them to select their own body image from a range of body images on the computer. Patients normally select larger images than their own and so the extent of their distortion can be measured. Patients with schizophrenia lack the cognitive ability to self-monitor, i.e. recognise their thoughts as self-generated, and cognitive psychologists have devised ways of measuring this lack of self-monitoring, e.g. asking them to draw a picture that they cannot see and then seeing if they can recognise their own drawing from a sample of pictures. Patients experiencing hallucinations and delusions are less able to recognise their own drawings than are controls and schizophrenics without hallucinations or delusions.

> **?** **Outline and assess the cognitive explanation of psychopathology.** **8, 10, OR 12 MARKS**

> **EXAM HINT**
> Make sure you include detailed examples of faulty cognition to access the high mark bands on AO1. Candidates often perform poorly because they keep repeating the same point in slightly different ways, i.e. that the abnormality is due to faulty thinking. You need to use examples to move beyond this.
>
> 10-mark question: Leave out the example of schizophrenic thinking to reduce AO1 and leave out the last point about reductionism.
>
> 8-mark question: Leave out the example of schizophrenic thinking and condense the content on "should" statements to reduce AO1 and leave out the last point about reductionism and the point about cognitive-behavioural therapy.

Paragraph 1 AO1

A breakdown in cognitive processing explains abnormality, according to the cognitive model. The computer is used as an analogy because the individual is seen as an information processor and so a breakdown in processing leads to irrational, i.e. abnormal, thinking. An example of such a breakdown is when the individual fails to distinguish between imagination and reality, leading to psychosis. Beck's cognitive triad explains depression as an example of faulty thinking whereby the individual's thoughts about the self, world, and future can lead to depression. For example, "I'm old and fat, everyone is horrible to me. I will never have a chance of happiness in life or have a boyfriend". The more negative and hopeless the cognition, the greater the risk of depression. Other examples of faulty thinking include "musterbating" or "should statements" where the individual's thinking is very inflexible and negative: "I should achieve an A grade otherwise I'm a failure". This cognitive bias suggested by Beck is also known as "all or nothing" thinking, e.g. "I must be liked by everybody otherwise I'm unlikeable". Another example is a person with schizophrenia may hear voices and think "people are communicating with me and about me". They ask others who deny it and so assume this is part of the conspiracy, leading to persecution delusions. Faulty thinking can affect emotions and behaviour and so, according to the cognitive approach, the cause of the abnormality is rooted within the individual—it is their thought processes causing the abnormality.

Paragraph 2 AO2

The model has validity (i.e. truth) as there is no doubt that distorted and irrational thinking does characterise mental disorders. However, the cognitive approach may be more relevant to anxiety and depression than other mental disorders, particularly in the treatment of abnormality as it is difficult to challenge the faulty cognitions of schizophrenics when they have completely lost touch with reality and have no insight into their disorder, although they are not in an acute stage all of the time and so may have more insight into their cognition some of the time. A key weakness is cause and effect because the faulty cognitions may be an effect of the disorders rather than the cause. It is difficult to establish whether the faulty cognitions come first or after the disorder develops because mostly people are researched after their abnormality has developed. Key strengths of the model include the fact that the cognitive-behavioural model has developed from it and this combination has proven even more effective at treating mental disorders than either model on its own because both cognition and behaviour are treated. A further strength is that responsibility is placed on the patient and this can empower patients to take control of their mental wellbeing. On the one hand, it is a positive that responsibility is placed on the individual because, according to the cognitive model, they have the power to treat their abnormality by changing their faulty cognitions. However, on the other hand, this is a negative because the individual could feel to blame for having the faulty cognitions, and so this raises ethical issues. A further weakness is that it ignores other important factors such as genetics and social factors. This means the model is too reductionist and so would be better integrated into a diathesis–stress approach.

If asked to give a criticism use REDUCTIONISM as all models can be criticised as too simplistic (reductionist). This would be worth 3 marks.

The _____ model is reductionist (too simplistic) as it focuses on only one level of explanation, *the gene, the unconscious, learning, cognition* and so ignore s o ther alternative explanations . . . *and then identify the other explanations as alternatives.* Thus, to fully explain something as complex as abnormality we need to move beyond a reductionist singular explanation and take a multi-dimensional approach, which accounts for both nature and nurture. For example, the diathesis–stress model suggests that we need to consider the interaction of genetic predisposition (diathesis) and environmental triggers (stress). The diathesis–stress model provides a more comprehensive explanation because it considers the interaction of nature as the "genes load the gun" and nurture because the "environment pulls the trigger".

See the Essay question answers for further criticisms of each model/approach to psychopathology/explanation of abnormality.

Application of knowledge questions

? **The following are four approaches to the understanding of mental disorder.**

A   Psychodynamic

B   Behaviourist

C   Cognitive

D   Biological

In the table below, write down which approach, A, B, C, or D is associated with each assumption.   **3 MARKS**

Assumptions about abnormality	Answer
People become ill because of negative thoughts	*C*
People become ill due to imbalances of neurotransmitters	*D*
People become ill due to unresolved unconscious conflicts	*A*

EXAM HINT

Four options with three assumptions— you do have to be able to select only the three that are relevant.

EXAM HINT

Identify three or four concepts and elaborate each to access all of the marks. Don't worry about being too specific. The example answer considers the nature of the unconscious conflict but you don't need to be this specific if you can't come up with this in the exam. Instead stick to three key concepts— unconscious forces drive behaviour; conflict between the id, ego, and superego; the role of traumatic childhood experience—and you should easily access the marks.

? Sarah has always been attracted to men that are older than her. However, her relationships never last long, she constantly moves on to a new relationship, and this is making her feel anxious and depressed.

Use the psychodynamic approach to explain why Sarah might be attracted to these men even though it makes her unhappy. **4 MARKS**

Sarah is fixated at the phallic stage, due to under-gratification (lack of love) during the stage that has led to an unresolved female version of the Oedipus complex, in which she is in love with her father and views her mother as a love rival. This explains her attraction to older men as they are father substitutes. In the same way as the father relationship did not provide enough love nor do her adult relationships and so she keeps moving on trying to find a love that will make up for the lack of it during her childhood. Her succession of failed relationships is anxiety-provoking because she will question herself and how loveable she is and this can also lead to low mood and negative thinking, which characterise depression.

EXAM HINT

Make sure you do use one of the models of psychopathology and don't get confused and use the definitions. The cognitive model lends itself well to the stimulus but you could consider the psychodynamic approach and fixation at the anal stage if you prefer.

? Ryan is a perfectionist. He is obsessive about his appearance to the extent that he spends over an hour getting dressed in the morning. He is equally particular about his school work and takes real pains to make sure his notes are as neat as possible and his books are kept as good as new.

Using your knowledge of the approaches to psychopathology, use one of them to explain why Ryan's behaviour is abnormal. **3 MARKS**

Ryan's abnormal behaviour can be explained by the cognitive approach because his perfectionism may be due to faulty thinking. Such thinking can lead to cognitive distortions such as "musterbating" or "should statements" whereby the individual's thinking is very inflexible and negative. So Ryan may be so obsessive over his school work because he may think, "I should achieve an A grade otherwise I'm a failure". This cognitive bias suggested by Beck is also known as "all or nothing" thinking and would explain why Ryan's behaviour is so obsessive.

TREATING ABNORMALITY

Drug therapy

> **[?]** **Explain drug therapy as a treatment of abnormality.**
> **6 MARKS**

Drugs are a chemical approach to treatment as they act upon the brain chemicals (neurotransmitters) and try to balance these to treat and reduce the abnormality. For example, anti-depressants act upon low levels of the neurotransmitters serotonin and noradrenaline. The most common drugs used to treat depression are the serotonin re-uptake inhibitors (SSRIs); Prozac is the best known. These drugs are more selective in their functioning than the tricylics, in that they increase serotonin activity by blocking the re-uptake of serotonin without influencing other neurotransmitters such as noradrenaline. Anti-anxiety drugs act upon the body's response to stress. For example, benzodiazepines, such as Valium, increase the activity of the neurotransmitter GABA and GABA decreases serotonin activity. As serotonin is linked to arousal, low serotonin activity reduces arousal and so reduces the stress response. Drugs work by reducing the symptoms of abnormality, but do not necessarily address the causes.

EXAM HINT
Use specific examples. Note the use here of SSRIs and benzodiazepines.

> **[?]** **Evaluate drug therapy as a treatment of abnormality.**
> **6 MARKS**

EXAM HINT
This answer focuses on the negatives. But it is just as appropriate to use evidence of effectiveness as a source of evaluation.

Key concerns with drugs as a therapy are the fact that there can be problems of drug dependence, with patients finding it very hard to cope without the drugs. Side effects are often experienced. Nearly all drugs have unwanted side effects. Some of these side effects can be extremely unpleasant. For example, tardive dyskinesia is a chronic disorder of the nervous system characterised by involuntary jerky movements of the face, tongue, jaws, trunk, and limbs, which is an effect of taking anti-psychotics for schizophrenia. The side effects lead to a high drop-out rate, which of course limits the effectiveness of drugs as a treatment. Perhaps the key issue is that drugs are criticised as treating the symptoms not the causes of the abnormality because drugs don't deal directly with the problems underlying any given mental disorder, e.g. faulty cognitions, conflicts from childhood. A further issue is that it is difficult to know how much of any improvement is due to the particular drug and how much to the placebo effect, i.e. the patient improves because they *expect* the drug to work.

Electroconvulsive therapy

? **Explain electroconvulsive therapy.** **6 MARKS**

EXAM HINT

It's useful to include how the approach has changed over time as this adds extra detail to your answer.

AO ADVICE

Note this is an "explain WHAT" question because it asks you to describe the therapy.

Electroconvulsive therapy (ECT) involves an electric current being passed through the head. In the past, ECT used to cause broken bones, patient terror, and memory loss. However, various changes in treatment have been introduced so that these problems have been almost eliminated. First, strong muscle relaxants are given to patients to prevent or minimise convulsions. Second, the current is generally only passed through the non-dominant brain hemisphere rather than through both hemispheres. This is called unilateral ECT; the traditional form of both hemispheres is called bilateral ECT. Third, anaesthetics are used to put patients to sleep during ECT, thus substantially reducing anxiety. The exact mechanism of ECT is not fully understood but it is thought that the electric current alters the levels of neurotransmitters in the brain and this alteration is responsible for the improvement in symptoms.

EXAM HINT

If you are going to use research as the answer here try to include the % statistics to give your answer added detail.

? **Evaluate electroconvulsive therapy (ECT) as a treatment of abnormality.** **6 MARKS**

Electroconvulsive therapy (ECT) has been found to be effective in the treatment of depression. Petrides et al. (2001) reported that between 65% and 85% of depressed patients had a favourable response to ECT. Pagnin et al. (2004) carried out a meta-analysis in which the effectiveness of ECT was compared against various types of anti-depressant drugs and simulated ECT. ECT was more effective in the treatment of depression than anti-depressant drugs or simulated ECT. However, a key concern is that we lack understanding of how ECT works and some argue that we should not use ECT if we do not know how it works because we cannot be sure about the damage it may cause. Also, whilst unilateral ECT reduces the danger of memory loss, this also on average reduces the effectiveness of treatment. ECT is associated with various side effects including memory loss and other cognitive impairments, although most of these problems seem to be short term rather than long term. Another issue is that ECT does not work well for all patients. It is less effective in the treatment of depression among patients who are below 65 years of age, who respond poorly to anti-depressants, and who have a psychotic depression and a personality disorder (de Vreede et al., 2005).

> **?** **Discuss the effectiveness of biological therapies.**
>
> **8, 10, OR 12 MARKS**

> **EXAM HINT**
>
> Note this essay does not follow the usual AO1 in paragraph 1 and AO2 in paragraph 2 format. Instead each paragraph has both AO1 and AO2 because drugs and ECT are outlined and evaluated in each paragraph.
>
> 10-mark question: To reduce AO1 condense the description of ECT in paragraph 2 and leave out the point about not understanding how it works.
>
> 8-mark question: Reduce the description of ECT, leave out points about not understanding how it works, and condense the point about side effects.

Paragraph 1 AO1/AO2 Outline and evaluate anti-depressants.

Drugs are a chemical approach to treatment as they act upon the brain chemicals (neurotransmitters) and try to balance these to treat and reduce the abnormality. For example, anti-depressants act upon low levels of the neurotransmitters serotonin and noradrenaline. The most common drugs used to treat depression are the serotonin re-uptake inhibitors (SSRIs), of which Prozac is the best known. These drugs are more selective in their function-ing than the tricyclics, in that they increase serotonin activity by blocking the re-uptake of serotonin without influencing other neurotransmitters such as noradrenaline. This means the SSRIs have fewer side effects than the older types of anti-depressants. Key concerns with drugs as a therapy are the fact that there can be problems of drug dependence, with patients finding it very hard to cope without the drugs. Nearly all drugs have unwanted side effects, for example, the SSRIs have been linked to an increase in aggression and suicidal thoughts in some patients. Perhaps the key issue is that drugs are criticised as treating the symptoms not the causes of the abnormality because drugs don't deal directly with the problems underlying any given mental disorder, e.g. faulty cognitions, conflicts from childhood. Another issue is that relapse is more common after drug therapy than other types of therapy; the drop-out rate is high possibly due to people's aversion to drugs.

Paragraph 2 AO1/AO2 Outline and evaluate ECT.

ECT involves an electric current being passed through the head. First, strong muscle relaxants are given to patients to prevent or minimise convulsions. Second, the current is generally only passed through the non-dominant brain hemisphere rather than through both hemispheres. This is called unilateral ECT. Third, anaesthetics are used to put patients to sleep during ECT, thus substantially reducing anxiety. The exact mechanism of ECT is not fully understood but it is thought that the electric current alters the levels of neurotransmitters in the brain. Pagnin et al. (2004) carried out a meta-analysis in which the effectiveness of ECT was compared against various types of anti-depressant drugs and simulated ECT. ECT was more effective in the treatment of depression than anti-depressant drugs or simulated ECT. However, a key concern is that we lack understanding of how ECT works and some argue that we should not use ECT if we do not know how it works because we cannot be sure about the damage it may cause. A further concern is that ECT is associated with various side effects, including memory loss and other cognitive impairments, although most of these problems seem to be short term rather than long term.

Psychoanalysis

> **?** **Explain psychoanalysis as a treatment of abnormality.**
> **6 MARKS**

This treatment is based on Freud's theory and so focuses on the dynamics of the mind. It is known as the "talking cure". The therapies are based on Freud's key assumption that abnormality is due to internal conflicts that are repressed, and that lead to regression, i.e. going back to an earlier stage of psychosexual development. Psychoanalysis seeks to uncover the repressed memory so that patients can gain insight into their mental disorder. To do this the patient has to access the unconscious. The insight gained from accessing repressed material can extinguish the neurotic symptoms of the abnormality. Free association is one method used to access the unconscious whereby the therapist tells the client to respond with the first thing that comes into his/her mind. It is thought that encouraging the client to talk without censorship will reveal the individual's unresolved and unconscious conflicts. Another method used by Freud to uncover repressed memories was the analysis of dreams. Freud argued that the mind has a censor that keeps repressed material out of conscious awareness. This censor is less vigilant during sleep, and so repressed ideas from the unconscious are more likely to appear in dreams than in waking thought. The repressed ideas are in a disguised form and so the therapist has to work with the client to decide on the true meaning of each dream.

EXAM HINT
Explain the basics of the psychoanalytic treatment before moving on to the specific techniques.

? Outline two techniques used in psychoanalysis.
2 + 2 MARKS

EXAM HINT
This question requires you to describe specific techniques, not to describe psychoanalysis in general.

(i)   Free association is one method used to access the unconscious, during which the therapist tells the client to respond with the first thing that comes into his/her mind. It is thought that encouraging the client to talk without censorship will reveal the individual's unresolved and unconscious conflicts.

(ii) Another method used by Freud to uncover repressed memories was the analysis of dreams. Freud argued that the mind has a censor that keeps repressed material out of conscious awareness. This censor is less vigilant during sleep, and so repressed ideas from the unconscious are more likely to appear in dreams than in waking thought. The repressed ideas are in a disguised form and so the therapist has to work with the client to decide on the true meaning of each dream.

? Evaluate psychoanalysis as a treatment of abnormality.
6 MARKS

Psychoanalysis has a very important place in the history of therapy. It was the first systematic form of psychological treatment for mental disorders, and it has strongly influenced several subsequent forms of therapy. However, some of the concepts of central importance to psychoanalysis are very vague and so cannot be operationalised (measured). This means it is hard to test concepts such as "insight" and "transference". It is impossible to test how much insight contributes to recovery and transference does not seem to have the positive effects Freud attributed to it. Studies in which attempts have been made to manipulate or to measure transference have mostly failed to find any evidence that it facilitates recovery from mental illness and so psychoanalysis as a treatment lacks scientific validity. Psychoanalysis has too narrow a focus. Insufficient attention is paid to the individual's *current* problems and the difficulties he/she has at the social and interpersonal level as there is too much emphasis on the past (childhood) and sexual factors. Another issue is that psychoanalysis is very time consuming, some patients undergo the therapy for years, and so it can seem less effective than other therapies. On the other hand, it may be that clients treated by behaviour or cognitive therapy often have less serious symptoms than those treated by psychoanalysis.

? Outline and evaluate psychoanalysis.
8, 10, OR 12 MARKS

Paragraph 1 AO1 Outline the key features of the treatment.

This treatment is based on Freud's theory and so focuses on the dynamics of the mind. It is known as the "talking cure". The therapies are based on Freud's key assumption that abnormality is due to internal conflicts that are repressed, and that lead to regression, i.e. going back to an earlier stage of psychosexual development. Psychoanalysis seeks to uncover the repressed memory so that patients can gain insight into their mental disorder. To do this the patient has to access the unconscious. The insight gained from accessing repressed material can extinguish the neurotic symptoms of the abnormality. Free association is one method used to access the unconscious whereby the therapist tells the client to respond with the first thing that comes into his/her mind. It is thought that encouraging the client to talk without censorship will reveal the individual's unresolved and unconscious conflicts. Another method used by Freud to uncover repressed memories was the analysis of dreams. Freud argued that the mind has a censor that keeps repressed material out of conscious awareness. This censor is less vigilant during sleep, and so repressed ideas from the unconscious are more likely to appear in dreams than in waking thought. The repressed ideas are in a disguised form and so the therapist has to work with the client to decide on the true meaning of each dream.

Paragraph 2 AO2 Consider strengths and weaknesses of the treatment.

Psychoanalysis has a very important place in the history of therapy. It was the first systematic form of psychological treatment for mental disorders, and it has strongly influenced several subsequent forms of therapy, such as Jungian therapy and play therapy. However, some of the concepts of central importance to psychoanalysis are very vague and so cannot be operationalised (measured). This means it is hard to test concepts such as "insight" and "transference". It is impossible to test how much insight contributes to recovery and transference does not seem to have the positive effects Freud attributed to it. Studies in which attempts have been made to manipulate or to measure transference have mostly failed to find any evidence that it facilitates recovery from mental illness and so psychoanalysis as a treatment lacks scientific validity. Psychoanalysis has too narrow a focus. Insufficient attention is paid to the individual's *current* problems and the difficulties he/she has at the social and interpersonal level as there is too much emphasis on the past (childhood) and sexual factors. Another issue is that psychoanalysis is very time consuming, some patients undergo the therapy for years, and so it can seem less effective than other therapies. On the other hand, it may be that clients treated by behaviour or cognitive therapy have less serious symptoms than those treated by psychoanalysis.

Systematic de-sensitisation

? Outline systematic de-sensitisation as a treatment of abnormality.   6 MARKS

EXAM HINT

Make sure you include how the technique is based on classical conditioning so that you do make clear how it is a behavioural therapy.

Systematic de-sensitisation is based on classical conditioning, i.e. the theory that behaviour is learned through association (classical conditioning). It was developed by Wolpe (1958, 1969) and it is used to treat phobias that have been learned through the association of the feared stimulus with something unpleasant. The counter-conditioning of systematic de-sensitisation involves unlearning the association of the object with fear by replacing the fear response with relaxation. This is based on the theory that fear and relaxation are opposed to one another and so in a relaxed state the patient cannot feel fear. Wolpe called this reciprocal inhibition because the relaxation response inhibits the fear response. The first stage is to provide clients with relaxation training in which they learn how to engage in deep muscle relaxation. In the second stage clients construct a fear hierarchy with the assistance of their therapist. A fear hierarchy begins with exposure to the feared stimulus that causes only a small amount of fear and moves on to those that cause increasingly greater levels of fear. At the bottom of the hierarchy the client uses the relaxation techniques whilst imagining the objects or situations they fear. The client then places himself/herself in progressively more frightening real-life situations between sessions. Finally, the client experiences the feared object, known as in vivo de-sensitisation. So a client with a phobia of spiders may have a picture of a spider in their head, then look at a real picture, then a TV clip, then a spider in the room with them but whilst in a tank, then out of the tank, and then within a metre of them, and this may end with the client holding the spider.

> **[?]** Evaluate systematic de-sensitisation as a treatment of abnormality. **6 MARKS**

> **EXAM HINT**
> A weakness of this technique is related to the behavioural theory, and the fact that it ignores cognition and emotion, but to make this relevant you must explain how this limits the treatment.

The success of systematic de-sensitisation played some role in the subsequent development of related techniques, such as exposure therapy and virtual reality exposure therapy. It can be evaluated as a successful treatment of phobias. Denholtz, Hall, and Mann (1978) evaluated it as effective in the treatment of flying phobia, although others have concluded it is only moderately effective. This is because systematic de-sensitisation has restricted usefulness; it is specifically designed to reduce anxiety, and in particular phobias, and so does not work for a range of disorders, such as depression, schizophrenia, and personality disorders. Another issue is that simply exposing the client to the feared object and allowing extinction to happen is often more effective than systematic de-sensitisation (Choy et al., 2007). However, such exposure is very stressful and so systematic de-sensitisation has the strength of being more humane and so raising fewer ethical issues. Perhaps the greatest weakness is that the underlying causes are ignored because the behaviourists refuse to investigate internal processes. This means they treat only what is observable and measurable, i.e. symptoms not causes. Cognitions and emotions are often the motivators of behaviour and these are ignored, so the systematic de-sensitisation is only dealing with symptoms not the underlying causes, and this of course limits its effectiveness because the real problem is not dealt with. This can lead to symptom substitution, so even if the phobia is cured the anxiety may be expressed in another way and so present as another symptom.

> **[?]** Critically consider the effectiveness of systematic de-sensitisation. **8, 10, OR 12 MARKS**

> **EXAM HINT**
>
> Make sure you include an example in paragraph 1 and consider how behaviourism limits the effectiveness of the treatment in paragraph 2.
>
> 10-mark question: To reduce AO1 leave out the point about reciprocal inhibition and to reduce AO2 leave out the point about symptom substitution.
>
> 8-mark question: To reduce AO1 leave out the point about reciprocal inhibition and condense the example given at the end of the paragraph, so just include the first and last stage. To reduce AO2 leave out the point about symptom substitution and the restricted usefulness of the therapy.

Paragraph 1 AO1 Outline the key features of the treatment.

Systematic de-sensitisation is based on classical conditioning, i.e. the theory that behaviour is learned through association (classical conditioning). It was developed by Wolpe (1958, 1969) and is used to treat phobias that have been learned through the association of the feared stimulus with something unpleasant. The counter-conditioning of systematic de-sensitisation involves unlearning the association of the object with fear by replacing the fear response with relaxation. This is based on the theory that fear and relaxation are opposed to one another and so in a relaxed state the patient cannot feel fear. Wolpe called this reciprocal inhibition because the relaxation response inhibits the fear response. The first stage is to provide clients with relaxation training in which they learn how to engage in deep muscle relaxation. In the second stage clients construct a fear hierarchy with the assistance of their therapist. A fear hierarchy begins with exposure to the feared stimulus that causes only a small amount of fear and moves on to those that cause increasingly great levels of fear. At the bottom of the hierarchy the client uses the relaxation techniques whilst imagining the objects or situations they fear. The client then places himself/herself in progressively more frightening real-life situations between sessions. Finally, the client experiences the feared object, known as in vivo de-sensitisation. So a client with a phobia of spiders may have a picture of a spider in their head, then a real picture, then a TV clip, then a spider in the room with them but whilst in a tank, then out of the tank, and then within a metre of them, and this may end with the client holding the spider.

Paragraph 2 AO2 Consider strengths and weaknesses of the treatment.

The success of systematic de-sensitisation played some role in the subsequent development of related techniques, such as exposure therapy and virtual reality exposure therapy. It can be evaluated as a successful treatment of phobias. Denholtz, Hall, and Mann (1978) evaluated it as effective in the treatment of flying phobia, although others have concluded it is only moderately effective. This is because systematic de-sensitisation has restricted usefulness; it is specifically designed to reduce anxiety, and in particular phobias, and so does not work for a range of disorders, such as depression, schizophrenia, and personality disorders. Another issue is that simply exposing the client to the feared object and allowing extinction to happen is often more effective than systematic de-sensitisation (Choy et al., 2007). However, such exposure is very stressful and so systematic de-sensitisation has the strength of being more humane and so raising fewer ethical issues. Perhaps the greatest weakness is that the underlying causes are ignored because the behaviourists refuse to investigate internal processes. This means they treat only what is observable and measurable, i.e. symptoms not causes. Cognitions and emotions are often the motivators of behaviour and these are ignored, so the systematic de-sensitisation is only dealing with symptoms not the underlying causes, and this of course limits its effectiveness because the real problem is not dealt with. This can lead to symptom substitution, so even if the phobia is cured the anxiety may be expressed in another way and so present as another symptom.

? **Outline cognitive behavioural therapy.** **6 MARKS**

Cognitive behavioural therapy

Cognitive behavioural therapy (CBT) combines cognitive and behavioural therapy and so treats mental illness with a combined approach, in which both maladaptive behaviour and dysfunctional thoughts are treated. Challenging patients' thinking about themselves and the world, in particular their interpretative bias (a tendency to interpret ambiguous situations in a negative way), and changing their behaviour are the key goals of therapy. In Beck's (1976) CBT he argued that therapy should involve more than simply changing dysfunctional thoughts and replacing them with

EXAM HINT

Make sure you explain through the example the cognitive and behavioural basis of the therapy.

more appropriate and positive ones. He emphasised the use of homework assignments requiring clients to behave in certain ways they find hard. For example, a client suffering from social anxiety might be told to initiate a conversation with everyone in his/her office over the following few days. A crucial ingredient in such homework assignments is hypothesis testing. Clients typically predict that carrying out their homework assignments will make them feel anxious or depressed, and so they are told to test their predictions. The clients' hypotheses are generally shown to be too pessimistic and the discovery that many of their fears are groundless speeds recovery. Thus, the therapy involves a cognitive element, because the behavioural homework challenges negative thinking, and a behavioural element, because the homework assignments help the client learn more adaptive behaviours.

EXAM HINT
Use the comparisons to other therapies and make sure you consider reductionism and determinism.

? Evaluate cognitive behavioural therapy. **6 MARKS**

Cognitive behavioural therapy combines features of cognitive therapy and behaviour therapy. As such, it is broader and more effective than either of the forms of therapy from which it arose. However, this does mean we lack understanding of which aspects of it are most effective. Cognitive behavioural therapy has been found to be more effective than anti-depressants in the treatment of major depressive disorder especially in terms of long-term beneficial effects. Cognitive behavioural therapy has shown itself to be clearly effective (and generally more effective than other forms of therapy) across a range of disorders. However, the effects of changing faulty cognitions may be exaggerated. Many clients develop more rational ways of thinking about important issues with no beneficial changes in their maladaptive behaviour. Also the negative cognitions may be realistic to patients' difficult lives rather than being distortions of that reality! There may be too much emphasis on the individual's cognition being "wrong". Perhaps the focus is too narrow and so we need to consider social and cultural factors, not just the individual. The treatment is less reductionist in the sense that it combines two approaches but it still ignores other influential factors, for example, little attention is paid to biological processes, and the emphasis is on current problems rather than traumatic childhood experiences. A key strength of the therapy is that it is not deterministic: it acknowledges the individual's free will through the emphasis placed on the individual's ability to control his/her thoughts.

> **?** **Describe and assess the effectiveness of cognitive behavioural therapy.** **8, 10, OR 12 MARKS**

EXAM HINT

Use an example to illustrate the technique and do consider how there is too much emphasis on the individual in the cognitive approach.

10-mark question: To reduce AO1 leave out the last sentence of paragraph 1, and to reduce AO2 leave out the point about not understanding which aspect, cognitive or behavioural, has more effect.

8-mark question: Condense the description of the homework assignments to reduce AO1 and leave out the point about not understanding which aspect, cognitive or behavioural, has more effect, and the point about how thinking rationally does not always cure the abnormality.

Paragraph 1 AO1 Outline the key features of the treatment.

Cognitive behavioural therapy (CBT) combines cognitive and behavioural therapy and so treats mental illness with a combined approach, in which both maladaptive behaviour and dysfunctional thoughts are treated. Challenging patients' thinking about themselves and the world, in particular their interpretative bias (a tendency to interpret ambiguous situations in a negative way), and changing their behaviour are the key goals of therapy. In Beck's (1976) CBT he argued that therapy should involve more than simply changing dysfunctional thoughts and replacing them with more appropriate and positive ones. He emphasised the use of homework assignments requiring clients to behave in certain ways they find hard. For example, a client suffering from social anxiety might be told to initiate a conversation with everyone in his/her office over the following few days. A crucial ingredient in such homework assignments is hypothesis testing. Clients typically predict that carrying out their homework assignments will make them feel anxious or depressed, and so they are told to test their predictions. The clients' hypotheses are generally shown to be too pessimistic and the discovery that many of their fears are groundless speeds recovery. Thus, the therapy involves a cognitive element, because the behavioural homework challenges negative thinking, and a behavioural element, because the homework assignments help the client learn more adaptive behaviours.

Paragraph 2 AO2 Consider strengths and weaknesses of the treatment.

Cognitive behavioural therapy combines features of cognitive therapy and of behaviour therapy. As such, it is broader and more effective than either of the forms of therapy from which it arose. However, this does mean we lack understanding of which aspects of it are most effective. Cognitive behavioural therapy has been found to be more effective than anti-depressants in the treatment of major depressive disorder, especially in terms of long-term beneficial effects. Cognitive behavioural therapy has shown itself to be clearly effective (and generally more effective than other forms of therapy) across a range of disorders. However, the effects of changing faulty cognitions may be exaggerated. Many clients develop more rational ways of thinking about important issues but this does not cure their abnormality. Also the negative cognitions may be realistic to patients' difficult lives rather than being distortions of that reality! There may be too much emphasis on the individual's cognition being "wrong". Perhaps the focus is too narrow and so we need to consider social and cultural factors, not just the individual. The treatment is less reductionist in the sense that it combines two approaches but it still ignores other influential factors, for example, little attention is paid to biological processes, and the emphasis is on current problems rather than traumatic childhood experiences. A key strength of the therapy is that it is not deterministic, it acknowledges the individual's free will through the emphasis placed on the individual's ability to control his/her thoughts.

Application of knowledge question

EXAM HINT
You must meet two requirements: explain the treatment and relate it to Sarandeep.

? Sarandeep is very socially anxious. She experiences panic when meeting new people and often avoids social situations rather than deal with her anxiety.

Explain how cognitive behavioural therapy could benefit Sarandeep.   **3 MARKS**

Beck's (1976) cognitive behavioural therapy (CBT) involves home-work assignments requiring clients to behave in certain ways they find hard. So to help Sarandeep overcome her social anxiety she might be told to initiate a conversation with one new person per day. A crucial ingredient in such homework assignments is hypothesis testing. Clients typically predict that carrying out their homework assignments will make them feel anxious or depressed, and so they are told to test their predictions. Sarandeep's fears will hopefully be shown to be too pessimistic and the discovery that many of her fears are groundless will speed recovery.

How Science Works questions

> **?** Some patients, especially children and those with mental impairments, may not be able to give informed consent for treatment of their mental disorders.
>
> Explain how informed consent could be gained in an ethical manner for these types of patients.
> **3 MARKS**

EXAM HINT
Consider that informed consent can be given on behalf of individuals if they are considered sufficiently incapacitated to give it themselves.

A parent can give consent on behalf of a child and, similarly, a family member or caregiver can give consent if the individual is incapacitated. However, a person with mental impairments may be capable of giving their own consent after a suitable period of treatment.

> **?** A psychologist wants to research the effectiveness of different psychological treatments for depression, including psychoanalysis, cognitive behavioural therapy, and psychoanalysis.
>
> (a) Suggest how the psychologist could measure the effectiveness of the treatment. **1 MARK**
>
> (b) Give one criticism of the measure you suggested in (a). **2 MARKS**

(a) The psychologist could time how long it takes before the individual has made a recovery.

(b) The problem with the above measure is that recovery is not an objective thing, it is open to interpretation, and so the timings may lack reliability if recovery has been interpreted to mean different things.